NETWORKED POETICS

A Volume in the Series
PAGE AND SCREEN
Edited by
KATE EICHHORN

Networked Poetics

THE DIGITAL TURN IN SOUTHERN AFRICAN POETRY

SUSANNA L. SACKS

University of Massachusetts Press
AMHERST AND BOSTON

Copyright © 2024 by University of Massachusetts Press

The electronic version has been made freely available under a Creative Commons (CC BY-NC-ND 4.0) license, which permits noncommercial use, distribution, and reproduction provided the author and University of Massachusetts Press are fully cited and no modifications or adaptations are made. Details of the license can be viewed at https://creativecommons.org/licenses/by-nc-nd/4.0/.

This book will be made open access within three years of publication thanks to Path to Open, a program developed in partnership between JSTOR, the American Council of Learned Societies (ACLS), University of Michigan Press, and The University of North Carolina Press to bring about equitable access and impact for the entire scholarly community, including authors, researchers, libraries, and university presses around the world. Learn more at https://about.jstor.org/path-to-open/.

All rights reserved
Printed in the United States of America

ISBN 978-1-62534-767-1 (paper); 768-8 (hardcover)

Designed by Sally Nichols
Set in Minion Pro
Printed and bound by Books International, Inc.

Cover design by adam b. bohannon
Cover art by Elson Kambalu, *Code: Sixth Sense*, painting © 2022.
Courtesy of the artist. https://www.elsonkambalu.art

Library of Congress Cataloging-in-Publication Data

Names: Sacks, Susanna L., author.
Title: Networked poetics : performing digital cultures in southern African poetry / Susanna L. Sacks.
Other titles: Page and screen.
Description: Amherst : University of Massachusetts Press, 2024. | Series: Page and screen | Includes bibliographical references and index.
Identifiers: LCCN 2023027639 (print) | LCCN 2023027640 (ebook) | ISBN 9781625347671 (paperback) | ISBN 9781625347688 (hardcover) | ISBN 9781685750435 (ebook)
Subjects: LCSH: Southern African poetry (English)—21st century—History and criticism. | Poetry, Modern—21st century—History and criticism. | Digital media—Social aspects—Africa, Southern. | Social media—Influence. | Literature and the Internet—Africa, Southern.
Classification: LCC PR9342 .S23 2024 (print) | LCC PR9342 (ebook) | DDC 821.9209968—dc23
LC record available at https://lccn.loc.gov/2023027639
LC ebook record available at https://lccn.loc.gov/2023027640

British Library Cataloguing-in-Publication Data
A catalog record for this book is available from the British Library.

Portions of chapter 2 were published in a previous form in "Evan Mawarire's #ThisFlag as Tactical Lyric," in *African Studies Review* 50, no. 1 (Summer 2018): 238–57. Reproduced with permission of Cambridge University Press. Portions of chapter 3 were published in a previous form in "Moving Forms: Individuals, Institutions, and the Production of Slam Poetry Networks in Southern Africa," in *ASAP/Journal* 5, no. 1 (January 2020): 153–79. Copyright © 2020 Johns Hopkins University Press. Published with permission by Johns Hopkins University Press.

Contents

List of Illustrations vii
Foreword ix
Acknowledgments xi

INTRODUCTION
Poetry in Motion
Reading for Performance for the Digital Age **1**

CHAPTER 1
Hashtags Become Chants
The Collective Poetics of Protest **23**

CHAPTER 2
Commenting in Community
Poetry's Regional Digital Aesthetic Networks **55**

CHAPTER 3
Institutionalizing Algorithmic Aesthetics
Slam Poetry's Regional Networks **90**

CHAPTER 4
Migrating Movements
Poetry Festivals and the Limits of Digital Cosmopolitanism **121**

CHAPTER 5
But Canons Continue
Koleka Putuma's *Collective Amnesia* and the Digital Fight over Cultural Capital **153**

CODA
Digital Poetry and the Global Creative Economy **182**

Notes 189
Index 215

Illustrations

FIGURE 1. Protesters outside the state house in Boston, MA.   xiv
FIGURE 2. Student protesters in Zomba, Malawi.   24
FIGURE 3. Hear My Voice's Poetry Relief Fund paid poets honoraria to perform online during the pandemic.   56
FIGURE 4. Zimbabwean poet Morset Billie uses image macros to capture audience attention on social media.   75
FIGURE 5. impepho press's "Virtual World Poetry Day" brought poets together to provide relief during COVID.   80
FIGURE 6. Siphokazi Jonas first posted her poem to Twitter before posting a screenshot of the Tweet on Instagram.   84
FIGURE 7. Vusumuzi Mpofu shared his poetry on Facebook before performing it live a few days later.   91
FIGURE 8. Malawian poet Muyanga performing at the KwaHaraba Open Mic.   100
FIGURE 9. Map from the *Spoken Word Project*.   106
FIGURE 10. Lingua Franca perform *Umzila ka Moya* at the Poetry Foundation, Chicago, IL on 4 April 2017.   117
FIGURE 11. Malawian musician Faith Mussa performing at Tumaini Festival in 2016.   122
FIGURE 12. Koleka Putuma launched *Collective Amnesia* in popular poetry spaces that spanned digital and live events.   154
FIGURE 13. Poets online pair text with image to tie the author's personal brand to their words.   173

Foreword

LITERARY FORM TEACHES how to be and how to behave. It models the relationship between the individual and their community, and its representations of the social world can open up alternative forms of behavior and being. As literary production and reception move online, though, literary networks shift, and new forms emerge in turn. In *Networked Poetics*, I ask: What kind of communities form around poetry online? What is the relationship between literary form and algorithmic curation? How do artists use the platforms available to them to imagine new literary forms? What work do those forms do, circulated globally? And, more broadly, what would a theory of poetry that accounts for YouTube and Instagram publication look like? The book focuses on poetry from Malawi, South Africa, and Zimbabwe: three countries where performance and literature have historically been tied to political movements of resistance and nationalism and where new youth networks have built paravirtual networks to imagine new ways of being in the world—and new literary forms to imagine with.

This project grew out of conversations with young writers in southern Africa, for whom digital networks opened crucial new artistic and cultural possibilities in the face of limited publishing opportunities. I began the project interested in better understanding how the nationalist traditions of the mid-twentieth century emerged today; I soon learned that studying poetry through national formations was itself a limiting paradigm, challenged by long histories of migration and the rapid spread of digital communication. In September 2016, for instance, I asked Maclean Mbepula, a poet whose work I admired, where she found inspiration. She explained how Rudy Francisco, a Black American spoken word poet whose work she had found on YouTube, inspired her performance style. Mbepula shared his videos with me via Bluetooth, before inviting me to join a Pan-African poetry WhatsApp group where she frequently shared her own work. In southern Africa, where print publishing opportunities are dominated by multinational corporations, leaving little room for literary publishing, social media has transformed the process by which literature is produced, published, circulated, and evaluated.

That change, I argue, is mediated by two emergent processes in the social production of poetry. The first, "networked poetics," draws on Mizuko Ito's conception of the networked public sphere to suggest that the connective logics of digital media communication inflects contemporary artistic production offline as well. The second, "algorithmic aesthetics," refers to a secondary effect of that process: the aesthetic norms established by and in response to the curatorial algorithms that organize social media newsfeeds. These processes follow global patterns: WhatsApp groups offer continuous forums for literary debate; live tweeting remediates prior broadcast patterns; live streaming transforms the audiences for local open mics. But they unfold in locally specific ways: WhatsApp groups in Malawi debate the relationship between poetic form and generational concerns, while South African groups consider the role of local identity. Studying these global trends and local patterns together reveals the interplay between literary form and digital culture in the twenty-first century.

Ultimately, in *Networked Poetics*, I argue that contemporary African poetry is shaped, from inception to canonization, by social media's growing influence. Poetry, a form whose brevity and allusiveness have made it uniquely suited to digital publication, has flourished on social media: Instagram poetry, tactical poetry, and spoken word are on the rise around the world. But the conflation of communication and publication on social media platforms places new pressures on literary form, which increasingly reflects the forms of digital conversation. These changes, in turn, challenged elite processes of valuation, forcing literary institutions like prizes, festivals, and curricula to account for and accommodate those works that draw popular attention. Even as the flexible networks of communication purport to democratize literary art worlds, then, the quantitative gatekeeping of algorithms reward works that are brief, popularist, and didactic. *Networked Poetics* demonstrates that digital media publication has shifted processes of cultural capital formation: today, cultural markets are driven by the promise of quantitative success, rather than by the putative removal from material concerns.

Acknowledgments

THIS BOOK—LIKE ALL, but perhaps more than many—is the work of many minds and conversations. I am grateful to everyone who shared time and space with me over the past decade, listening to my questions and teaching me new ways of asking. This work would never have come to fruition if not for the generosity of the incredible thinkers alongside whom I have had the fortune to learn.

The most important contribution has been, of course, the creativity and insight of the writers, thinkers, and arts organizers who took the time to speak with me about their work. Lily Banda, Shadreck Chikoti, Robert Chiwamba, Q. Malewezi, Benedicto Malunga, and Yankho Seunda introduced me to the contours of contemporary Malawian literature; Siphokazi Jonas, Roché Kester, Malika Ndlovu, Mbongeni Nomkonwana, Javier Perez, and Palesa Sibiya each illuminated the power and possibility of spoken word in addressing contemporary inequities; and Morset Billie, Mbizo Chirasha, Chirikure Chirikure, Linda Gabriel, and Tongai Makawa helped me appreciate the incredible resourcefulness of poets in finding avenues to speak truth. Their work is the reason this project exists.

I have had the good fortune, as well, to learn from teachers who were both intellectually generous and personally supportive. Evan Mwangi, Wendy Griswold, Andrew Leong, Harris Feinsod, and James Hodge: your insight, care, and faith gave this project shape and argumentative purpose. Aleck Bwanali, Arnold Mboga, and Mario Thodi, at the University of Malawi's Centre for Language Study, expanded my vision of what literary form can do and demonstrated the worlds opened up through language study. Kim Benston's belief in the power of Black radical poetics to make new historical meaning, and in me, bolstered this work against my own doubts.

Over the span of this project's many lives, I have found tremendous support and community across a range of institutions. Erin Andrews, Anne

Boemler, Kellen Bolt, Hannah Chaskin, Corrinne Collins, Misty de Berry, Meghan Fritz, Claudia Garcia-Rojas, Stephen Hudson, Carli Leone, and Ashlie Sandoval offered crucial feedback in the book's early stages. Kate Beutner, Iemanja Brown, Claire Eager, Jennifer Hayward, Christopher Kang, Tom Prendergast, Siavash Samei, and Desiree Weber helped me shepherd the book through some of its most challenging phases. Yasmin DeGout, Nkonko Kamwangamalu, Emily Kugler, James Purcell, Tony Medina, Sheshalatha Reddy, Christopher Shinn, Dana Williams, and Jennifer Williams helped orient the work through critical transitions. And, throughout, Shola Adenekan, Carli Coetzee, Tosin Gbogi, Stephanie Bosch Santana, Kristin Stern, and Nathan Suhr-Sytsma provided inspiring models of what critically engaged scholarship can be.

Thanks are due, as well, to Marc and Naomi Sacks, for reciting poetry at bedtime and teaching me the power of performance to change lives; to Deborah and Dan, for always being there first; and to Ethan, for everything.

Research for *Networked Poetics* was supported by funding from the US Department of Education's Foreign Language and Area Studies Program; Northwestern University's Department of English, Graduate School, African Studies Program, Alice Kaplan Institute for the Humanities, Buffett Institute for Global Studies; and the College of Wooster.

NETWORKED POETICS

FIGURE 1. Protesters outside the state house in Boston, MA, use poetry to connect their demands to a global movement. Image courtesy of Norrie Gall.

INTRODUCTION

Poetry in Motion
READING FOR PERFORMANCE IN THE DIGITAL AGE

No one leaves home
unless home is the mouth of a shark.

THE WORDS APPEAR over and over: in visual representations on Instagram; written on protest signs; in the titles of news stories and opinion pieces. They proliferate in the repetitive logics of the digital, taking on new valences in each iteration, chant, and image. One of the most widely circulated poems of the decade, Warsan Shire's 2012 "Conversations about Home (at a Deportation Centre)," has become shorthand for the trials of migration. The poem draws on interviews that Kenyan-born, Somali British poet Shire conducted with refugees in Rome and London. Their words now circulate globally, digitally deracinated through poetic license (see figure 1). They enable protesters, readers, and writers to mark their own political and affective investments. Across the phrase's republications and repetitions, the poem takes on new valences, drawing connections with the migrant crisis in the United Kingdom and the Trump administration's inhumane policies against migrations in the United States. Shire's "Conversations about Home"—broken into its component parts and recirculated piecemeal—spawned a world of adaptations: performances, visualizations, and rewritings. It has become many poems at once, an asynchronous, multivocal collaboration.

Over the past twenty years, poetry has entered global discourse on an unprecedented scale, facilitated by publication and distribution on social media platforms. These changes have been especially significant for poets from Africa, where shifting communication technologies in the early twenty-first century facilitated new, youth-oriented, South-South literary and activist networks, disrupting the extractive structure of many mainstream publishing industries. The rapid spread, evaluation, and celebration of poetry online creates new literary communities, linked by a common investment in particular literary forms and platforms.

Poetry circulates rapidly online because it is, generally, shorter and therefore easier to reprint and repost than other literary forms: as Nathan Suhr-Sytsma writes of print poetry's recirculation in the postcolonial era, "Poetry's typical concision meant that it could be composed more quickly than long-form fiction and reprinted more widely, whether in little magazines, weekly papers, or mass-print anthologies"—or, comparably, on X (formerly Twitter), in protest, or on the nightly news.[1] Digital poetry operates in parallel with the forms of humor that James Yékú argues mark "cultural netizenship" in Nigeria: by participating in a shared discourse, members of a digital community claim a political belonging that operates within the nation, yet unconfined by the state.[2] Poetic rhetoric roots individual auditors in a shared community across cultural and political spaces.

Networked Poetics tracks the effects of digital publication on poetry's publics in southern Africa. It asks, first, how poetry creates publics; how those publics, in turn, use poetry to launch their claims to political agency; and, finally, what these claims mean for poetry's place as a marker of cultural capital. Throughout southern Africa, poetic forms have historically been used to critique leaders, define social norms, and tell collective histories. During independence movements, poetry offered a rhetoric of affiliation for dissident groups.[3] In the early twenty-first century, as mobile phone subscriptions on the continent rose nearly sevenfold, poetry publication exploded online.[4] The new generation of "born free" writers—a generation who had not known colonialism and apartheid but had lived the failed promises of independence—seized on the transnational coordination enabled first by internet forums and blogs and later by social media platforms.

Digital platforms support and extend literary communities, creating aesthetic networks dedicated to poetry. Their conversations span WhatsApp groups, hashtag channels on Twitter, and open mic nights in city bars. Performance poetry, in particular, draws together diverse literary traditions and formal norms to foster new communities and aesthetic forms. In Africa, where publishing centers were maintained in colonial metropoles and prize programs reflect the values of judges and organizations based in the Global North, social media fills a key gap in arts production, promising popular publication spaces with relatively high levels of authorial control.[5] But at the same time, it imposes new constraints, rewarding only that poetry which can circulate widely, decontextualized, across vast networks.

Even as social media promises to democratize publishing, then, the poems that "win"—from spoken word to Instapoetry and Twitter "micro-poems"—reflect the aesthetics of digital algorithms: they are brief, full of allusions to global popular culture (often US-focused), and often didactic. The rise of digital publication encodes what I call "algorithmic aesthetics": the form literary production takes in response to digital selection pressures created and reinforced by technological sorting structures. Algorithmic aesthetics reinforce the "echo chamber" effect of network platforms, encouraging both look-alike poems and literal re-formations of the same lines. It makes poetry into globally circulatable memes.

Focusing on Anglophone poetry from Malawi, Zimbabwe, and South Africa, *Networked Poetics* argues that social media's aesthetics and logics shape both poetic production and social organization today—that the two are, in fact, inextricable. I examine poetic forms and performance as they intersect with the lived experience of politics and power. In doing so, I track how the logic of social media publication has shaped poetic production across the region, even as the poetry itself has offered new forms of affiliation for ever-mobile, increasingly urban and transnational communities. Doing so reveals poetry's enduring power to call together communities within the confines of digital structures, while raising questions of curation and technological gatekeeping. Where poetic forms have historically been tied to communal formations in southern Africa, poetry today—reshaped in the movement between media yet recognizable in its artistic force—carries collective expectations for community behaviors, articulated and mobilized through public language that operates simultaneously locally and transnationally. Literary form has material consequences: it teaches modes of interpretation and offers means of imagination. Platform-specific presumptions about the circulation and consumption of knowledge shift literary form. And the communities heralded by those forms shift as well.

The Political Uses of Poetry in Southern Africa

I begin this study with a brief overview of the regional history of political poetry in order to emphasize the way digital poetry builds on locally specific poetic forms with much longer histories. In some ways, poetry's digital renaissance is ironic. Poetry in Africa is rooted in orature, intimately tied to the body and performance: F. Abiola Irele writes, "For all their undoubted diversity, the manifestations of the imagination in our traditional societies have one common denominator: they rely primarily on an oral mode of realization. It is this that accounts for the pervasiveness of the spoken word in traditional African cultures," a consequence of which is "the social significance of the literature in the face-to-face situation of traditional societies, which provide the context of its performance."[6] In orature, Ngũgĩ wa Thiong'o argues, "the production line [of imagination] runs from orality straight to aurality; the mouth produces, the ear consumes directly. Historically this goes back to time immemorial and it is still an integral part of the contemporary African reality."[7] Poetry's reliance on sound and rhythm ties it to performance and to the body, even more intimately than other verbal arts. American poet Robert Pinsky writes, "The medium of poetry is a human body: the column of air inside the chest, shaped into signifying sounds in the larynx and the mouth."[8] The shape of the art itself draws on lived experience, built into the bodies of its readers. And its connection to performance makes it a participatory medium, which connects writer and audience in a shared space.

Literary production, and poetry in particular, relies for its meaning on a culturally specific encounter between artist and audience—a specificity that digital publication promises (or threatens) to unmoor. Yet it is precisely that focus on copresence, participation, and synchrony that fits poetry to digital publication. Although many studies of digital literature have highlighted the performative assertions of identity online, I analyze digital publication through the qualities of performance it takes on: its emphasis on shared temporality; the importance of participatory or interactive reception; and broader questions of archival records. Performance charts a space of interactive possibility, within which cultural norms are established and contested: as Ngũgĩ wa Thiong'o describes, "It was in performance and the conditions surrounding it that a well-developed system of oral aesthetics was perpetually generated. The conditions of the performance were themselves inseparable from the very aesthetic they helped to generate"—and remain so. Performance becomes, in April Sizemore-Barber's words, "a method of refraction—of seeing differently." Sizemore-Barber proposes a model of "prismatic performance" that "reflects and refracts the emotional investments projected onto it by varied audiences."[9] If poetry is tied to the body, then online it reminds us of the connection between fingers and screens, individuals and collectivities. Attending to the continuities rather than the disjunctures between poetic media highlights the ways poetry's historical power expands through its encounters with digital media—and the significance of performance to the production of meaning.

Performance focuses attention. And, moving across media, it can act as communal focal point to catalyze frustration into change. This is the power of the chant. In August 2014, the Economic Freedom Fighters (EFF) Party brought South Africa's parliament to an early close as they chanted "Pay back the money," demanding President Jacob Zuma return public funds he had appropriated to build a vacation home.[10] Protesters and citizens throughout the country soon took up the chant to express their discontent with Zuma's administration. The rhythmic chant transformed a dissenting public into a cohesive unit whose voices, together, overpowered Zuma's own microphone-enhanced responses. In 2017, as the extent of the president's corruption became clear, the chants returned, this time reminding the public that impeachment efforts had lasted nearly four years. "Pay back the money," as a poetic speech act, created a community whose shared rhetoric enhanced its participants' political agency, helping to launch the EFF as a major opposition party.

"Pay back the money" drew on a longer tradition of politically active poetry in southern Africa, a tradition that binds individuals within a community through their investment in the poem's message and the repetition of its rhetoric. Performance poetry offers an authorized space of popular critique: the Ndebele praise form of *izibongo* rhetorically enacts a community's political agency; as a praise poet reciting a community's lineage, the *imbongi* establishes the community's bounded existence. And the poem itself asserts a historical precedence for self-organization—an existence defined and reified through izibongo. Given his power to define the community, the imbongi works as both adviser to and single authorized critic of the chief, a mediating voice between the people and their leader.

Popular poetry encodes collective memory, which in turn carries shared values and norms. For Lupenga Mphande, writing of Tumbuka poetic traditions in Zambia, Malawi, and Tanzania, "Memory is considered a collective phenomenon of the individual, and private memory is viewed as suspect. Narratives about the chief's heroic deeds may refer to deeds of individuals, but these deeds are always depicted as collective."[11] Poetic narratives invest the individual voice in communal activity, creating a public through collective claims to belonging. The doer's identity is less important than the narrative in which their deed is embedded and the community addressed in its retelling.

The historical strength of poetic forms like izibongo speaks to the cultural significance of poetry in southeastern Africa. Its spread through southern Africa in the nineteenth and twentieth centuries demonstrates that each of these nations came into being in conversation with the others. During the Mfecane ("crushing" or "scattering") in the early nineteenth century, Ngoni peoples migrated widely throughout the region. Communities that had started out on the southeastern tip of the continent moved as far north as Malawi and as far west as Botswana, unsettling cultural norms across the regions and spreading Ngoni artistic forms.

Migration intensified in the latter half of the nineteenth century, furnishing cheap labor for South African and Rhodesian mines. Migrant laborers didn't simply labor, though: as Lupenga Mphande, Ari Sitas, and others have shown, they brought musical and poetic forms with them to the mines, returning home with new ones.[12] When anti-colonial struggles took hold in the mid-twentieth century, fighters from across the region organized in training camps in Mozambique and Tanzania. During the labor movement in South Africa in the 1970s and 1980s, izibongo entered urban life as an organizing tool. When workers in Durban went on strike for equal rights, and rallies and protests dragged on with little relief, the poet and organizer Alfred Temba Qabula took the stage, performing isiZulu praise poems in support of the strike, entertaining workers and maintaining morale.[13] His work, together with that of fellow labor poets Nise Malange and Mi S'dumo Hlatshawayo, was published in the 1968 anthology *Black Mamba Rising*—one of the few anthologies to highlight the collective, workshop-oriented nature of public poetry. And, although *Black Mamba Rising* could not circulate openly in South Africa at the time of its publication, it was never banned either. The bilingual English-isiZulu text helped disseminate the protesters' rhetoric, promoting the integration of izibongo into a wider array of political events and rallies.[14]

Artists and politicians alike build on recognizable forms to draw together new communities, connected by their shared investment in literary form. Independence leaders across southern Africa adapted literary forms to anti-colonial struggles: in South Africa, *izibongo* connected urban anti-apartheid activists to rural performance traditions. The *pungwe* forms embraced by Chimurenga fighters in Rhodesia blended dance, music, and song to spread the fighters' rhetoric to the villages whose support they required.[15] The *mbumba* developed by the Nyasaland African Congress spread the anti-colonial rhetoric before being used by the Malawi Congress Party to ventriloquize popular support.[16] In Tanzania, poets debated the future of the nation, while *taarab* dances celebrated it.[17] These forms moved with activists: as Rhodesian and South African liberation fighters trained in Mozambique, they shared musical lyrics and chants.[18] Their productions supported the independence struggle, entertaining crowds at protests and disseminating the logic of the movement beyond its urban centers. They used recognized genres to build new communities, inscribing national logics in traditional forms.

Shared poetic genres facilitated the establishment of national counterpublics in key moments of political struggle, but they also fostered the production of coercive national rhetoric in the late twentieth century. In the 1970s in Malawi, President Hastings Kamuzu Banda commissioned songs, poems, and dances as spectacle of popular support; in Zimbabwe at the turn of the millennium, as Robert Mugabe lost popularity following massacres and a failing economy, Zimbabwe African National Union-Patriotic Front *chimurenga* and national festivals, broadcast on the radio, created a shared language of regime support; and in South Africa in the 2010s, as Jacob Zuma struggled to hold power for an increasingly unpopular African National Congress (ANC), his imbongi appeared incessantly alongside him: as Raphael d'Abdon describes, "Some of the oral poetic practices that have survived colonization and apartheid (like *izibongo*) are sometimes commercialized and trivialized by pragmatic, business-oriented artists like [celebrity poet] Zolani Mkiva, and manifest themselves in caricatured renditions of the art of their ancestors."[19] Mkiva's performances strip the laudatory poem of critique and communal responsibility. They become, in d'Abdon's terms, "commercial poetry": appealing to as wide an audience as conceivable while (and by) making as few controversial claims as possible.

Nationalist poetry binds an imagined public through commercial broadcast on state-sponsored television and radio networks. In Malawi, for instance, one radio station served the entire country for nearly the whole of the one-party era, creating a shared rhetorical and temporal experience.[20] These media retained their power well into the twenty-first century. As Winston Mano writes, "Radio has remained the top medium in Africa in the global era because of its ready adaptability to rapidly changing living conditions on the continent. [...] In Africa, radio's main advantage is its ability to overcome communication barriers on the continent: poverty, illiteracy and linguistic diversity."[21] The relatively centralized networks of radio and television broadcast enable a single national rhetoric to emerge in conversation with poetic norms.[22]

Where the Mfecane intensified regional cultural connections and shared media infrastructure solidified them, English colonial rule established common legal forms and education systems—along with shared resistance movements. Today, each is shaped by the cyclical migration of people and the flow of information between them. To speak of one nation in isolation would therefore obfuscate their connections: how social change, political activism, and artistic expression in any one country affect the others. The three countries' independence movements all culminated in an extended period of minority rule (by white settlers in Zimbabwe and South Africa and by implicit Chewa dominance under Banda in Malawi). Malawi, South Africa, and Zimbabwe are formally bound through their commitment to the Southern African Development Community (SADC) in facilitating regional economic and social engagement.[23] All three share English as an official language of governance and education. They share, as well, a postindependence legacy of disappointment and a youth-driven spirit of protest and hope. In each place, a flourishing of music and performance poetry accompanied youth dissent in the early twenty-first century: South Africa's "Fallist" movement led to university and government shutdowns in 2015–16 and encouraged Jacob Zuma's resignation in February 2018. Zimbabwe's intensifying protest movements, perhaps most notably the #ThisFlag movement, facilitated President Robert Mugabe's deposal in November 2017. And, in Malawi, artists placed an increasing emphasis on poetry criticizing the role of international governmental organizations (IGOs) in the country's governance.

Nonetheless, the three countries differ substantially in their ethnic composition, infrastructural investments, and postindependence history. Malawi, which gained independence in 1963, embraced a monoethnic nationalism in its first thirty years. The Malawi Congress Party government, led by President Banda, privileged a Chewa national identity and suppressed others.[24] While opposition politicians in the multiparty era have curried favor with

Lomwe, Tumbuka, and Yao communities through more liberal language policies, the monolingual norms H. K. Banda established have persisted. Since independence, Malawi has retained a predominantly agricultural economy but has become—in part due to the lingering effects of World Bank–enforced structural adjustment policies—one of the lowest income countries on the continent, with among the lowest internet penetration rates in the world.[25] Even though the country has officially embraced English as its language of instruction beginning in primary school, poetry remains predominantly Chichewa, with Anglophone poetry popular in urban areas.[26] Today, Malawi has a multiparty democracy with full enfranchisement, but high levels of corruption have depleted trust in the government and generated nostalgia for Banda's single-party dictatorship.

Zimbabwe, in contrast, has a bifurcated ethnic nationalism under single party rule. Since the advent of majority rule in 1980, the country has been led by the Zimbabwe African National Union—Patriotic Front (ZANU-PF). Mugabe headed ZANU-PF for forty years, until his deposal by military coup and the subsequent installation of President Emmerson Mnangagwa, whose reelection in 2018 was, itself, contested. In his efforts to centralize power and cement his power during periods of unrest, Robert Mugabe capitalized on the tensions between Shona and Ndebele peoples—tensions fomented under British systems of imperial favoritism. Though Zimbabwe exports tobacco and nickel, it regularly faces severe cash and fuel shortages. Its once-strong agricultural economy all but collapsed following farm seizures and international sanctions beginning in the late 1990s. Nonetheless, the strong centralized government allowed the country to invest in mobile infrastructure across its urban areas, with over twice the internet penetration rate of Malawi.[27] Additionally, Zimbabwe has one of the best educational systems on the continent, with a literacy rate of 89.7 percent as of 2021.[28] However, ongoing voter intimidation, media suppression, and limited rural infrastructure have left its citizens effectively disenfranchised.[29] The combination of high literacy and internet penetration with widespread media repression and voter intimidation has made social media and poetry discussions especially important channels for community organizing.

Finally, South African activists, in the fight against apartheid during the 1960s to 1980s, sought to unite the country's diverse ethnic communities under an Anglophone rhetoric that resisted both the Afrikaans language of the apartheid government and the dominance of any one Afrophone language.

This marked a direct resistance to the cultural and linguistic segmentation the apartheid government sought through its Bantustan system.[30] Today, although the country offers instruction in all twelve of its official languages, English is the primary language of instruction, with home language education offered only until Standard 4, or approximately age 9.[31] Following the end of apartheid in 1994, the country retained its growing industrial and mining base. Released from international sanctions, it quickly became one of the strongest economies on the continent, second only to Nigeria.[32] The country's influence has expanded with its economy, as South African companies from fast-food chicken chain Nando's to the media conglomerate Naspers and the financial services group Standard Bank spread around the world. It has also become an educational hub, home to six of the continent's top ten universities.[33] Its cultural influence is commensurate with its economic and educational power: an increasing range of literary celebrities and international festivals are based in South Africa.

The three countries together reflect the broader diversity of SADC: its political leadership, economic inequality, and national diversity. The "mobile revolution" of the twenty-first century has both deepened their connections and accelerated their divisions. The rise of mobile communication decentralizes media networks, launching multiple, overlapping public spheres. Where radio requires direct access to physical waves, digital connection relies only on the shared knowledge of an IP address, the passive complicity of a government uninterested in actively blocking internet access, and corporate interests invested in expanding their consumer base. Digital communication promises to connect rural communities to urban centers and to link urban areas within and between nations. Poems like "Conversations about Home" jump between protest sites around the world, without recourse to its original print publication context. At the same time, old anxieties about national exceptionalism, literary form, and community establishment persist online, in WhatsApp groups and Twitter debates: as Meg Arenberg shows of the Facebook group Umoja wa Washairi ("The Poets' Fellowship"), each of these groups balances "a worldwide audience" with a "wariness of cultural contamination."[34]

Digital networks open a broader audience to more voices within an otherwise limited cultural market. But the digital, as Stephanie Bosch Santana argues, is neither global nor universalizing; instead, it facilitates regional networks of audiences invested in a single story or institution.[35] Performance and poetic forms, in particular, create embodied affiliations that extend the rhetorical strength of literary connection. And even as digital publication has opened more markets to more writers, performance remains a dominant mode of literary reception: most writers find their first audiences at local open mic nights and workshops, where they build a community that can position them in large aesthetic networks. These local spaces afford microcosmic glimpses into the formation of poetic networks. They illustrate how people and words move across nations to create transnational publics with a shared investment in form and agency. And, most important, they show the novel networks that digital media supports: regionally specific communities through which artists develop and promote new literary ends.

Studying literary form in the digital age requires a transnational approach, highlighting regions and networks over borders and spaces. Social media platforms intensify and expand these local connections—most notably for poetry that intersects with issues of national and transnational importance.

Listening for the Poetic Voice in a Networked Public Sphere

Poetry online blends political rhetoric with poetic form, intensifying its connection to social causes. In late 2016, a Lilongwe-based poetry group organized a "Poetry for a Cause" event in support of people with albinism whose lives were under threat. Every week for months, newspapers had carried a new story of a murder or attempted abduction of a person with albinism. The crisis in Malawi was part of a larger trend across Mozambique and Tanzania.[36] The event, organized on a WhatsApp group, advertised across platforms, and hosted in one of the African Bible College's largest auditoriums, was standing room only. In the poems they composed for the event, writers built on terminology developed by people with albinism across the continent and offered a new framework for the issue through which a sympathetic audience could signal its support. The event suggests the ongoing importance of poetry—and particularly performance poetry—in forging communal connections. Poetry, in performance, invested its audience in the language and experiences of the performer. It broadened the affective community engaged at the theater and offered new urgency to a potentially abstract issue. The physical stage became one node through which poetry moved, linking together international problems, cosmopolitan audiences, and local forms within the digital spaces in which it was rebroadcast.

Poetry's ability to call communities together reflects the broader capacity of performance and literary forms to elicit fellow-feeling. As Karin Barber writes, "It is well known that coming together as spectators or auditors of collective cultural events can have the effect of making people aware of the things they share. [. . .] But specific forms of address to dispersed audiences of readers can also play a part in constituting new forms of sociality—forging bonds, generating cleavages or developing people's awareness for their common condition."[37]

Poetry's formal structure, in conjunction with its historical uses, make it an especially potent form for engaging communities and forging bonds online. Its rhythms and sonic aesthetics beg to be read, and to be heard, aloud. Its lyricism offers a unique rhetoric through which disparate groups may find unity or identify their differences. And the particular emphasis on allusion and indirection in poetry invites its audience to invent their own meanings, projecting themselves into its narrative. In performance, poetry highlights the relationship between artist/speaker, audience, and community; in print, it carries their traces. Together, these qualities make poetry a networked form, one that relies on an engaged audience to make its meaning and, in turn, offers its audience new ways to create meaning and communities.

Scholarship on African poetry tends to emphasize literary form's imbrication within broader media networks and institutional systems. In his foundational study of Anglophone African poetry, Emmanuel Ngara argues for a reading practice that accounts for the "complex interaction of historical and social factors, subject matter, theme, ideas and the ideological element"—structures that require critical attention to form, as well as content.[38] It therefore behooves us to attend simultaneously to poetic form, social norm, and aesthetic network, as exemplified in Nathan Suhr-Sytsma's history of twentieth-century poetic networks and decolonial movements across Africa, the Caribbean, and the UK. Focusing on the social factors that influence form, Suhr-Sytsma highlights the role of small magazines, university workshops, and international arts festivals in establishing such poets as Christopher Okigbo, Derek Walcott, and Derek Mahon, whose work would come to define postcolonial canons.[39]

Poetry's remediation carries it through unknowably multiple audiences—the multiple publics to whom African literature has long been addressed, navigating between imagined inside and outside worlds, high- and lowbrows, and the real audiences in between. Poetry is an implicitly public and political form, establishing communities, claiming rights, and performing the nation for a transnational audience. It uses its multicentric address and uneven mediation to create its audience, enacting the role that Eileen Julien has ascribed to the "extroverted African novel." Caught up in "what is assumed to be European or global discourses" so as to "express our common differences," contemporary poetry travels widely, telling stories of difference in order to appeal to an imagined universal human experience.[40] In the mid-twentieth century, poets across Africa, from Christopher Okigbo to David Rubadiri, made use of performance poetry's sonic qualities and communal capacities to compose print poetry that spoke to emerging nations. Where broadcast media stayed under state control, the poetic voice—mediated through print—offered alternative models for communal organization.[41]

Networked Poetics highlights works that, like Okigbo's and Rubadiri's, bridge the live and the mediated. In this, it expands on recent work demonstrating the power of digital cultures in African literary production. Moradewan Adejunmobi's work on poetry in Mali, for instance, convincingly suggests that the rise of mobile networks has supported a shift away from the primacy of print in poetry. Comparing the attitudes of storytellers, slam poets, and rappers, Adejunmobi illustrates the complex interactions between print and performance in contemporary literary culture. The artists she describes "tended to define their activity as verbal artists mainly in relation to the written composition of texts. First, they did not present themselves first and foremost as performers but as composers of texts. Second, their creative texts circulated only through performance, whether such performance was live or digitally mediated. Digitally mediated performance was especially popular with younger male verbal artists. Third, all three types of composer-performer strongly objected to any comparison of their performance with that of the griots/jeli, traditional bards of Mande society. Fourth, they all emphasized the centrality of writing to composition and textual production."[42] Adejunmobi's findings suggest the limitations of an oral-written divide. They encourage us to engage their interstices and overlaps. Digital production enhances the complexity of performance forms.

Of course, poetry has always been networked, responding to a range of influences and addressing multiple publics. These multiple levels of address reflect the "multicentricity" that Jahan Ramazani has identified in postcolonial poetry. Ramazani, insisting on attending to the way postcolonial poetry responds to a range of cultural norms and codes, suggests that we read it in terms of its dialogic capacity: "Cross-cultural poems cannot be reduced to Bakhtin's putative lyric homogeneity: instead, they switch codes between dialect and standard, cross between the oral and the literary, interanimate foreign and indigenous genres, span distances among far-flung locales, frame discourses within one another, and indigenize borrowed forms to serve antithetical ends. [...] Poetry—pressured and fractured by this convergence—allows us to examine at close hand how global modernity's cross-cultural vectors sometimes fuse, sometimes jangle, sometimes vertiginously counterpoint one another."[43] The poem, for Ramazani, is simultaneously local and global: at once the ultimate expression of cultural particularity and an ideal way to transcend difference. Reading poetry as both form and movement, Ramazani offers a method to evaluate how individual works respond to a range of influences to address diverse rhetorical publics.

Adapting Ramazani's vision of transnational poetic productions, I read poetry as vectorized movement: rather than frozen nodes, poems function as links between nodes. I argue that poetry's ability to span in-person and online media makes it a networked art form. My concept of "networked poetics" responds to sociologist Zeynep Tufekci's provocation that the contemporary public sphere is, at all levels, networked. She contends that "as technologies change, and as they alter the societal architectures of visibility, access, and community, they also affect the contours of the public sphere, which in turn affects social norms and public structures. . . . I use the term . . . 'the networked public sphere' as a shorthand for this complex interaction of publics, online and offline, all intertwined, multiple, connected, and complex, but also transnational and global."[44] Tufekci postulates that the contemporary public sphere is implicitly networked—that digital media, and especially social media platforms, have so shaped our everyday experiences that even those publics drawn together without direct recourse to digital networks are, nonetheless, shaped in their wake. All social organization and cultural production is simultaneously digital and grounded.

Tufecki's framing of networked publics expands Michael Warner's reconceptualization of Jürgen Habermas's public sphere. For Habermas, the European enlightenment was enabled by shared access to public spaces of discourse. Warner, in contrast, emphasizes the role of attention over conversation in defining publics. Sharing discursive space invests individuals with a shared community. It creates "talk values" that "allow a structured but mobile interplay between the reflexivity of publics (the talk) and the reflexivity of capital (the value)."[45] In digitally mediated, networked publics, popularly circulated phrases become cultural currency: using a hashtag in the right context, to share a recognizable reference at the right time, marks the speaker's affinities and builds community with the audience they address. Deploying poetic rhetoric (whether Shakespearean or slam) in the proper time and context online positions the speaker as what Yékú calls a "cultural netizen," through "the online performance of citizenship through popular cultures by digital subjects."[46] Similarly, engagement with popularly circulated phrases like "No one leaves home" creates a sense of shared cultural values, invoking a broader public who understand its significance.

Participating appropriately in a hashtag campaign, recirculating a poetic refrain in the right context, or sharing the right moment of connection are means of marking one's knowledge, connections, and rhetorical capacity—in other words, a means of marking one's access to cultural capital. These links between literary rhetoric, community structure, and cultural capital help explain why shifting media technologies have always, seemingly inevitably, provoked cultural panics and shifted literary forms: rising literacy rates in late eighteenth-century England prompted anxieties about gender norms and class divisions, while the rise of community radio and newspaper publishing facilitated the emergence of Pan-Africanist anti-colonial movements in the mid-twentieth century.[47] In each case, new literary forms emerged to address and examine changing social structures. Lynn Hunt, for instance, has argued that changing reading patterns in the late eighteenth century led to the rise of the realist novel, which in turn engendered a shift in human rights discourse; Brian Larkin, similarly, has argued that cinema technologies shaped new modes of leisure in northern Nigeria.[48]

I want to argue, though, that social media represents a change not merely in the quantity of text and readership but also in kinds of distribution. It merges technologies of publication and communication, blurring lines between public and private speech. Algorithms, following functionally unknowable logics, lead poets to emulate one of only a few models for success. The networks that support artistic work change in response to shifting affordances of communication technologies. And aesthetic forms themselves change in response to the networks and platforms that produce and stage them. Poetry has been transformed in the wake of shifting media technologies; understanding its social role and ideological impact demands new analytic modes, from models of mediated virality to frameworks of immediacy and embodiment.

While these phenomena unfold globally, focusing on southern Africa highlights the interplay between local, regional, and global aesthetic networks.

Infrastructure, industry, and individual preference intersect to shape local literary forms. My opening example of "Conversations about Home" is exceptional in its spread across regional networks. More typical, perhaps, is the movement of the slogans #ThisFlag and "Pay Back the Money" through extant communities and local networks, drawn together by overlapping participation at open mics and arts festivals. Poets in local spaces build on shared knowledge and concerns to broaden their audiences and create new communities. For instance, when Malawian poet Qabaniso "Q" Malewezi performed in Durban at Poetry Africa in 2014, his poem "Wikipedia" drew cheers and laughter when he said:

> Power is one of the most addictive drugs
> But is also something Escom
> Doesn't have.[49]

Malewezi's references to Malawi's perpetually failing power services (run by the Electricity Supply Company of Malawi, or Escom) evoke the local power outages in South Africa (where the electricity public utility is called "Eskom"). The allusions give his international audience a seemingly unlikely stake in his message. Through the performance, the borders of Malawian national experience bleed into the South African experience. The poem itself is shaped in its movements across digital media and live performance: influenced by slam poems circulated on WhatsApp, advertised on Twitter, and eventually published to YouTube.

Analyzing digital media's influence on poetry and aesthetic networks reveals how changing media norms influence audience-performer interactions. For Malewezi, the poem's publication on Poetry Africa's YouTube page opened a door to commentary by Malawians living in the diaspora, who otherwise have few opportunities to interact with his work. Today, Malewezi's performance is archived on Poetry Africa's YouTube page. One of the largest archives of African poetry performance online, Poetry Africa's videos are nonetheless subject to YouTube's and Alphabet's terms of use—terms that provide for their removal, should the parent company decide the videos go against its best interest. Platform-specific presumptions about the circulation and consumption of knowledge shape emerging literary forms. The structures of social media platforms, including the newsfeed, the friend list, and the "update," establish rhetorical norms of circulation and iteration. These norms then determine what form rationed discourse and aesthetic products must take online. Facebook's newsfeed, for instance, highlights and expands posts that solicit interaction, emphasizing interactivity; Twitter's search function does not return results older than seven days unless they have been retweeted and thus made new, demanding contemporaneity. On nearly every site, images and videos take up more space than words, so more users embrace multimodal publication to promote their messages.

Although individual platforms' specific affordances may change, the logics inscribed through social media aesthetics are consistent, and they are transforming cultural production globally: writing now emphasizes repetition, interactivity, urgency, and multimodality. Reading poetry in the digital age therefore requires reading for what Safiya Noble has called "algorithms of oppression," opaque structures that privilege certain ways of knowing at the cost of others.[50] Those structures, as Nick Seaver's recent ethnographic work dramatizes, reflect the implicit norms and attitudes of their designers—disproportionately white and Asian men based in urban centers in the United States.[51] And, as the release of Twitter's algorithm in March 2023 indicated, these decisions are not merely the consequence of attention-seeking programs: some, like a bias toward Anglophone writing and generically consistent themes, are hard coded into the programs. Algorithmic curation reinforces American cultural hegemony: those same algorithms affect how a poem circulates, whose networks it enters, and to whom it remains invisible. Poets may find topical freedom publishing to Facebook, but they must contend with the platform's algorithms to get attention. They fit form to platform, for instance by appending images and hashtags to make their work more visible to more people. They prioritize English, reflecting digital anglonormativity, despite the local popularity of Afrophone poetry. Networked poetics, as an analytic method, reveals the strategies with which poets manage the networked media landscape in which their work is inevitably embedded.

Rather than see poetry as either divorced from or the inevitable product of its social environs, then, I consider the range of circulating influences and forces that poets engage or dismiss in their creative processes. Examining very contemporary work through its mediation reveals the continuities between twentieth- and twenty-first-century poetry networks while simultaneously underscoring how poetry's confrontation with new media publication transforms those same networks. The complex circulation of aesthetic form across cultures and regions is not new, nor is artistic collaboration.[52] But, in the context of the networked public sphere, poetic movements incorporate a new type of audience, developing a diffuse yet highly specific address in response to shifting media aesthetics. The digital does not transcend the embodied. Instead, digital interactions, logics, and aesthetics are immanent in lived experiences, even as local networks remain paramount in making meaning.

Site-Based Readings of Networked Poetics

Networked Poetics is organized in five chapters following popular sites of poetic reception: protest rallies, digital platforms, poetry slams, arts festivals, and, finally, the interchange between bookstores and classrooms. If poetry is the matter of my analysis, these spaces are its medium, shaping its form and meaning. Each site constitutes an "edge" of the network, connecting individuals both within a given space and across time. In each space, I combine formal analysis of individual poems with ethnographic observations of its production and reception contexts in order to elucidate the shifting relationship between literary form and reception.

The first chapter explores digital poetry's power to build and bind rhetorical communities across platforms. I examine three youth protest movements that, from 2015–16, constructed alternative forms of national affiliation: South Africa's Fallist movement, Zimbabwe's #ThisFlag movement, and Malawi's university shutdown. All three movements were organized online and realized on the ground. But what sets them apart is their use of popular poetry and poetry videos to promote the cause. Through primary research into the organizing networks on Facebook and WhatsApp, textual and performance analysis, and rhetorical analysis, I maintain that the power and success of these movements demands a circulation-first reimagining of contemporary poetry. In this chapter, I evaluate the chants and hashtags that unite each movement, along with the poetry that emerged from and motivated the movement, to illustrate poetry's rhetorical capacity to establish communities. The chapter lays the groundwork for my argument that poetry online merges with the community it addresses.

The second chapter digs into three of the most popular social media networks to examine exactly how these platforms are used by poets and how they affect the poetry published on them. Each section examines a different, clearly defined group: WhatsApp groups dedicated to Malawian poets; a Facebook group for politically active Zimbabwean poets; and Instagram poetry competitions that sought to support artists during South Africa's lockdowns. Each platform assumes a different community structure and degrees of publicity: WhatsApp's closed groups and private circulation, for instance, contrasts with the open networks and publication norms of Twitter. I use comparative netnography to examine the influence of digital networks and algorithmic structures on literary style.[53] Formal analysis, in turn, illustrates how poets develop and innovate on those structures. These three case studies introduce my argument—elaborated and expanded in the following three chapters—that digital media publication has enforced a form of algorithmic aesthetics across platforms.

As artists seek digital platforms for publication, new strategies for managing audience relationships emerge on the ground. In the third chapter, I argue that formal norms developed and enforced online increasingly shape poetry offline. I trace the development of poetry slams and spoken word organizations in the region, tracking the long influence of Harare's House of Hunger poetry slam on urban poetry communities in Lilongwe and Johannesburg. My ethnographic and performance analysis of specific poetry performances and slams illustrates how poets respond to changing trends and norms, as individual works transform across digital and grounded iterations: the KwaHaraba open mic night in Blantyre, for instance, emphasizes local themes, whereas the Cape Town–based Lingua Franca Spoken Word Movement offers a wholly new, collaborative structure for poetry performance. Slam poetry's popularity and power reflect the complex relationships between literary production and global norms, as forms established on the ground and circulated online are transformed in their movement between spaces.

Digital media heightens the tension between desires for universalist works that address a wide range of audiences and demands for artists to perform locally specific authenticity. These tensions come to the fore in the international arts festival, the focus of my fourth chapter. Examining audience-artist interactions at festivals in Malawi and South Africa, I argue that the imagined cosmopolitanism of the contemporary poet comes into conflict with audience's expectations of an "authentic" performance at arts festivals, staging anew the poet's conscription into the collective logics of the nation. The chapter works through examples of three international arts festivals—Poetry Africa, Lake of Stars, and Tumaini Festival—each of which stages the confrontation between the local and the cosmopolitan, or the national and international, in a different way. Poetry Africa draws poets from across the continent and the world to a South African audience, who are trained and moderated by ushers. At Lake of Stars, in contrast, audiences from around the world gather on the shores of Lake Malawi to see the best the country has to offer—implicitly made to perform their Malawianness for international audiences. Finally, the Tumaini Festival in Malawi's Dzaleka Refugee Camp offers the refugee-artists who perform the opportunity to tell their diverse stories to an audience of Malawians. The arts festival exposes the limits of the cosmopolitanism imaginary in the digital age, as it simultaneously engages with ideals of globalism and fetishizes the national and the exotic.

My final chapter maps the routes by which digital media publication's support of popular reception processes enables the redistribution of cultural capital. Global market forces, mediated through online discourse, have empowered youth poets as cultural mediators. Although a few specific institutions (and poets) still play gatekeeping roles, the distribution of those institutions and roles has shifted. Bringing together literary analysis and social history, I demonstrate how contemporary canons respond to digital norms of engagement. I focus on Koleka Putuma's debut collection, *Collective Amnesia*, which broke through prior barriers in poetry publication and circulation, to illustrate how popular modes of circulation now shape elite forms of valuation. Digital publication has made poetry popular again. But it has done so by enforcing digital norms—demands for quantifiable markets and advertiser viability—on the literary sphere. Rather than removing the elite from the material, digital publication means that material success now legitimizes elite institutions.

Finally, the coda extends the argument's geographic scope to suggest that these phenomena, which are so pronounced in southern Africa, echo worldwide. Through discussions of protest poetry in Ghana, the integration of Instagram poetry into university curricula, and even the appearance of slam poetry at a presidential inauguration in the United States, I argue that the rise of digital self-publication has, however gradually, effaced boundaries between popular and elite literary spaces. I therefore suggest that the popular poetic forms described in the book, shaped as they are by algorithmic forces and global networks, herald a new form of artistic engagement. Popular poetry links its readers to regional literary marketplaces, forcing elite institutions to revisit adjudicatory processes.

A Note on Scope

In addition to the geographic and formal focuses outlined above, this project has two further limitations to note: chronological and linguistic.

First, I limit this book primarily to the period from 2008 to 2020, with occasional reference to longer histories and later resonances as appropriate. My goal in doing so was to attempt a "record of the present," one that tracks the relationship between changing media paradigms and cultural formations as it unfolds.[54] In or around 2008, mobile penetration in Africa crossed 50 percent.[55] By 2020, that number had reached 82 percent across the continent, with 55 percent smartphone adoption within SADC. A relatively smooth, upward trend was suddenly disrupted, in March 2020, by lockdowns in response to the global COVID-19 pandemic. Lockdowns concentrated social, cultural, and economic energies online, driving rapid mobile uptake and dramatically increasing consumer spending on mobile and digital technologies.[56] Poets who were already active online grew that activity; those who were not were often forced to find new ways to engage with audiences.[57] I take the effect of those lockdowns into account, but understanding their long-term consequences exceeds the scope of this book.

To encourage digital development in the latter half of the 2010s, government-, IGO-, and corporate-sponsored projects, from the World Bank's Digital Economy for Africa Initiative to Facebook Free Basics, pushed mobile adoption as a solution to all of the continent's woes, from underemployment to medical infrastructure. The vast majority of these initiatives focused on importing technologies developed in the West (especially in the United States) and in China. In doing so, they implicitly reproduced hegemonic cultural norms—including an Anglocentric bias. The internet is, primarily, based on English. In this, it mirrors global education and economic systems.

This book, unfortunately, reproduces that bias. Although I do seek out and reference poetry in African languages, especially isiXhosa, Chichewa, and Shona, the majority of the poetry and discourse analyzed is in English. There are two primary reasons for this: personal and structural (though, of course, these are entwined). First, my own linguistic limitations and biases, as an English first-language speaker, led me to seek out Anglophone spaces early on. Additionally, as an academic trained and employed in English literature departments in the United States, my professional networks were readily connected to Anglophone literary networks. Second, the global economic and technological structures outlined above, and throughout this project, engender an Anglocentric bias that is especially prominent among educated urban youth—the people with whose poetry and activism this project is concerned. My personal limitations are, of course, enmeshed with the global structural limitations that they reproduce—and to which this project seeks to draw attention. Nonetheless, I hope the outcome does justice to the poets whose work and thinking have guided it.

Poets and Their Publics

Together, these case studies offer a new way of reading poetic production in the digital age—one that takes seriously the fact that digital means of publication and circulation are shaping poetic discourse everywhere, even as most consumers of poetry remain offline. Poetry online connects the screen to the body on the ground. Despite persistent visions of a placeless "web" or "cloud" connecting the globe, as Stephanie Bosch Santana writes, "The fact that distinct digital forms have emerged in different locations tells us that real geographies are still important for understanding their production, circulation, and consumption."[58] The sites of poetry's reception—online or on the ground; popular or elite; hyperlocal or broadly transnational—demand increasing attention precisely because the emergence of the digital threatens to obfuscate their significance. These spaces create communities linked by their attachment to particular poetic forms. The shift in poetry's address has broader implications for all its forms, reconfiguring local works as translocal, mediatized ones; repositioning the audience as active producers in poetry's meaning; and intensifying poetry's already-multiple address. The poems are themselves shaped by site-specific audience expectations, whether in the precarious intensity of the protest, the sociable chaos of regular open mics, or the sacred hush of the arts festival. The digital cosmopolitanism of contemporary poetry thus registers the changing shapes of poetic reception and of cultural diffusion around the world.

CHAPTER 1
Hashtags Become Chants
THE COLLECTIVE POETICS OF PROTEST

THE HASHTAG MAY be the paradigmatic marker of digital discourse. Compounding symbol with word, it renders human connection algorithmically legible. Converting between text and speech, it bridges ground and cloud. Hashtagged and hashtaggable communications extend bodily action from street to screen and, crucially, back to the street. They invite global attention to local discourse. Since 2011, when protest movements around the world consolidated their messages through hashtag channels, the shape has come to emblematize broader debates about changing cultural norms and the rise of new communicative frameworks. Protest poetry today draws on the connective logic of the hashtag to address a networked national public sphere.

Networked poetics, as a form of collective rhetoric, bridges digital organizing and grounded action, mediated by the hashtag. Protest movements illustrate poetry's function as a networked and networking form. On 18 July 2016, hundreds of students marched through the University of Malawi's flagship Chancellor College after the government announced an unprecedented fee increase of nearly 300 percent. Blocking the main tarmac road leading from the college into town, they chanted a direct threat to the Malawian government: "Tinapha Bingu ifeyo / apolisi anapha Chasowa" (We killed Bingu ourselves / the police killed Chasowa) (see figure 2). The students asserted their political power in just two lines, claiming responsibility for the death of the late president, while recalling suspicions surrounding the 2011 death of student activist Robert Chasowa. The regular rhythm of the lines makes them easy to repeat, and the parallel stress patterns of "iféyo" and "Chasówa" make them easy to remember. The chant appeared again and again during

FIGURE 2. Student protesters in Zomba, Malawi, use lines from South African protest movements on their signs. Image from "Mutharika Orders Unima Fees Reduction, Opening of Chanco," *Nation Online*, 4 August 2016.

Facebook as #FeesMustFall, the digital channels that students established to advertise their case, and later, as the movement gained steam, through news reports and stories. Three months later, as Zimbabwean strikers rallied against Robert Mugabe's government and the failing economy, they echoed the student protesters' language. Inspired by Pastor Evan Mawarire's video-poem "This Flag," protesters in Zimbabwe and the diaspora joined their stories through the hashtag channel #ThisFlag. In a media landscape dominated by radio and television, poetry and song produced a rhetorical community unified by a shared investment in the language and proceedings of the nation.[1]

Online, chants and poetry enter into conversation with a youth-oriented, regionalist imaginary of aesthetic production. In southern Africa, social media is mostly used by urban, university-educated youth—a group in whom hopes for national futures are invested. Levi Obijiofor argues that this group is "classified as elite because they hail from elite backgrounds and also because university education is seen as a gateway to securing high-profile jobs and higher social status in society."² Throughout much of sub-Saharan Africa, university education symbolizes the nation's promise, and educated urban youth represent its future. Their disappointment is thus an indictment of the current government.

Concerns about youth activism have crystallized in anxieties about social media, as Rekopantswe Mate identifies in her analysis of "youth lyrics." "In most of sub-Saharan Africa," Mate writes, "there is a fairly common fear that disenfranchised youth might constitute a 'natural opposition' to incumbent governments."³ Mate argues that, faced with seemingly inevitable unemployment, many youths turned to the performing arts as a way to make a living without governmental oversight or interference. Some turned to YouTube and other social media sites to promote and spread their work, building an international audience and promoting dissident messages.⁴ Digital spaces extend their messages both to a local audience excluded by state-controlled media and to a diasporic audience excluded from the state's address.

Since Twitter introduced the hashtag in 2008, popular protest movements have increasingly followed a shared pattern: organized online and realized on the ground, they rely on the mass organization and careful rhetorical management enabled by social media's many platforms. As Elizabeth Losh argues, "Any hashtag always poses a question to the audience. The question that the hashtag asks is 'are you listening?' or 'are you there?'"⁵ Whether hashtag or chant, call-and-response speech gives a mass of people—already invested in an event and a cause but otherwise disconnected from one another—the ready rhetoric of a common language. Chanting creates an embodied connection to the imagined community alongside which protesters chant. Similarly, hashtag channels operate as the primary linking apparatuses that allow disconnected, discontented individuals to come together. Each enables protesters to voice collective complaints about the status quo.

The hashtag helps discourse communities to organize across platforms. By providing a shared language, hashtags enable individuals to mark their positions in a broader community, much as chants and other forms of collective speech do. It operates, then, as a poetic speech act: mobilizing language's symbolic functions to will new communities into being. Like chants, hashtags evangelize: they advertise a cause, idea, event, or affiliation to a broader audience. Yet the hashtag's algorithmic legibility renders them ironically manipulable by broader structures: as Eunsung Kim has shown, the concept of the "trending topic," whose claim to popular opinion validates much contemporary reporting and journalism, is itself controlled by the deliberate curation of Twitter programmers.[6] Hashtags thus mark (and demand) the negotiation between activists and social media platforms. These poetic speech acts bridge digital and grounded communities to produce new spaces of collaboration and paravirtual networks.

In networked protest, the hashtag merges with the chant to offer a rhetoric of affiliation. Together, these two form a new kind of "tactical poetry" that, following Thomas McGrath's framework, is "about some immediate thing" or cause. Tactical poetry, as McGrath describes it, is "not there to *expand* consciousness, but to *direct* it, point it, give it focus." Tactical poetry should have "as much clarity and strength" as possible "without falling into political slogan, clichés, and so on," but "it can at its very worst turn into simply slogans."[7] If hashtags and chants are slogans, though, their success relies on their ability to link the bad tactical poetry with the good. In these contexts, poetic language—its assonance, rhythm, and repeatability—takes on heightened importance. Poetry, hashtags, and chants together produce a rhetoric of affiliation that enables the flow of protest movements between online spaces of organizing and publicity and offline spaces of action and building community.

In this chapter, I follow the rhetoric and forms of poetry, chants, and hashtags across online and offline settings to evaluate their influence on the affective communities of protest. I begin by situating the chant and the hashtag in a longer history of protest poetry in southern Africa, before turning to examine three youth protest movements that mobilized digital rhetoric to organize grounded action. Together, South Africa's #Fallist movement, Zimbabwe's #ThisFlag movement, and Malawi's university crisis model the use of poetic expression in the growth and circulation of grounded protest networks. These movements took advantage of social media's apparent ungovernability and youth culture to launch critiques of the state. The chants and the hashtags of these movements demonstrate poetry's capacity to span the distance between digital organizing and grounded action. Poetry offered a collective language of power and demand that was succinct, rhythmic, and repeatable, linking offline communities to produce networked protests and collective agency. The form's power to connect a diasporic community behind a national cause has been enhanced by the hashtag, which links a collective narrative through specific phrases.

Tactical poetry, acting as a rhetorical link for diverse groups of protesters, sets the stage for understanding the broader social and cultural changes precipitated by digital platforms. The rise of the hashtag as a dominant means of organizing transnational and diasporic protest movements enhanced protest poetry's spread, even as it made protest rhetoric more readily surveilled. Poetic refrains offer a concisely repeatable message by which the protest can be recognized. The hashtag digitizes those refrains to publicize rising protest movements. The chant offers a sense of connection between protesters separated by geography and even underlying motives. And the poetry that accompanies and grows out of it offers a language of affiliation and motivation for those already involved. Through a shared investment in poetic rhetoric, communities formed online can find a voice on the ground, and those taking place on the ground find audiences online. Together, the hashtag, the chant, and the poem operate as tactical poetry. They consolidate grassroots movements by developing a terminology and rhythm through which protesters can identify themselves, recognize one another, and present their demands to the world.

The Tactical Poetics of Protest: The Chant and the Hashtag

Poetic language, including raps, songs, and chants, provides a rhetoric of affiliation. It helps individuals both to name their concerns and to identify others with shared concerns. These diverse forms are linked by their tendency toward repetition, sparse phrasing, and a sense of rhythm and musicality—all of which suit them to mass circulation. Attention to poetry's tactical role highlights the form's social effects: generic references, musical rhythms, and repetition work together to "focus consciousness" to particular ends.

Poetry's rhetorical and political significance comes from its broader capacity to call communities together, innovate on speech genres, and offer new modes of voice connection. Under the British colonial regime, poetry provided a protective discursive space to register complaint and build national pride. In southern Africa, the poet was "entrusted with the divine calling to bless various occasions of significance [and to . . .] notate[] ontological and epistemological histories of certain communities."[8] As Leroy Vail and Landeg White detail, poetry encodes standards for good governance and rightful leadership. *Izibongo*, for instance, offers praise and critique of a leader's ability in terms that connect him to the broader community history. *Mbumba*, in turn, allows subordinate groups to complain about ill-treatment, inscribing norms for proper behavior.[9] Lupenga Mphande describes such forms as "strategic tools for societies in their consolidation and socialization processes. [...] For centuries, singing praises of rulers has been a way of legitimating power and regulating the community in Africa."[10]

The historical power of orature lent strength to independence movements, which adapted oral forms to gather an imagined national community, connected through its collective ethics and its leaders' histories, and to project that community into the future postcolonial nation-state. In Zimbabwe, "popular forms like the *chimurenga* songs of the Zimbabwean guerrillas could be used coercively to ensure peasant compliance even while articulating a liberatory message."[11] Oppositional forces in South Africa's anti-apartheid movement drew on song and poetry, where "poetry as a medium gained popularity after the 1960 Sharpeville massacre."[12] The African National Congress (ANC) began officially supporting performance productions in the mid-1980s, when it launched the cultural outreach group Amandla.[13] Performance brings independence movements into "immediate contact with the public," which, as Augusto Boal writes, enhances "its greater power to convince."[14]

That "power to convince," combined with the mnemonic power of alliteration, rhythm, and rhyme, has made performance poetry a particularly potent organizing tool. Nationalist poetic forms, in particular, offer a rhetoric of affiliation through which marginalized voices could claim political power and through which political power could be consolidated. These forms were taken up by political leaders, who, Mphande argues, "appropriated and deployed the performance skills of song singers and praise poets for political expedience."[15] During his thirty-year rule from 1963 to 1993, Malawi's "President for Life" Hastings Kamuzu Banda solicited both izibongo and mbumba to suggest public support.[16] Under Robert Mugabe's Zimbabwe African National Union–Patriotic Front (ZANU-PF), chimurenga music became a form through which the state co-opted popular support and silenced potential dissidence.[17] In 2017, even as President Jacob Zuma lost his grip on ANC leadership, his *imbongi* introduced each public appearance with his praise.[18] These genres activate a host of cultural norms embedded in both everyday interaction and artistic production. By building on well-known forms tied to the telling of collective history, the issuance of grievances, to the organization of community action, nationalist leaders claimed the support of the people and invented histories for the nation. In turn, dissident activists built on nationalist rhetoric and its familiar forms to create imagined possible futures for the nation—relying on older verbal genres to integrate a possible listening public.[19]

As Benedict Anderson argues, the performative nature of the popular public sphere strengthened developing national imaginaries, which were secondarily inscribed and disseminated in print. Though scholars tend to emphasize the print elements of his imagined national community, for Anderson the nation is a performative undertaking. He writes, for instance, that the imagined collective performance of national anthems ties together an imagined community across the unfathomable space of the country: "There is a special kind of contemporaneous community which language alone suggests—above all in the form of poetry and songs. Take national anthems, for example, sung on national holidays. No matter how banal the words and mediocre the tunes, there is in this singing an experience of simultaneity. [. . .] How selfless this unisonance feels! If we are aware that others are singing these songs precisely when and as we are, we have no idea who they may be, or even where, out of earshot, they are singing. Nothing connects us all but imagined sound."[20] The imagined unisonance of the anthem expands the effect of proximity to incorporate the "imagined community" of the modern nation. The anthem, like the chant and the hashtag, requires many voices for its audition. Singing establishes collective effervescence, bringing the individual along in the felt force of the crowd. It demands a dissolution of the self into the communal, an engagement with collectivities that may be imagined in print but are embodied in the present audience of a performance.

The embodied collectivity of song evokes a harmonious affective community. Like Anderson's prayers and sports cheers, chants bond individuals engaged in a collective endeavor. Such collective speech acts create sympathy between speakers: participants in a conversation become physically entwined, their breath and gestures mirroring each other's. In joint speech, such as chants or prayers, "repetition also serves to accentuate and exaggerate the rhythmic properties of utterances, while repetition of a short phrase can also induce a change in perception from speech to song," creating what Fred Cummins refers to as "collective intentionality."[21] The chant offers individual speakers collective intentionality. Unmediated, it creates physical connections between the individuals inhabiting a space; mediated, as in a radio broadcast or digital discourse, it interpolates new potential publics in its address.

The chant broadens the active community to include those who might share in its "imagined sound." This sound is structured by contemporaneity: occupying the same affective mode at the same moment of time with an unseen other. Poetry's "imagined sound"—whether the internal monologue of the reader or the imagined chorus of the individual singer—binds a local audience through their shared sense of time and space. New communication technologies shift the relationship between publics and rhetoric but retain a focus on shared time. They expand the temporal logic of the newspaper, which Benedict Anderson argued created a shared sense of time for a geographically dispersed, potentially global community. The all-present concept of the "trending topic," for instance, intensifies the temporal logic of the newspaper: it creates a shared time frame through which a digital community engages in shared conversation. In doing so, it ironically shifts the timescale for news reporting, providing journalists a convenient shorthand—"important events"—while obscuring the algorithmic curation that structures their selection.

The chant unifies many voices in a single pronouncement. Its over-enunciated rhythm facilitates participation. Negotiated in real time, between human and nonhuman actors, hashtags "perform the work of assembly as well as the work of speech."[22] They enable protesters to voice their collective complaints about the status quo. And, although their linking function is typically limited to a single platform, their linking logic "push[es] the boundaries of specific discourses," as Nathan Rambukkana has argued of what he calls "hashtag publics": "They expand the space of discourse along the lines that they simultaneously name and mark out." Hashtags—endlessly repeatable, highly malleable, and almost-entirely allusive commentary—shift the logic of coordination, enabling decentered movements to emerge. When hashtags and chants intersect, each works "as a uniting thread of discourse that allows those who use it to feed into an ongoing and evolving conversation."[23] In each case, the language of protest enables the direct interpenetration of online and offline spaces, allowing communities formed on social media to bring action to the ground.

Digitally mediated movements gain traction on the ground through poetry: through the shared investment in the rhetoric of poetry, communities formed online can find a voice on the ground, and those taking place on the ground find audiences online. A close examination of the organizing rhetoric of recent protest movements reveals how poetry—as allusive, repetitive, rhythmic, and sonically oriented verbal art—reasserts its political power in the context of these new media dynamics. The hashtag promises to coordinate conversations, operating beyond the digital realm as a rhetorical move to denote, variously, solidarity, ongoing conversations, or irony. In protest movements, the network effects of the hashtag (its ability to engage a broader crowd than would be privy to any one message) combines with the affective power of poetic speech (the words that define the hashtag) to create collaborative speech-acts.

#FeesMustFall: The Hashtag as Poetry

For nearly four weeks, from 20 March to 13 April 2016, students occupied and shut down the University of Cape Town's administrative offices in the central Bremner Building. In the renamed "Azania House," students—who were protesting rising university fees—reimagined what the university could become. They tutored one another, offered impromptu lectures, and—most striking of all—shared their experiences through poetry. For activist Khumo Sebambo, Azania House "refused external forces of these exclusively [white], mapped space—it promised spatial safety to black identities, which are otherwise formed on precarious grounds. That spatial safety allowed for the imagination of blackness to flourish."[24]

During the Fallist movement, which recurred from 2015 to 2017, students shut down university campuses across South Africa, demanding lower fee levels, decolonial pedagogies, and the decolonization of campus symbolism. They called for Afrocentric knowledge systems that could stand against the university's Eurocentric epistemologies—and they found them, in part, in one another's poems. Poetry's translanguaging, its collective address, and its allusivity marked an alternative to the prosaic forms of the Western academy, which, as Leketi Makalela writes, has historically "operated as extensions of colonial outposts to serve the interests of the former colonisers, while simultaneously stripping the local communities of intellectual stimulation and relevance to solve local issues."[25] For the Fallist protesters, chants established a connection to the nation's celebrated past, while hashtags connected their actions to global movements. Digital media facilitated tactical poetic forms appealing to historical models of national action.

The largest protest movement since the end of apartheid, Fallism drew together a range of disparate concerns—from workers' rights at the University of Cape Town (UCT) to the language of instruction at Afrikaans institutions—to demand labor and human equity in the context of higher education.[26] Following months-long protests at individual schools, the movement expanded nationally in October 2015, after students at the University of the Witwatersrand shut down campus in protest of fee increases. #FeesMustFall protests spread to Rhodes University and UCT the next day, and to universities throughout the country over the following week, as students across the country mobilized through Twitter and WhatsApp to demand that "fees must fall." Their demands quickly gained national attention through the hashtag channel #FeesMustFall, while communication via Facebook groups allowed rapid organizing. The phrase "hashtag fees must fall" became verbal shorthand for the movement. The hashtag trended on Twitter, bringing the movement international attention. On 23 October, after weeks of protest and poor press coverage, then-President Zuma announced there would be no fee increase that year. Schools reopened within a few days, only for protests to begin again a year later, when national fee hikes were threatened on 19 September 2016.

For many protesters, the call of "Fees must fall" was part of a revolution, an inheritor to the anti-apartheid movement of the late twentieth century. One common protest T-shirt read "#feesmustfall" and "#decolonizeeducation" on the front; on the back, it bore the words "The revolution will be black-led and intersectional—or it will be bullshit."[27] Far from acting against the national ideal, however, the protesters presented their actions as enacting those ideals: they often called "Amandla!" (power), a popular rallying cry of the anti-apartheid movement, and even sang the national anthem—a uniquely affiliating rhetoric and rhythm for the nation.[28]

Students' chants drew on historical referents to bind the movement to the nation's history and create an affiliation between the twenty-first century student protesters and their twentieth-century counterparts. Poetry had been a critical part of the anti-colonial and anti-apartheid movements in South Africa, stretching back to railroad strikes in the early twentieth century.[29] During the labor movement of the 1970s, poet and trade unionist Alfred Qabula updated this tradition in his own izibongo, effectively adapting the praise form for an urban environment. His poetry alleviated boredom during strikes while offering a connective logic for the workers' struggles.[30] Qabula drew on workers' calls that dated back to miners' strikes in the 1920s. His work, published in the 1986 anthology *Black Mamba Rising*, together with poetry by fellow unionists

Mi S'dumo Hlatshwayo and Nise Malange, gave rhetorical voice to the frustrations of Black laborers in apartheid South Africa.[31]

Black Mamba Rising also fortified the country's emerging poetry of protest. In the 1970s and 1980s, exiled activists used poetry and drama to build international support. Workshop theater programs integrated poetry, song, and monologue to tell stories barred from official histories.[32] They narrativized the apartheid regime's oppressive effects on individual lives. Programs like the London-based *Poets to the People* relayed these stories to international audiences in the United States and Europe.[33] It was not until the mid-1980s, though, that the ANC officially invested in the arts. With the establishment of Amandla in the early 1980s, poetry, song, and chant—relayed internationally—became a major component of ANC policy. Through the 2000s and 2010s, song and poem were increasingly integrated into mainstream South African politics, as the ANC drew on this politically potent art to present a rhetoric sympathetic to the increasingly unpopular leadership.

Fallist protesters drew on the rhetoric of the anti-apartheid movement in order to suggest that the ANC government under Zuma had betrayed its predecessors' promises. Students directly repeated historically potent chants. They referenced key moments in South African history: at the march on the South African Union Buildings on 23 October 2015, for instance, one sign read, "We will do to the ANC, what the youth of '76 did to the apartheid government," referencing the year that apartheid security forces shot student protesters in Soweto, launching months of violence. The Fallists positioned their movement as successor to the anti-apartheid movement: the ANC government's slow progress, they suggested, hampered their opportunities much as apartheid policies had harmed their predecessors. Chants and songs condemned the year 1994 as an empty promise. The 2012 Marikana Massacre, the first and largest murder of civilians by government forces since apartheid, appeared frequently in chant. In each case, the protesters positioned themselves on the side of dissidents and linked the current administration to the apartheid structures that national leaders had once fought.

Although many of the students' grievances were local to individual campuses, the general frustrations of #FeesMustFall allowed the hashtag and movement alike to circulate broadly and expand rapidly. As Daniel de Kadt has shown, between 19 and 22 October 2015, the hashtag #FeesMustFall expanded nearly fourfold, from 50,000 to 200,000 tweets per day.[34] The channel trended on national Twitter circuits in South Africa, bringing it into dialogue with mainstream broadcast media networks like the South African Broadcasting Corporation (SABC). Such networked attention has an outsized effect: Twitter celebrities' huge followings transform them into virtual megaphones.[35] And these "trends" become, themselves, reportable events: as Kim notes, trending topics increase their visibility, justifying journalistic attention (which fails to account for the recommendation algorithms that determine which topics and terms rise to trend) and thus driving discourse from the closed coteries of the digital realm into the public sphere of broadcast and print media.[36]

The hashtag is "neither fully material nor fully symbolic but rather [. . .] an important agency in the construction of power relations, events and knowledge," one that transforms live speech into networked discourse.[37] As a discursive medium, the hashtag enabled a community with little access to broadcast media to organize local movements and advertise their cause to national onlookers. It carried the rhythm and rhetoric of the chant into the multivocal organizing sphere of Twitter. At the same time, its detechnologized circulation—represented at protests and in poetry—created an affective community across local and national bounds. The chants and images of the protests draw on the rhetoric of the network, reflecting the protest community's formative spaces. As a rhetorical link, the hashtag channel #FeesMustFall spilled over from Twitter to Facebook and even onto such material objects as protest signs and T-shirts.[38] The virtual gathering place it produced extended the discourse of the campus community into a broader national sphere.

The language of decolonization suffused both the protest chants and the poetry performed at fundraisers, in protests, and on videos circulated on Facebook and Twitter. Performance poetry connected the networked discourse of the hashtag to the institutional spaces the protesters occupied. In places like Azania House, politically explicit poetry was interspersed with pieces about personal pain, drawing the individual protesters together in an affective community of dissent. The performance space brought the audience into the poem, demanding either verbal action or visual attention. Recorded by friends, repeated by spectators, the poems continued to reverberate beyond the moment of their performance. In each space, the audience's responsiveness shapes the poem, their reception mingling with the poet's performance in an essentially collaborative production.

Such performance poetry expresses the urgency of the movement itself. In our personal conversations, poets suggested that writing for performance could address much more urgent issues than print, perhaps because it allowed less time for reflection. Poet and theater-maker Siphokazi Jonas, who was a postgraduate student at UCT during the Fallist protests, described the difficulty of crafting thoughtful, reflective poetry during the urgency of protest. "Spoken word, especially in South Africa, is accompanied by this militancy, the urgency of the moment. It's this militant poetry and it's very in your face. It is kind of this second wave of protest poetry, because there is that energy of rallying and creating a community that says, okay, this is how we'd like to forge the present and the future."[39] Performance encourages rapid production, letting poets improvise as necessary to speak with their audiences. Performance poetry, in particular, melds the urgency of chants with the public responsibility of social media.

During the strikes, Jonas collaborated with fellow poet Kyle Louw on the poem-video "Books Not Bullets," which they published on YouTube barely six weeks after protests began.[40] The piece was written and recorded in under seventy-two hours, to be shared when it was most needed. Much like the protests themselves, "Books Not Bullets" was conceived for and through an online community, realized on the street, and propagated digitally. The poem-video tactically renews the story of the South African nation as one of resistance, focusing students' energies through a series of slogans and anecdotes. Through the title—a reference to Nobel Laureate Malala Yousafzai's slogan in her work for women's education in Pakistan—Louw and Jonas's poem situates the violence unfolding at South African universities against the global backdrop of unequal access to education.[41] Evoking the pressing rhythms of slam poetry, the poem actively claims the audience's attention, summoning "the energy of rallying and creating a community" that would respond to the rhythms of the poem and support the emerging struggle.

The poem-video traces the connection between bodies, sound, protest, and hashtag, suggesting that a new wave of protest poetry, one that spans the physical and the virtual, is the proper response to the hashtag activism of Fallism. Throughout the video, Louw and Jonas occupy important spaces on campus, beginning with the iconic steps of the campus's Jameson Memorial Hall. Named after British colonial officer Leander Starr Jameson, Jameson Plaza and Memorial Hall recall the growth of English colonial presence beyond Cape Town. The stairs are the main gathering point on campus and the central focus of every publicity shot. To occupy them is to situate oneself at the campus's physical and operational center. Renaming it, along with other key buildings on campus, was a major demand of the UCT #FeesMustFall campaign's drive to decolonize education. The poets thus occupy colonized territory to map the university along the grounds of contention.

Before the poem begins, shouts and gunshots ring out over a black screen, noises that conjure the disorienting sounds of protest. Against this soundscape, Jonas's voice calls out, "P-p-p-pages." The aspirated *p* mimics the sound of automatic gunfire. Louw repeats the sounds, and the two trade the word back and forth, sounding out its possibilities. Throughout, the rhythm of their speech evokes the rhythm of chants, with unusually strong emphasis on unaccented syllables and a trochaic pattern typical of Anglophone chants. Strong rhymes and assonance make the lines both memorable and repeatable, even as they engage with the rhythms of slam poetry. Jonas opens the poem: "Bookbags, like bookshelves, clutched the spine of a lead magazines, knees / At 45, 60, then 90 degrees," Jonas enhances the aggression of the opening lines by aspirating the hard *b*'s and *k*'s, using her voice to evoke the invasion of "lead magazines." Jonas's performance embodies the threatened student who, under pressure to leave her educational institution, stands her ground.[42]

As the poem develops, Jonas's and Louw's voices entwine in an escalating rhythm that mimics the escalating violence protesters faced, from armed guards on campuses to tear gas and rubber bullets at parliament. South Africa's history of apartheid and present of inequality entwine in a critique of the neoliberal ideology that allows liberation leaders to prosper while maintaining structures of inequality shaped during apartheid. In the poem's final segment, the speakers claim the legacy of the liberation struggle by asserting that police brutality

> will reveal how a liberation after-party betrayed them
> with the blade in their backs. And yet
> It took 39 springs from '76 for revolution's children
> to bloom.

Jonas's breaths interrupt the thought, defamiliarizing the common image of the 1976 uprising, to create suspense as the listener rushes to fill in the line. The audience's imagined responses organize even the static filmed performance.

The video ends back outside Jameson Hall. The speakers block the door as they stare directly at the camera. Jonas gestures emphatically downward and declares,

> These
> fees
> will fall—

Louw joins his voice to hers:

> While we stand tall.

Transforming the slogan's imperative "must" to the declarative "will" situates the movement as an unstoppable force, its collective demands irresistible. Every word is emphasized, every syllable punctuated, pressurizing the phrase's meaning even as the speakers' merged voices evoke the larger protesting public. The poem's conversational rhythm turns to a chant, a call to action. By directing their piece to the audience and using a style typical of live interactive pieces, Jonas and Louw demand their audience invest in their message. They nonetheless claim membership in the national narrative, and their direct gaze constitutes both a challenge and an invitation to the audience: join us.

The poem creates its own public, interpellated through the circulating phrase "Fees Must Fall." The hashtag inaugurates an individual into a community while defining the community's structures and values. It functions as what Judith Butler calls "excitable speech," or speech that incites action without acting itself. For Butler, excitable speech, like the insult and the nickname, situates the addressee within a collectivity: "By being called a name, one is also, paradoxically, given a certain possibility of social existence, initiated into a temporal life of language that exceeds the prior purposes that animate the call."[43] The hashtag allows users to identify themselves within an aspirational community, which has been shaped by shared values, experiences, or emotions. Tagging a tweet, an image, a video, or a poem positions the object, its author, and its viewers alike in a conversation delimited by collective uses of the hashtag's unique linguistic marker. Constituted within a community and within the limitations of censorship, the individual is empowered to name and thus shape the community within which she operates.

"Books Not Bullets," in this context, augmented the familiar songs of struggle to offer a rhetoric of affiliation through which protesters could mark their support.[44] It connected the legacy of the anti-colonial struggle with ongoing global struggles for educational equality. The hashtag links the affective community of a national—and, eventually, international—protest movement. Separated geographically, the protesters found motion through the mediatized language of the hashtag, which draws them together rhetorically and links them digitally. South Africa's Fallists show the power of a hashtag to call a community to action, as well as the importance of poetry in maintaining community support.

#ThisFlag: Poetry as Hashtag

The nationalist message of the Fallist poems was central to their success: they claimed to better realize national ideals, rather than break them down. By aligning their demands with the government's professed goals, they suggested that national policies ran contrary to their official goals—and they did so through the poetic refrains of hashtags and chants. This structure typifies twenty-first century protest movements: Zimbabwe's "This Flag" movement and Malawi's university crisis of 2016 similarly used poetry to call for a national future that aligned national ideals to the experiences of urban youth. Like protest movements in the United States and Nigeria, these demonstrations called out the state for its failures to enact its own promises. Their chants and hashtags offered alternative visions for organizing social life. Such poetic rhetoric articulates a national counter-imaginary. Hashtags, in turn, broadcast that rhetoric to a transnational public. The #ThisFlag movement—one of the most sustained threats to ZANU-PF leadership in the twenty-first century—began with a single video-poem posted to Facebook. Pastor Evan Mawarire's poem-rant seized on broadly recognized national symbols to insist on a populist revision of governmental policy. This Flag's symbolic reclamations launched a viral hashtag movement that transformed national politics in a famously repressive national space.

Unlike most protest movements, #ThisFlag began with a poem. On 19 April 2016, Mawarire sat down at his desk in Harare, fed up. Despite his success offering marital counseling, Mawarire had been struck by the country's cash shortage and was left unable to pay his children's school fees. He wrapped the nation's flag over his shoulders, sat down in front of his computer, and recorded a video he titled "This Flag: A Lament for Zimbabwe."[45] The three-minute video he then posted to Facebook went viral, gathering over one hundred thousand views in its first week.[46] Later that day, the poem was published to YouTube, where users offered their interpretations and posted response videos. As the post's popularity grew, Mawarire organized a twenty-five-day series of protest videos, each one airing grievances or documenting the state of the country. Others posted response videos and tweets linked through the hashtag channel #ThisFlag. Those responses soon overtook Mawarire's original post to guide the conversation. The social media strategies of the protesters extended the movement beyond the borders of the nation and beyond the control of the state, linking protesters across Zimbabwe and the diaspora. Their direct action, culminating in a series of protests and boycotts in July 2016, brought Mawarire's rhetoric to the ground. As a poem, "This Flag" builds on traditions of politically active poetry in Zimbabwe; as a social media link, #ThisFlag builds on contemporary organizing trends; and as both at once, the refrain created a unique rhetoric of affiliation through which a collective poetry of resistance emerged.

The poem's spread, popularization, and transformation demonstrate poetry's capacity to motivate collective action by reframing national rhetoric. Since 2000, Zimbabwean President Robert Mugabe's ideological campaigns, combined with his regime's practices of censorship and political suppression, had made his leadership a crucial part of Zimbabwean national identity. His leadership, in turn, came to stand in for the broader legacy of the anti-colonial struggle, framing any resistance to the ruling Zimbabwean African National Union-Patriotic Front as anti-independence. These images were cemented in musical galas and songs that "mediated a narrow national imaginary that served to legitimize continued reign of the ruling party."[47] Broadcast over radio and television, songs in support of Mugabe created a ubiquitous language and rhythm of support for the party in power. Mawarire's poem offered an alternative vision of the nation, one that Zimbabweans picked up and responded to in their own pieces before rallying together in multinational protests.

"This Flag" is instructive not only in its use of social media to promote collective action but also in its use of formal norms to encourage audience interactions and feedback. Mawarire subtitled his video, "A Lament for Zimbabwe," suggesting that the nation's story was one of tragedy and that his words would be an expression of his personal grief at the nation's fate. But in the video itself, he doesn't simply mourn Zimbabwe; instead, he offers an alternative vision for its future, providing hope even as he tears down the narrative promoted by Mugabe's regime. His refrain, "this flag," punctuates the poem, recentering his claims after each emotional peak. It is simultaneously slogan and prayer, condemnation and supplication. Like the piece itself, the refrain is simple, multilayered, allusive, and deeply hopeful, enabling the audience to find themselves in his narrative.

Mawarire's poem resists dominant partisan narratives, which imagine ZANU-PF as either the heir of the anti-colonial movement or a monolithically oppressive power, so as to break through what another poet called "our culture of silence" on political concerns and frustrations.[48] The piece's first half breaks down the flag's official symbolism, which projects a rosy picture of Zimbabwe at odds with many of its citizens' experiences. Pointing to the strip of red dividing the flag, Mawarire complains: "The red, they say that that is the blood. It's the blood that was shed to secure freedom for me, and I'm so thankful for that. I just don't know, if they were here, they that shed their blood and saw the way this country is, that they would demand their blood be brought back. This flag." Even as he accepts certain elements of the national symbols—the importance of the flag, the meaning of its colors, the value of memorializing martyrs—Mawarire rejects the official reading of those symbols. His rhetoric focuses on the future he imagines for the country, rather than the present he rejects: "they" who tell at the outset become "they" who have passed, subtly transferring authority from the false prophets of the regime to the true martyrs of the nation and, thence, to the speaker who imagines and ventriloquizes their responses, and from him to the protesters who would take up his call.

Having vacated the nation's symbols of their official meaning, Mawarire substitutes his own. The poem's second half reclaims authentic patriotism by reframing what the country could be. It begins by asserting the speaker's own interpretations of the flag: "I look at the green and think to myself that it is not just vegetation, but the green represents the power of being able to push through soil, push past limitations and flourish and grow. This is me, my flag." Accepting the color's official meaning while rejecting its implications, Mawarire reimagines Zimbabwe's future in order to reinterpret its present. The writing evokes the country's post-2000 struggles with floods, droughts, and political disaster leading to famine and rising prices. But Mawarire finds pride in Zimbabwe's present as a site of resistance: through his symbolic reclamations, the green becomes "the value of this land," the red "the will to survive," and the black "that . . . which we emerge from and shine." By focusing on the people of the nation rather than on the land of the country, Mawarire empowers a Zimbabwean nation to "flourish and grow" beyond the boundaries of the state. Although the original "they" still hold authority, "we" are Zimbabwe's true resource—and, reminded of that, "we" secure the power to resist.

As it ends, the poem enacts its own central proposition, forming a collective "we" from an alienated "I" and "they." It thus produces an alternative image of the nation's past, present, and future. Mawarire closes the poem by calling explicitly for mass action: "Quit standing on the sidelines and watching this flag fly and wishing for a future that you are not at all wanting to get involved in. This flag, every day that it flies, is begging for you to get involved, is begging for you to say something, for you to cry out and say why must we be in the situation that we are in. This flag. It's your flag. It's my flag. This flag." The closing makes Mawarire's experiences parallel to those of his viewers and reframes "this flag" as "my," "your," and thus implicitly our flag—not an abstraction of the state but a possession to be claimed and managed by its people.

For Mawarire, poetry offered an especially apt response to Mugabe's regime. The president had gradually, over his thirty-five years of rule, co-opted anti-colonial and independence-era poetry for his cause.[49] Throughout the twentieth century, music and song furthered the demands of the fighters by affectively engaging a broader community in the language of their movement. As John Kaemmer describes: "Songs in the [guerrilla] camps served to instill in the guerrillas a clear idea of the goals of the struggle and the requirements of being a disciplined fighter. [. . .] Music was thus an important means of mobilizing the energies of the guerrilla fighters."[50] The combatants used the music to draw local communities into their cause. Music, song, and dance functioned as symbolic markers of the cause and helped further their goals. Stephen Chifunyise suggests, "This dynamic use of the diverse and popular forms of indigenous performing arts, for instance traditional dance, ritual dances, poetic recitation, chants, slogans, songs and story-telling, enabled the combatants to mobilise the peasants to articulate their opposition to the settler white minority regime."[51] Blending traditional rhythms and instruments with contemporary melodies and lyrics, chimurenga music promised to link Zimbabwe's diverse peoples. The lyrics themselves helped define an emergent Zimbabwean national identity against the remnants of Rhodesian rule.

Following independence, ZANU-PF used these songs to claim the legacy of the independence struggle. Writing about Zimbabwean hip-hop and censorship in the early 2000s, Wonderful Bere argues: "Taking its cue from the chimurenga music of the frontline, the government turned to music to raise morale in the impoverished country, publicize government programs and rally people behind ZANU-PF. We, thus, continue to see music used as a tool for communication and mobilizing support for a political cause. Even government ministers recorded their own music supporting the government and ZANU-PF."[52] The Zimbabwean state didn't merely co-opt this tradition: they formalized it. Beginning in the early 2000s, annual national galas used poetry, theater, song, and dance to celebrate the state. These galas frame contemporary events in the state's favor, as Stephen Chifunyise details, to produce "drama that appeals to a wide cross-section of the Zimbabwean society as well as one that is easily adaptable to the theatre-in-the-round formation dictated by the structure of the Harare International Conference Centre where the gala is presented annually."[53] They form part of a broader apparatus of state control—not merely suppressing unfavorable works but actively producing, promoting, and disseminating favorable ones. The Zimbabwean state transformed artistic practice into political spectacle, a performance both of its power and of popular support.

Mawarire's poem-video builds on a performative image of the nation, one tied to the musical and poetic traditions that Mugabe's regime had appropriated. The refrain was so effective that it was adapted by his opponents, who rallied around the rival hashtag channel #OurFlag. Online, #OurFlag was popularized by Jonathan Moyo, then minister of education, who was among the most prominent defenders of the ZANU-PF government on social media. Moyo's tweets declaimed, for instance, "It's #OurFlag, the #PeoplesFlag vs #ThisFlag campaign founded & funded by #US & #EU Ambassadors. *Hande tione* [Let's see]!"[54] Moyo inverted the common phenomenon of political resisters adapting state rhetoric to suit their own ends to suggest ZANU-PF's more direct claim on the flag.[55] By offering an alternative performance of national identity, Mawarire invites a dialogic imagination of the national community, one that depends as much on the citizens' performance of connection as on the state's presentation of it.

In many ways, social media itself—its ungovernability, its supranational address, and its attachment to youth cultures—heightened the threat of the #ThisFlag movement. Through social media networks, Mawarire could reach rural areas and diasporic citizens to address a national audience that exceeds the geographic boundaries of the country and the peripheries of state censorship. As the movement took hold, Mawarire called for a two-day national strike through the hashtag channel #Tajamuka (We Rise). Protesters organized their work through the encrypted texting service WhatsApp and publicized their complaints and protest through Facebook and Twitter. Social media was such an effective organizing tool that the government restricted access to many social media sites, including WhatsApp, in the hours leading up to the 6 July demonstrations.[56] The organizing channels #ZimShutDown2016, #Tajamuka, and #ThisFlag, which spoke respectively to the protest's action, its goal, and its symbol, trended on Twitter, making them more visible to more people.

Protests continued on 7 and 8 July. Banks and shops were closed, and dozens of protesters were arrested. President Mugabe called for them to stop, claiming that Mawarire himself was an agent of Western governments. After the national strike, government attention turned against Mawarire, who was arrested and jailed on charges of inciting violence. Threats against and arrests of politically dissenting artists were not uncommon in Zimbabwe under Mugabe, but Mawarire's international fame and popularity aided his release, as people rallied outside the courthouse to support him. Following his release, Mawarire left for South Africa—by 2017, home to between 100,000 and 2 million Zimbabweans. He remained there for several months, giving speeches at many of the major universities, rallying support and assuring conationals that the movement continued.[57] Carrying the flag on his back, his movement across nations echoed the poem's movement across social media channels, enacting the digital cosmopolitanism of his political claims.

The movement's use of social media enabled diasporic Zimbabweans, scattered as far as South Africa, Great Britain, the United States, and Australia, to participate. Many even organized satellite protests on "national stay-away day." Social media, as well as the language of the movement, appealed to an important sector in Zimbabwean resistance politics: urban youth groups, frustrated with the country's "predominantly gerontocratic" mainstream politics looking for "their own counter-publics, where they can openly articulate their socio-economic and political grievances, as well as counter the hegemonic political publics."[58] Mawarire has repeatedly asserted that social media is both a natural and the dominant form of communication for young Zimbabweans. In an interview with SABC, Mawarire said that he started the movement on social media because, "for my generation, it's a very natural way of connecting and of communicating."[59]

YouTube, in particular, emerged as a key platform for protest in the #ThisFlag movement. Privileging the individual content-creator, YouTube linked each hashtagged concern to a potentially infinite movement. Between May 2016 and June 2017, over seven hundred videos tagged #ThisFlag were posted to YouTube. These include Mawarire's own recorded statements, news reports trying to explain the events, and sympathizers' responses to Mawarire's call.

Comments on these personal videos are nearly universally supportive of the movement, typified by verbal applause like "wow" or "kkkkkkk."[60] And where the news videos are primarily in English and Mawarire's personal videos are in English with sprinklings of Cheshona, the personal responses tend to be Cheshona and Sindebele, as are the comments in response, marking users' diverse cultural investments.[61] The use of local languages enables a continued attachment to the specificity of the national project amid the transnational circulation of these digital objects. It suggests outreach toward and engagement with a digital diaspora. Even as the hashtag mutates with its many authors' engagement, its underlying connection to the poetry of protest and to the building of community inheres in all its uses, creating an overarching lyrical connection for its many publics.

Popular personality Amanda Habane's video, "Feeling emotional. Being tear gassed in my own country. #ThisFlagzw," is typical of responses to Mawarire's video.[62] The title—simultaneously confessional, emotional, descriptive, and connective—puts the video in conversation with the #ThisFlag protests even as it maintains her individual experiences working to drive the country forward. The video features a lone speaker, framed in close-up, who speaks directly into a camera which she appears to hold herself. She uses few gestures, except for emphasis, and directs her attention to a listening and attentive "you." Alongside its title, the video's form imagines the content-producer as an everyday citizen, with access to the same limited technologies and platforms as her viewers. Somewhat unusually, Habane's video calls out Mugabe directly—not for his failed policies but for his age. She looks into the camera and demands: "How do you run a nation with outdated—outdated minds. [. . .] How do you run a nation when you are an old bag, an outdated version, and you actually refuse to update yourself. The world is going this way—the world is becoming digital. This is a new era. You need fresh minds that can work better, that can see better."[63] Here, Mugabe's blindness to digital technologies marks his obsolescence: Habane suggests the country cannot operate properly in the modern, digital landscape with such old, "outdated" leaders. For many protesters, like Habane, social media offered rhetorical weapons that rejected Mugabe's leadership as out of touch. As a gathering place for those looking to resist Mugabe's rule, social media became a symbol for an imagined, youth-oriented, democratic nation.

The #ThisFlag movement showcases poetry's power to produce grounded action and broaden the scope of national publics. Through the networked authorship of the hashtag, #ThisFlag channeled national anxieties, fears, and angers into a single international movement—one linked through social media and mediated through poetry. The hashtag organized previously isolated concerns under a single umbrella; it provided a rhetoric of affiliation broad enough to incorporate a wide range of sympathizers; and it created a literal link to bring them together. The human microphone effect of social media and protests—where each post and each voice becomes audible as people share it, repeat it, and use their own reach to promote it—quickly spread Mawarire's poetic call to arms, producing a potentially democratizing movement. The piece's lyricism kept it alive at home: in a country that had around 25 percent social media penetration, the direct hashtag channel was insufficient to build a movement's strength.[64] The slogan "This Flag" was a deeply poetic one: its brevity and allusiveness make it broadly relatable. In its poetic malleability, the refrain becomes an identity and a marker of affinity. Social media's organizing strategies and connections to poetic logics extend offline to shape protest movements on the ground.

Malawi's University Crisis: The Chant as Networked Poetics

The entwining of digital media and popular politics speaks to broader shifts wrought by the networked public sphere: as Zeynep Tufekci writes, "The whole public sphere, as well as the way movements operate, has been reconfigured by digital technologies [. . .]. This reconfiguration holds true whether one is analyzing an online, offline, or combined instantiation of the public sphere or social movement action."[65] Digital technology doesn't simply shift communication structures: it changes expectations about public relationships, whether the functioning of democracy or audience/artist relationships.[66] In Malawi, which had less than 10 percent social media penetration, the strategies of social media protest—emphasizing affiliatory rhetoric, youth empowerment, and populist nationalisms—shape the poetry and position of protest.[67]

In late June 2016, Malawi's struggling Ministry of Education announced a rise in university fees from K275,000 (USD 379) to K400,000 (USD 551). The new fees would take a third of an average Malawian family's annual salary.[68] Since 1969, when "President-for-Life" Hastings "Kamuzu" Banda first opened the national university, official discourse in Malawi had emphasized higher education as key to success. The fee hike represented an attack on economic progress and social mobility. In response, students at Chancellor College staged a protest against Malawi's President Peter Mutharika, bringing the fees crisis into the public eye.

Barely three months after #ThisFlag had shaken Zimbabwe's political landscape and a year after #FeesMustFall had first challenged South Africa's higher education systems, student protesters in Zomba blockaded the entrance to Chancellor College carrying signs that called for a "NATION WIDE CAMPAIGN" and read "#UNIMA University Education 4 All, Fees Must Fall" (see figure 2). Adopting the language and symbolism of digital protest, the students aligned themselves with a global resistance to austerity policies and international pushes for free education. In their responses to the events, students used strategies derived from social media movements, alongside poetic imaginations of community formations, to transform traditional media communications. This shift reflects a trend Philip Auslander observed, wherein "the general response of live performance to the oppression and economic superiority of mediatized forms has been to become as much like them as possible." Their chants and protests put the hashtag to rhythmic purpose, using the threat of digital attention to pressure the Malawian government into rolling back the fee hike that would have further threatened their already-limited access to higher education.

Prior to the students' action, the *Maravi Post* and *24News Malawi*, the nation's two major online news sources, had each carried one article noting the fee hike; the *Daily Times* and the *Malawi News*, print news sources with high market penetration, had each carried two articles. Following the protests, however, each publication featured front-page articles on the fee hikes across multiple days, and online publications promised hourly updates on the breaking news.

The broadcast and print news outlets' coverage reflected the social media logics of the protesters: they published popular voices and even quoted Twitter in their regularly updated discussion of the events. Older media forms acceded to the more intensive mediatization of digital platforms. Contemporary broadcast news responds to social media just as twentieth-century theater responded to film: first by imposing older forms on the new, and later by incorporating new forms into the old.[69] New media discourse penetrates traditional media and performance forms. As students compelled Malawian citizens to confront the nation's future, they turned to a globally ascendant media form. Becoming "as much like [digital forms] as possible" entails structuring discourse to enable ready incorporation into digital formats: protesters use hashtag phrases in everyday speech; print media reproduce digital logics by emphasizing popular opinion as itself news.[70]

The students' movement, which was largely organized through WhatsApp groups, brought together protesters and their supporters by way of a shared poetic language and the urgent, interactive logics of social media, as reflected in the offline hashtag campaign. The poetry of student chants carried with it the Malawian legacy of politically resistant poetry. At the same time, the movement reimagined poetry and protest alike through new media paradigms, offering novel strategies for reinvigorating a legacy of youth protest through poetry.

Politically active poetry is woven into Malawi's history, its legacy continually evoked in government sessions, corporate board meetings, and even commercials. During his thirty-year rule, H. K. Banda co-opted praise poetry traditions to craft a political image in line with his desire to return to an imagined, neotraditional Malawi.[71] The Censorship Board, established in 1966, placed strict limitations on the materials that could be published or disseminated. In this space, the Malawi Writers' Group—founded in 1970 by a group of young poets at the University of Malawi—offered a surprising outlet for political dissent. Such Writers' Group poets as Felix Mnthali and Jack Mapanje developed a rhetoric of dissent that partially protected them from the president's wrath even as they mocked him. At the same time, the Traveling Theatre—founded by scholar David Kerr and dramatist Christopher Kamlongera in 1970—brought these discussions beyond the university through a "Drama for Development" model. They worked with local communities in southern and central Malawi to create theater that spoke to pressing concerns. The company would submit partial scripts with the Censorship Board, but "since the actors were all very skilled at improvisation, during performance they would ad lib lines that were not in the script submitted to the Censorship Board."[72] Such improvisation drew on work songs and shared metaphors to make its meaning.

These artists expanded the tradition Vail and White identified by using the relatively sanctified space of song to launch their critiques. The poetry of the Malawi Writers' Group—a writers' workshop originally formed at Chancellor College to encourage the production of Chichewa poetry under Kamuzu's own instructions[73]—famously built on local forms while making use of the obscuring tendencies of high modernist poetry. Then censored and now canonical, Malawi Writers' Group poets took advantage of poetry's ambiguity and layered meaning to produce an alternative image of the nation's present and future. The poetry of the group, along with the popular songs and dance of dissident musicians, inspired protest movements in the 1990s, creating a political culture mediated through poetic discourse.[74]

Following the beginning of multipartyism in 1993, though, print poetry embraced "universal" themes: praising God, admiring the nation, and instructing children.[75] Popular twenty-first-century "newspaper poetry" promises a prescriptive life: respect your parents, study hard, worship God, and your life will come out well—promises belied by the country's official unemployment rate of over 20 percent.[76] As Kerr writes, "It was no longer necessary for Malawians to use the obscure allegory of poetry or drama," and John Lwanda even "speculates that the 'writers' tradition in Malawi' could 'only really thrive in adversity.'"[77] Print and broadcast media did embrace a more conciliatory and moralizing attitude, but politically critical poetry did not disappear. Rather, it turned to the stage.

In the twenty-first century, performance poets comment on current events and bring up topics that would be all but unprintable in Malawi's self-censoring publishing houses, which many writers feel will not publish materials that could offend the country's conservative Christian population. Despite low literacy rates and the bemoaned "dying reading culture," Malawi saw a surge in poetry performances and poetry radio shows in the 2010s. Performance poetry provides an inexpensive and accessible avenue for mass communication. Poetry's imagery shifted from obscure to transparent, and its presentation transitioned from written to performed, yet the form has retained its critical potential.

For younger poets, poetry's dual roles of entertainment and instruction are fruitfully melded in performance, producing easy-to-follow narratives with highly polemic messages, whether about proper sexual behavior, prejudicial superstitions, or domestic violence. Robert Chiwamba, among the best-known young Malawian poets, explained, "Whenever we need change, poetry can also be part of it, just like music."[78] For Chiwamba and his peers, poetry's connection to political change comes from its accessibility: poetry is part of the rhythm of everyday life, and its power does not benefit from interpretive difficulty. Much of the most popular poetry in Malawi takes a similarly conversational approach, suggesting that the power of poetic language derives not purely through its formal elements but also through its use and reception. In other words, poetry operates contextually: as Karin Barber has shown more broadly of the popular arts in Africa, the popular is typically understood as an "interstitial category—neither traditional nor modern, but hybridizing both and constantly inventing new things."[79]

Popular poetry in Malawi is marked by its repetition, allusive style, polemic messaging, and engaging performances, making it well suited to digital circulation and regular remediation. Yankho Seunda, a poet and radio DJ who runs an Anglophone poetry radio program in Malawi, described bringing his audience into a call-and-response poem "just to get people along with your performance," fully engaging the audience at every turn.[80] Because of Malawi's low internet penetration rates and social network use, most poems are first received in communal performances. These performances join the poet's and audience's voices to produce a collaborative poem. Audiences deepen their emotional attachment to a poet's message simply by being called on to repeat it. In this sense, the poem and the chant alike are drawn together in a call-and-response style of collaborative production reinforced in hashtag channels. When popular Malawian poets declined to record poetic commentary on the university crisis—many of them citing fears of political reprisals or informal blacklisting—the chants themselves became the poetry of the moment, moving forward both political rhetoric and aesthetic urgency in the development of communal protest practices.

In July 2016, in the first days of the university crisis, students massed together on campus, physically occupying the space they risked being financially forced out of. Their collective chanting offered a rhetoric that could unite them and their supporters against the government policies threatening their continuing education. Students chanted, "Timcheka-cheka Mutharika" ("We will chop down Mutharika")—both laying the blame for the fee hike at Mutharika's feet and suggesting that youth would determine the country's future. The chant is structured as a call and response: one student projects his voice above the shouts and drumming of his co-protesters to declare, "Timcheka-cheka" ("We will chop him down"), and others respond to confirm the target, "Mutharika." A threat to the president's body, understood as a vow to cut him down politically, became a way to confirm group commitment, a shared political rhetoric through which to shape group identity.

Most of the students' chants followed a similar call-and-response structure: one or two callers begin a phrase, and others pick it up, carrying the original message forward with their voices. The most successful chants are rhythmically simple, with one dominant foot repeating; lyrically repetitive, no longer than four or five words per line; and sonically compelling, with hard consonants that encourage over-enunciation. In Felicia Miyakawa's words, protest chants must be "sung or performed *by* protesters, not *at* them."[81] Social media content production and reproduction mirrors the chant structure: an originator proposes collaboration, and its success or failure relies on others' willingness to build on it, to lend their own social and bodily presence to give it meaning. Such call-and-response forms, whether performed live or online, invest the audience in a received message, maintaining an ongoing interaction as in conversation, whereas those chants no one repeats fade on the basis of that failure.

The students' chants illustrate the power of poetics in protest. "Timcheka," for instance, is brief. It voices a collective "we." Its rhythm—three trochees that carry across the call and the response—urge the chant forward, landing on an upward inflection. It has few repeating sounds, so that newcomers can join easily. And it has an empowering message, declaring a collective agency that overpowers established political structures.

The chant, as speech act, enacts its promises. The collectively chanted "we" produces a counterpublic whose existence challenged President Mutharika's power to frame national narratives. As "tinapha Bingu ifeyo / apolisi anapha Chasowa" ("we killed Bingu ourselves / the police killed Chasowa") calls attention to the state's failures, "Timcheka-cheka Mutharika" imagines a future within the present moment. The present-future of the chants grants the speakers discursive power where, politically and materially, they have very little. The immediate future tense of "timcheka," combined with the historical memory of "anapha," produces an alternative narrative of Malawi's national structure and political circumstance. In chanting "Tinapha Bingu ifeyo / apolisi anapha Chasowa" and "Timcheka-cheka Mutharika," students launched a direct challenge to Peter Mutharika's government, reminding him of the specific power of protests to destabilize his party and his presidency.

These chants offered internal critiques of Malawian governance, yet others marked students' attention to a transnational community of protest. Cycling through the chants was the inevitable refrain that "Fees must fall." "#FeesMustFall" was also printed on many of the signs students carried, alongside the more specific, "We say no to fee hikes at UNIMA." The signs, like the English chants, were at least partially outward looking. They occurred most frequently in highly public moments, as when then-Second Lady of the United States Jill Biden attempted to visit the Chancellor College campus. The English chants and signs, in conversation with the Chichewa ones, signal a general engagement with and investment in a regional rhetoric of resistance. This rhetoric spread through and beyond social media sites to produce a transnational consciousness of generational change.

Even as it was primarily a grounded action, reported on and promoted through offline mainstream media outlets, the protests of the university crisis built on the strategies of movements organized and promoted through social media. Student protesters worked on the ground, but they levied their claims through an appeal to a shared national history and future, building on the transnational protest cry "Fees must fall" as well as older chants from protests against single-party rule in the 1990s. The students' chants evoked recent national embarrassments and suggested their position as intensely political agents. They thus furthered the claims of both transnational movements and immediately local imperatives.

Unlike the South African and Zimbabwean protesters, relatively few Malawian students turned to the frontstage, public-facing networks of Twitter and Facebook to voice their concerns. Instead, they used backstage channels to organize protests and establish shared rhetoric, via the peer-to-peer mobile messaging service WhatsApp. WhatsApp, unlike Facebook or Twitter, does not directly facilitate the development and maintenance of networks. It functions as an international, data-based service, allowing individuals to connect privately on mobile phones via text, much like SMS does. Before Meta acquired the messaging application in 2014, that privacy was WhatsApp's primary draw: its end-to-end encryption has made it a popular form of data transmission in general, particularly among organizers of protest movements across the world.[82] The groups are private and require an administrator to add each new member directly. WhatsApp provides channels for organizing and administrating closed groups—not publicity and marketing venues.[83]

The students used digital rhetoric and platforms to organize grounded action. But rather than use social media to publicize their work directly, they extended its logics—of immediacy, interactivity, and populism—into the traditional broadcast media that still dominated in Malawi. In addition to spectacles well-suited to television and radio broadcast, they gave interviews and encouraged reader-response publications in newspapers. News outlets invited alumni, students, parents, and other university affiliates to "weigh in," presenting their remarks as though without commentary. Their coverage of the events follows the interactive demands of social media, where countable interactions and constant updates are necessary to produce meaning. Major news websites promote such expectations: the *Maravi Post*, for instance, highlights newness and popularity in the right-hand column, with sections dedicated to "Latest Posts" and "Most Popular" embedded in the site's architecture and accompanying every article. These forms, along with the Twitter feed embedded directly below them, remind the news viewer of her position as part of a crowd and in a highly specific moment. The driving paradigms of social media—popularity and recentness—have made their way into traditional media paradigms, and it is these paradigms that the protesters made use of in their work.

Students' collective voices build on earlier models of poetic action to produce a new, socially mediated urgency in the offline Malawian public sphere. Social media and digital reporting remain a potent part of the offline protest community's imagined public, evoking international affinities even as individual chants focused on convincing a specifically Malawian audience. In his analysis of social media's effect on information architecture, Geert Lovink argues, "Real-time signifies a fundamental shift from the static archive toward 'flow' and the 'river.' Who responds to yesterday's references? Time speeds up and we abandon history. In a 24/7 economy, we transmit tweets while the visible part of the archive diminishes to the last few hours."[84] In their efforts to stay "up to date" with the chants and demands of the protesting students, traditional news media reproduce the logic of social media. The poetics of engagement which dominate hashtags and chants come, as well, to define traditional media efforts.

The Poem as Social Form

The viral circulation of poetry on social media enables grounded action for both immediately local and broadly transnational communities. Digitally mediated rhetoric changes public discourse nationally: in South Africa, the hashtag #FeesMustFall gradually became shorthand for an alternative vision of the nation's future. The hashtag—primarily a means of linking online conversations—functions in these contexts as both chant and poetic refrain. It calls into being a community that exists across on- and offline spaces. The tactical poetry of these movements can even shift the boundaries of the imagined national community: Mawarire's original poem inaugurated a vision of Zimbabwean nationalism beyond Mugabe's ZANU-PF; #ThisFlag, in turn, interpellated diasporic Zimbabweans into the core of the national community. Tactical poetry, whether chant or hashtag, redoubles the linking effect of digital media: it offers a connective rhetoric through which to find identity and mark popular support.

Poetic language creates a shared rhetoric of affiliation, allowing protesters to bridge backstage and frontstage arenas of action. Moving between spaces, sites, and applications, chants and hashtags finesse their address to alternately encourage those who already support them and seek support from onlookers. Hashtags jump across platforms and media, as the networked public sphere shapes national discourse offline. Social media networks and the hashtags that link them rearrange prior media forms. In Malawi, digital aesthetic norms shape traditional media discourse as well. The use of hashtag-inflected chants in protest and poetry brought youth demands to national attention. In a region politically dominated by older generations, social media platforms amplify youth voices. They shift the political balance of national identities by centering otherwise dispossessed communities in national conversations.

Poetry's allusiveness facilitates this movement, offering a doubled address that appeals simultaneously to insiders and outsiders, while its presence on social media produces an alternative community structure that relies on and assumes the mutual availability of grounded and digital interactions. By providing a shared name, hashtags enable individuals to mark their positions in a broader community, much as chants and other forms of collective speech do, while supporting cross-platform organizing. It operates, then, as a poetic speech act: mobilizing language's symbolic functions to will new communities into being. Their movement illustrates how poetic speech acts bridge digital and grounded communities to produce new spaces of collaboration and para-virtual networks.

Poetry—produced and circulated online; presented and received on the ground—can shape national discourse. But it is shaped, as well, through para-virtual literary networks that rely, in part, on social media platforms. These privately owned digital publication and communication networks increasingly play the role of media infrastructure: facilitating communication at a broad scale while controlling its shape. What do the affordances of messaging platforms like WhatsApp mean for the literary networks that rely on them? How do the curation algorithms of such publication spaces as Facebook and Instagram influence the form of poetry that circulates through them? In the next chapter, I turn my attention to the platforms themselves, exploring how poetry communities instrumentalize social media platforms and what their algorithmic affordances mean for literary forms. Digital media transforms the nature of literary reception and, with it, the publics poetry creates.

CHAPTER 2

Commenting in Community
POETRY'S DIGITAL AESTHETIC NETWORKS

THE RELATIVE EASE of publication on social media has opened up new opportunities for regular collaboration and communication, amplifying an ever-changing set of voices. At the same time, though, the aesthetics of digital media demand specific literary forms, in response to the particular structures and norms of individual platforms. If, as Howard Becker writes, print poets "depend on printers and publishers [...] and use shared traditions for the background against which their work makes sense and for the raw materials with which they work," digital poets depend equally on programmers and network cables that support a committed coterie of listeners, commenters, curators, and reposters.[1] How do mobile technologies influence the networks that form around poetry? What does it mean for those networks to move, in Stephanie Bosch Santana's words, "paravirtually"?[2] To what extent do social media algorithms determine poetry's audiences? And how has poetry itself changed as a result?

When I first met Zimbabwean poet and arts organizer Linda Gabriel in December 2016, I asked how she publicized the poetry she wrote and the events she organized. She told me she uses Facebook to reach colleagues she had met during international travels, WhatsApp to maintain those connections, and YouTube to publish videos of her performances. She relies on these digital networks, she explained, for their relative stability.[3] All poets survive on the strength of their networks, but in southern Africa, where uncertain economies render local networks unstable and often require that poets move internationally and, sustaining strong regional connections is vital. College-educated youth, who are among the most likely to write and publish poetry digitally, frequently move between areas and countries for jobs and

FIGURE 3. Hear My Voice's Poetry Relief Fund paid poets honoraria to perform online during the pandemic. Image provided by Hear My Voice.

education. That regular circulation of people limits the potential strength of geographically bounded networks. Instead, poets turn to the relatively constant connections of social media, where individual users' profiles remain stable and where even deleted interactions leave a trace in a broader network algorithm.

Digital platforms facilitate translocal aesthetic networks. "Aesthetic networks," following Eiko Ikegami's coinage, consist of individuals within a larger social group who are linked by their attachment to and training in a particular art form—training that allows them to enter an art-producing group.[4] Aesthetic networks embedded on social media platforms, though, produce art in relation to the platform's affordances. And, in a networked public sphere, group formation and artistic production alike are predicated on the algorithmic curation of social media platforms. This is not to say that digital platforms are the only space of organization: rather, as Santana writes of what she calls "paravirtual networks," often the "most important work happens offline, in a physical space, rather than a digital one."[5] Nonetheless, artists' interface with digital networks opens new possibilities for and places new constraints on cross-platform collaborations. Digital aesthetic networks cultivate shared social and literary norms on emerging media platforms.[6]

Social media platforms offer relatively stable and consistent points of connection. The network effects of individual platforms like Facebook and WhatsApp help writers connect to growing digital audiences by concentrating users in a few specific areas. In Malawi, Facebook contacts helped me find open mic nights and poetry performances. Each program, I soon learned, had its own WhatsApp group, which connected poets during the week or month between events. In 2020, when the COVID-19 crisis precipitated lockdowns and social distancing across Africa, digital platforms became the singular means of maintaining community and advertising poetry around the world. Poetry events and publications proliferated online: the South African independent publisher imphepo press, for example, hosted the "21 Days of Poetry" event series on YouTube, inviting poets to share poems of comfort. The daily videos offered a sense of rhythm in an increasingly disordered life under lockdown, as well as a feeling of comfort and connection amid displacement and isolation.[7]

In this chapter, I examine the interface between aesthetic networks and platform structures. To do so, I track digital aesthetic networks across three social media platforms, each of which represents a paradigmatic element of each of three countries' poetry scenes: WhatsApp facilitates the small groups that define Malawi's poetic networks; Facebook use highlights the need to circumvent governmental oversight in Zimbabwe; and Instagram's capacity to move works across platforms connects dispersed communities in South Africa. The three networks represent three models of social media publication networks: closed publication to closed networks on WhatsApp; semi-open publication to personal networks on Facebook; and diffuse publication to an unknowable audience on Instagram (IG). Each platform is extensively used in all three countries, and the divisions between them are far more porous than this chapter's structure implies (marked not least by the fact that they are all owned by Facebook-parent corporation Meta): poets often post identical content across platforms to foster as much interest as possible. By separating these platforms out, I seek to identify their particular connective capacities and aesthetic frameworks but do not want to suggest that they operate atomistically. Each platform alone provides an incomplete picture of each nation's poetic networks, but together, their differential use illuminates the role of social media platforms in contemporary aesthetic networks throughout the region.

This chapter positions social media platforms themselves as agents in aesthetic networks, emphasizing the influence of digital affordances and algorithmic curation on contemporary literary networks. Algorithmic sorting promotes poetry that mirrors social media's structure: fast-paced, immediately accessible, personal, and interactive. These poems, shaped by the aesthetics of their platforms, in turn influence audience expectations about how a poem should look and what a poem can do. On social media, regular engagement (through comments and likes) and recirculation (through shares and reposts) ensure that a successful poem will be repeated and renegotiated across individual interactions. Social media allows users to comment on, critique, recontextualize, and even revise the poetry they encounter. The platforms' multiauthorial and interactive capacities have enabled an alternative, extensively networked and intimately social, form of social media art. As art worlds become networked and aesthetic networks go digital, the poetry they produce and the worlds they imagine are increasingly shaped in conversation with the platforms that host them and the algorithms that structure them.

Digital Aesthetic Networks and Algorithmic Forms

Social media platforms do not simply offer new publishing outlets for African writers: they change the communities that form around literature and the cultural imaginaries that emerge from them. In 2015, when Malawian poet Qabaniso "Q" Malewezi sought to promote a new album, he turned to YouTube to publish and circulate teaser videos; solicited his Facebook community to find artists to perform at his launch tour; and advertised events on Instagram. Malewezi is a tremendously influential arts organizer in Malawi; his mentorship has inspired a generation of young performers.[8] To expand his mentorship networks and poetry audiences, he relies on digital platforms that place their own structural demands on literary form. For Malewezi's poetry to gain traction, he had to reconfigure its form for each new platform:

an audio recording became a stylized video on YouTube, a conversational request on Facebook, and an image macro on Instagram.[9] Through digital aesthetic networks, like the ones Malewezi organizes, artists collaborate to produce new literary forms—but those forms are constrained, in part, by algorithmic curation systems, which determine what content is shown, when, and to whom.

This is a shift from digital forums and listservs of the early 2000s, which promised to connect writers from across the Global South to new South-South networks of circulation. Binyavanga Wainaina, the founder of the influential literary space and magazine *Kwani?*, paints the listservs and blogs of the 1990s as spaces of freedom and expression, where writers could find one another across national and geographic bounds.[10] Those networks offered a new imaginary for literary production. "For most writers—regardless of their status in the literary world," Shola Adenekan suggests, "the digital space provides an alternative to mainstream ideologies, and an opportunity to create new forms of expression."[11] Early advances in digital publication promised three significant departures from traditional print publication: (1) wider access to new audiences; (2) new structures to experiment with; and (3) direct collaborations with other writers. Specifically, Adenekan argues that "the internet allows [African writers] to reach readers and lovers of African literature in ways that could not have been possible in the world of book publishing. These young people use innovative means to make the internet space theirs, and they are using new digital tools to enhance the potential of African literature."[12]

For African writers, marginalized in global publishing networks, digital networks advance a model of artistic production as fundamentally collaborative, emphasizing the collective far above the individual. Digital aesthetic networks, specifically, position the individual artist in a dynamic community of aesthetic production: in contemporary groups, like the premodern Japan that Ikegami describes, "the greater part of artistic and literary endeavors [. . .] consisted of group activities in which participants were at once producers and recipients of aesthetic productions."[13] The fantasy of horizontal communication online reflects this model: a group speaking together to produce new forms. Within the fluid openness of an art world, aesthetic networks presume and enact shared expectations of artistic production and reception—norms that delineate proper behavior and mark potential for innovation. Online, group expectations form in conjunction with platform affordances and algorithmic curation.

The "network," which Patrick Jagoda conceives as an aesthetic as well as social form, is "never a static structure [but instead] an active flow among interlocked vertices." The metaphor of the network renders tangible the "webs of linkage, fields of affective possibility" that draw individual cultural objects together.[14] The dominance of "network thinking" in the twenty-first century has led, seemingly inevitably, to a recursive power analysis: "If, in a 'networked world,' the most powerful are the most networked," Ben Etherington challenges, "then to focus on networks is [to] choose grounds of relation and comparison that favour the powerful. [. . .] Networks instantiated with the aim of bringing about transnational cultural empowerment either shine brightly before encountering the organizational fatigue that comes with a lack of resources or they are conscripted by the networks of power that they had hoped to circumvent."[15] Etherington's critique is twofold: first, that a focus on networks will inevitably reflect the futility of resistance; and second, that it freezes dynamic subjects into static nodes. The focus on nodal interactions makes authors into objects, caught in a hegemonic web.

These transformations have deepened with the rise of social media platforms. In contrast with other publication structures, social media combines communication with publication; lines between closed and open, public and private, communication dissolve. These platforms are especially important in Africa, where the extractive practices of colonial-era publishers based in London, New York, and Paris, together with international laws that limit the accessibility of books, resulted in what Sarah Brouillette calls "the underdevelopment of postcolonial publishing" in Africa.[16] The mobile revolution means more readers can access popular texts through mobile phones, decentering prior models of literary consumption. This expansion allowed literary communities across the continent to define digital norms of their own.[17]

But, beginning around 2003, corporate capture gradually concentrated audiences in fewer and fewer spaces. The network effects of such social media platforms as Twitter, Facebook, and Instagram launched the careers of poets like Rupi Kaur and Warsan Shire, who capitalized on the platforms' branding focus to build celebrity status. Unlike the relatively open spaces of early forums and listservs, though, social media platforms rely on algorithms to organize and curate the work they host, implicitly promoting some voices and muting others. These curatorial algorithms shape communication patterns: after Facebook began prioritizing images, poets began posting their work as image macros; after the platform stopped recirculating posts that received too many "angry" and "sad" reactions, users began responding to friends' stories with more "care."

Each of these functions—of prioritization, circulation, muffling—is enacted by algorithms that are, at base, unknowable. Most social media sorting algorithms use machine learning, which means that the programmers may set certain objectives and limitations, but the algorithm "learns," over time, what processes within those limitations will best achieve those objectives. Nonetheless, their goals and limitations will reiterate the values, norms, and presumptions that the programmers who define them take as a given—norms their users may not share.[18] The public release of Twitter's algorithm in March 2023 pointed to the influence of these norms: while the algorithm strongly weighted predicted user engagement in modeling how much to promote a tweet, other factors—including the tweet's language, its use of media, and its thematic similarity to the user's other tweets—suggest that the programmers bring their own. Twitter's release of its algorithm was a unique occurrence, confirming that previously perceived effects were, in fact, intentionally programmed. The effects of algorithmic curation are felt by all users but known to none.[19]

Together, these three aspects of algorithmic curation—its functional opacity, cultural specificity, and tremendous effects—have shaped literary norms online. As algorithms structure what posts are promoted when and to whom, these platforms create new, always-changing aesthetic norms. Aesthetic forms are intimately tied to the social worlds and networks that produce them—and these worlds are, increasingly, shaped by digital functions: as Facebook algorithms change, so does the poetry they recognize and promote. Poets decide how to structure their work not only to appeal to themselves and their audiences but also, increasingly, to the algorithms that will determine their circulation on each platform.

The fantasy of social media publication as a liberatory, or democratic, space persists: Mike Chasar argues that social media poetry "stems from this same matrix of impulses—the desire to recapture an authentic originality and to locate and curate source texts that are unencumbered by traditional authorship—while shedding the colonialist approach to composition and related acts of racial or cultural appropriation."[20] Digital publication, as Chasar argues, centers the relationship between reader and writer. Yet the "colonialist approach to composition" has not disappeared; rather, on feed-based platforms like Facebook and Instagram, it has been replaced by opaque algorithms that systematically reward work that elicits interaction.

Producers operating under such conditions of uncertainty guess at what work the algorithms will reward. The embrace of aphorisms and allegory to appeal to as wide an audience as possible; the use of visual forms to try to punctuate the flow of content online; the popularity of the fortune cookie-size "micro-poems" that fit on phone screens—these are all the outcome of writing contorted to suit algorithms. These changes have accelerated in the wake of COVID-19 lockdowns. As creative energies focus online, the power of recommendation algorithms grows to shape both literary form and the art world. Algorithmic aesthetics come to the fore in digital aesthetic networks. It is therefore imperative to understand how dominant media forms resonate in unmediated art and how algorithmic aesthetics can emerge. This comes through even in manually curated digital aesthetic networks like those of WhatsApp groups.

Networked Publics and Networked Forms in Malawian Poetry Groups on WhatsApp

WhatsApp, a mobile-first messaging application owned by Meta, is the most popular messaging application in the world. "A smartphone application that enables people to share information directly via their phones," WhatsApp has been critical in facilitating diasporic care networks globally.[21] But WhatsApp is not a social media platform per se but a messaging platform based on mobile networks, where an individual user's profile is defined by their cell phone number. Instead of using algorithms to curate user-created content on individual feeds and databases to facilitate connection between users, it enables those with direct links to one another to communicate individually and organizes their chats chronologically. The program's relative popularity comes from its early embrace of three key features: first, the link to cell phone networks; second, customizable data settings, which allow users fine-grained control over the application's costs; and third, its end-to-end encryption.

These features have made WhatsApp especially popular in Malawi, where unstable infrastructure and relatively strong mobile networks demand creative approaches to organizing. Malawi's struggling economy has led many of its educated youth to seek employment abroad.[22] Poets move between cities, make international connections through festivals and social media, and leave the country for months or years at a time. So at the same time as poetry appreciation, production, and promotion have grown, the communities that support it have dispersed. But mobile infrastructure, unlike physical infrastructure, is relatively strong. Poetry groups hosted on WhatsApp thus enable young Malawian poets to build community and gain support across increasingly dispersed regional networks.

These WhatsApp groups are highly active, posting dozens if not hundreds of messages each day that signal, debate, and help define the current position and future directions of Malawi's ever-growing youth poetry scene. Chats include organizing discussions such as "Kaya amwene [*And you guys*] . . . . . planning of publishing an anthology of real traditional Chichewa poems with all what people are talking about in it . . . . . Zikakhala za recorded zi ine ndi [*Everything that's recorded with me*] content and style based not adherence to strict rules and regulations . . . . . . These for me impede creativity."[23] These discussions abut utilitarian advertisements like "Oh so by the way please like the [Facebook] page and share with friends and family!"[24] WhatsApp provides a sheltered space for debating frequent claims by established poets that the youth have nothing to add, a community for innovating new poetic genres, and a forum for discussing literary practice.

The relatively tight network structure of WhatsApp groups encourages innovation within clearly defined constraints. They bring poetry to a broader audience and enable newly collaborative genres to emerge. As Karin Barber predicted in 2007, "Electronic media greatly expanded the potential public initially opened up by the press"—and fundamentally changed that public, as "this broad, all-encompassing address to an unknown, dispersed and heterogeneous audience required a new kind of textual transparency."[25] Such direct conversation between writers and readers places new demands on writers' time and potentially constrains them to their readers' demands.[26] Even though WhatsApp's publics are private, its international infrastructure expands poets' potential interlocutors. The platform creates closed circuits within a potentially infinite network. It opens texts to constant commentary and remediation, through near-instant editing, copying, sharing, and conversing. In this sense, the text enters a real-time dialogue through and within the interactive framework.

Online chats engrain patterns established in face-to-face interactions, even as they mediate group behavior and enable group formation between those interactions. The constraints WhatsApp places on communication structure new, networked aesthetic forms in dialogue with user expectations. The poetry that writers produce on and for WhatsApp follows the logic of the platform itself: closed, connective, and collaborative. The allusions are highly specific. Responses are rapid. Poems are short and easy to read. Though repetition is limited, quotation is regular. As more young poets capitalize on WhatsApp's connective capacities, the networked poem has begun to remap the connections on which the country's poetry relies. The interactive capabilities of WhatsApp—allowing users to define communal expectations, respond to one another's poems, and create collaborative poems—represent a mobile alternative to the face-to-face poetry and writing workshops that remain popular in Malawi.

These groups are quietly, almost invisibly, transforming a nation's poetry. Two contrasting but representative poetry WhatsApp groups—Lilongwe Living Room Poetry Club (Living Room) and Sapitwa Poetry's Artists (Sapitwa)—reveal the centrality of such discourse to contemporary Malawian poetry. Living Room's chats are organized around a weekly open mic night in Lilongwe; Sapitwa, by contrast, was organized around a poetry website, www.sapitwapoetry.com.[27] A small number of contributors guide each group, checking in multiple times a day and maintaining group expectations. But the two groups differ in their style and focus. Living Room members write almost exclusively in English, chat mostly about in-person events, and rarely share poetry. On Sapitwa, on the other hand, members write in Chichewa frequently, have conversations focused on disseminating information, and share or critique poetry in nearly a quarter of conversations. Together, these two groups indicate the range of opportunities that WhatsApp participation affords Malawian poets: from linking in-person groups during the offseason to providing entirely new venues for online groups, supporting collaboration across geographic space and temporal distance. In both cases, WhatsApp groups filled key gaps in communication and group formation, while reproducing many of the hierarchies—poetic, linguistic, and social—present in local networks.

The connections that WhatsApp draws across regions and maintains within local spaces mirror those of extant social networks: because the program lacks a searchable database, instead connecting users only through their phone numbers, it implicitly prioritizes one-to-one connections, solidifying relationships built on the ground. As it does so, though, it reconfigures the form that aesthetic networks take. In Malawi, this means that aesthetic networks are increasingly organized along class, generational, and linguistic lines, rather than primarily geographic ones. Additionally, the platform grants administrators the power to approve users and dismiss transgressors. They can manage the poetry posted in each group, giving users a template for proper styles and responses. This shared understanding transforms participants into an audience. They take on what Barber calls a "co-constitutive role" in producing the text's meaning, "made palpable by the audience's visible and audible participation."[28] Where live audiences provide immediate feedback, the close-knit personal connections of WhatsApp groups carry expectations of direct responses. The speed of reception and response directly engages the audience in its composition, as does the feedback that follows. WhatsApp's social and cultural affordances deepen generational divides in poetry while enabling youth artists to establish strong networks in a diffuse art world.

The conversation and feedback patterns in each group reflect their distinct positions within a broader Malawian poetry world: Living Room members tend to share poetry and receive feedback during their weekly meetings and therefore use WhatsApp to coordinate events; Sapitwa is a purely digital group, so its WhatsApp channel functions as a virtual open mic, where poets can share and receive feedback on early work. In places where geography, economy, and climate make in-person networks difficult to maintain, WhatsApp networks serve the purpose Heather Inwood has ascribed to in-person events in China, "giving geographic shape to poetry communities and generating aesthetic developments, one-off incidents, and long-running sources of content that have in some cases irrevocably changed the course of contemporary poetry."[29]

WhatsApp's always-on capacities create potential links between all users at all times, intensifying long-standing networks. Group members expect regular participation on the platform, so groups host a wider range of conversations than occurs at in-person events. Nonetheless, discussions of poetry tend toward straightforward support over critical feedback.[30] On 10 February 2017, for instance, when a Sapitwa participant posted a poem entitled "Intense Affection," three people responded within minutes: one with fire emojis, another complimenting the "Zabwino [*very good*] heavy" poem, and the third claiming "John wayambapo . . ." [*John is getting going*].[31] Some groups debate current issues in the poetry scene, asking what it means to be poets in this cultural moment, what counts as poetry, and what poets should be doing. In addition to these poetry-specific discussions, members use the groups to share and discuss regional news, sage or humorous advice, and philosophical concerns. The WhatsApp groups function as both issue-specific forums and general venues drawing together individuals invested in one another's well-being.

The platform's near-exclusive emphasis on written commentary underscores linguistic divisions in the country's poetry worlds. In Malawi, the official languages, Chichewa and English, have become lingua franca, to the disadvantage of nationally minor languages including Chitumbuka and Chiyao.[32] Yet Chichewa's use is slowly decreasing, or blending with English use, as more and more young people—who are officially educated solely in English beginning in secondary school—enter Malawi's poetry scene. Moreover, digital technologies globally tend to default to English, contributing to a broader Anglocentrism in technology discourse.[33] These mechanical and cultural structures have encouraged an increasingly Anglocentric poetry scene among youth poets in Malawi, even though a large portion of the country's population speaks little or no English, and indeed, attendance tends to be much higher at Chichewa poetry events.

Language use is of particular concern for Malawian poets, relatively few of whom write regularly in multiple languages. Their language choice marks concerns about their connections to literary traditions, broader audiences, and possible recirculation. Although none of the groups I worked with used one language to the exclusion of the other, patterns of language use marked broader demographic differences, reflecting larger trends toward Anglophone writing in Malawian literary production. Sapitwa and the Living Room, each of which is made up predominantly of young poets based in urban areas, represent this shift and its attendant anxieties remarkably well. On the Living Room, English dominated almost all conversations, with only occasional stand-alone interjections in Chichewa. On Sapitwa, in contrast, language changed with conversation topic, so that responders would continue in whatever language the initiator used, and language shifts often marked topic shifts. The difference in language use can, again, be traced to differences in the groups' poetic investments and origins. Sapitwa is organized by Robert Chiwamba, who founded the poetry website in part to promote Chichewa poetry. Living Room's founder, Q Malewezi, writes and performs primarily in English. Although Malewezi mentors younger poets in both English and Chichewa, the Living Room Poetry Club has remained a predominantly English event: on the six occasions I attended, chat and commentary moved smoothly between languages, but most of the poetry performed was in English.

Despite these differences, the two groups produced similar poetry and criticism, because each group constitutes one node in the overlapping networks that make up the broader Malawian poetry art world. Such overlapping networks require the cooperation of many actors to produce collective aesthetic productions and sensibilities through shared "conventions known to all or almost all well-socialized members of the society in which it exists."[34] WhatsApp groups rely on broader conventions, but they are themselves venues for developing and enforcing emergent poetic conventions. Along with enforcing conventions for proper behavior—no swearing, no gossiping, no forwarded spam—they also innovate conventions for poetic production and responses.

In each group, when participants posted the texts of their poems, at least three others responded with accolades, complimenting the author on their piece or representing their reading experiences with emojis of clapping hands and crying faces. For Sapitwa poets, the goal was critique and improvement. Readers pointed to specific elements of pieces they liked—individual words or evocative moods—and debated if a piece was more interesting or funny, sad or serious. If too many poems received only accolades, someone would speak up, decrying the lack of genuine feedback and insight. On 14 November 2017, for instance, one user commented: "When I was about to join this group a few months ago I was told that the people here discuss everything poetry and assist each other to become better. But honestly, I have not seen any of that happening here. I am not a pro but I know there are people here who have the ability to dissect poems and show you where you need to improve on or where nothing needs to be changed. Should we say everything posted here is too perfect and needs no critique? I know we all have lives to attend to and can't be here full time, but seriously what's the point of being a member of a group where silence can go for up to entire day at a time?" Her complaint—which presumed, first, that the group would work together to improve one another's poems and, second, that group members be active most days—indicated a collective understanding of the group's purpose and rhythm. Most interesting of all is the sense she conveys that the group should be integrated into members' lives: not full-time, perhaps, but with dedicated space for critique. In response to her post, other writers confirmed, "Mwina anthu amaopa kukhumudwitsana. Komano [*Maybe people are forgetting how to criticize. However,*] the group is cold now ... not as it used to be ... everyone for himself it seems," and "I feel like people, we don't love this anymore." The proclamations of doom marked the group's failure to live up to its promises and poetic expectations, suggesting a shared understanding of what the group was meant to achieve and fulfill.[35]

Still others jumped in to suggest the group get "back to business" and host a "poetry cycle tonight," a term with which the group's fifty-five participants were familiar. When they decided on the theme of "silence," ten participants contributed stanzas in sequence, together building a poem about the topic. The poem included stanzas in Chichewa and English, as well as one left blank, representing silence. The collective participation in the cycle, along with the poems they produced for one another, implied that the group has a common language for and expectations of poetic participation, and members regularly stepped in to correct failures. This sort of collective participation in both poetic production and the production of group norms is possible on WhatsApp because group membership is limited and closed, meaning that each member must have a direct personal connection to one of the group's administrators to be invited.[36] The presumption that group members share social connections also moderates the sort of content members are expected to share, which can vary from group to group.

Although members of the Living Room Poetry Club rarely anticipate criticism, poets do expect direct responses to their poems, and the group has a similar model for creating collaborative poems. In between their weekly meetings or during the rainy season when in-person meetings happen less frequently, group members rely on the WhatsApp group to maintain connections and continue their poetry-oriented socializing. During one joking interlude in October 2016, a new member made fun of the group name (which refers to the venue where they meet), commenting, "Now write abt the deading room." Together, the participants suggested poetic alternatives to the "living room," such as:

> I used to live. I existed in love. I cut off my poetry supply. Now I suffocate in the deading room.

Or

> the dead suck out all that is ... in the deading room ...

And later,

> This invitation to enter, too tempting for my soul, but sitting in here, the flow of rhythm, the lingering melody, this tune of a song of wickied [sic] evil masters, and lovers parade. I dance in this deading room, on tombstones of beautifully crafted verses, that lie unpublished.

Unlike Sapitwa's poetry cycles, which tend toward lineated stanzas of similar lengths, the Living Room Poetry Club's collective poetry evokes improvisation. Stanzas are written in full paragraphs, with line breaks implied by ellipses and dashes. In place of the deliberation suggested by lineation, the punctuation suggests pauses for breath and thought. Indeed, many of the contributions to the "poetry cycle" are highly repetitive, including one that begins: "For the love of the room of love, the love the room the love the room." The repetition creates a rhythm that carries into the rest of the lines, evoking the breathing room necessary for improvisation, manifesting the relationship between thought, breath, and word.

Digitally facilitated poetic production accelerates the production of new poetic genres that echo the call-and-response style of collaboration of the vernacular. The collaborative works, in particular, mirror the participatory logic of new media: in place of a relatively separate audience responding to the call of an independent artist, the group creates a poem together.[37] Even on an unsorted platform like WhatsApp, these participatory gestures reflect the logic of algorithmic selection that dominates social media publication. The collaborations of these two groups—one focused on critique and the other on accolades, one on the production of poetry and the other on its reception—encapsulates each group's purpose, its rules and norms, and its leadership. It also speaks to WhatsApp's capacity to host poetic collaborations and to shape groups that want, write, read, and share them. As a messaging platform, WhatsApp grants no post or individual a clear status above or below any other. Tracing conversations and separating the threads of a multiconversational group is challenging at best. In this seeming messiness—the lived sociality of the WhatsApp group, nested among so many other conversations unique to the individual user's social world—each WhatsApp group carves out its own poetics, its own expectations, and its own civility, so that a poetry cycle that crosses linguistic and modal boundaries signifies within the social boundaries of the group.

The collaborative, participatory, and urgent ethos of social media platforms simulates the collective effervescence typically limited to live events. Although they lack the physical copresence core to performance genres, these platforms presume a shared intellectual and emotional attention, one that requires listening—even if it is the distracted listening of a linked, hashtagged public. The half-attentive, scrolling listener may comment on others' poems without sharing their own, or they may not comment at all but instead contribute to a crowd of listeners, which is essential to the development of digital social networks. These "background listeners," as Kate Crawford shows, are "critical to the sense of affinity generated in these spaces. [. . .] The disclosures made in social media spaces develop a relationship with an audience of listeners. Further, those background listeners are necessary to provoke disclosures of any kind."[38] The silent audience provides a reason for writers to write and a social world for them to write into, facilitating cross-platform interactions and links.

Poetry—shaped by the boundaries of the network it addresses—offers a key form of address through which imagined networks emerge.

Securing the Publication of Zimbabwean Poetry in Facebook Networks

Digital conversations enable poets to reach an audience bound by poetic address and national affiliations, rather than geography. Where the simple, chronological organization of WhatsApp chats enables groups to have conversations in real time, the uneven sorting mechanisms on algorithmically curated platforms like Facebook enable poets to tailor their audiences, rather than their messages. Because it is a messaging application, WhatsApp discourages background listening, or lurking. Social media platforms like Facebook, Instagram, and Twitter, by contrast, are broadcast oriented, allowing publication to a silent audience with little expectation of direct interaction. On Facebook, large audiences, combined with the option to limit publication of certain posts, enables poets to cultivate new communities as they build a name for themselves. However, the platform also employs an aggressive algorithm to organize the barrage of posts that flow through each user's feed. Over time, this sorting mechanism has been increasingly responsible for filtering the flow of information across the site's many functions. Facebook's popularity has, gradually, encouraged the production of literary works specifically geared toward its algorithmic aesthetics. Understanding the platform's algorithmic priorities is crucial to understanding poetry on Facebook. And, because of the platform's popularity, understanding contemporary discourse about poetry requires accounting for Facebook poetry.

Facebook's customizable publication options have made it a potent platform for poets in Zimbabwe. In a country where, in 2016, WhatsApp was shut down to avert rising protests and, in late 2017, an American woman was arrested for tweets criticizing President Robert Mugabe, poets and activists take advantage of Facebook's closed publication circuits and open conversational platforms to refine their collective lens on political developments.[39] Occupying a middle ground between the closed groups of WhatsApp and the open publication of Twitter and YouTube, Facebook offers a relatively sheltered platform for Zimbabwean poets to share their work and seek sympathetic ears as they simultaneously address a diasporic, transnational audience and establish aesthetic networks.

Facebook offers a dual advantage to these artists: its large built-in audience allows poets to publish work with little direct censorship, while its closed groups and customizable publication settings let them determine who hears their broadcasts, within the margins allowed by the platform's algorithms. It thus facilitates semi-open publication such that poets can publish their work on the periphery of the state's gaze and the nation of sixteen million—as many as a quarter of whom live abroad—maintains a network of communication.[40] As Shepherd Mpofu argues, "New media play an important role by acting as 'connective tissue' among diasporeans [sic], with some online activities culminating in social or political activities and opening up restricted democratic space, while resisting state propaganda." For what Mpofu calls "suppressed communities" like Zimbabwe, social media provides spaces of resistance made inaccessible by distance and repression.[41] Such felt connections are complicated by Facebook's content distribution algorithms, which gives Facebook's users what it thinks they want and implicitly silences the rest.

As the most popular and widely used social media platform in the world, Facebook promises to create communities and "bring the world closer together."[42] Each Facebook user has a personal profile, representing a unique individual identified through their legal name.[43] Its broad base of users—nearly three billion as of June 2021—gives artists built-in audiences, findable either through individual acquaintance or affinity groups. Unlike WhatsApp, profiles and groups are public by default, with privacy options only available through multi-tier menu functions. Facebook presumes openness to an unknowable audience, for better or worse. Its relatively open access allows writers to publish work with little direct censorship. Users can create pages representing their professional interests or hobbies. Writers can use such interest and professional pages to cultivate communities akin to those on WhatsApp groups, while maintaining a broader audience across the platform.

The platform's self-broadcast format, combined with options to determine access on a post-by-post basis—to choose when to whisper and when to shout—have made it appealing for artists working in countries with media suppression like Zimbabwe, where saying the wrong thing too loudly too often can lead to retribution. For such prominent dissident poets as Mbizo Chirasha, who used his poetry to criticize Mugabe's regime, publishing means risking violent repercussions—and, in his case, led to exile. For Chirasha, Facebook and Facebook groups become a significant medium to stay connected with home. Yet Facebook's algorithms implicitly promote certain voices over others, a division that can be ascertained only through indirect observation. In contrast with Chirasha, poet Morset Billie has built a presence online by working with the demands of the platform, using hashtags and images to increase his work's traction online. For both Billie and Chirasha, the key challenge is bringing attention to your work. Billie addresses this challenge by publishing image macros, which Facebook will generally circulate more widely. Chirasha, in contrast, builds closed groups, which increase his circulations within an audience that shares his concerns—selected, in this case, through their participation in the group 100,000 Poets for Peace-Zimbabwe. Comparing these two poets' publication strategies on Facebook illustrates the relationship between the platform's aesthetics and the poetic forms it promotes. Comparing the works they share on their individual pages to those posted in the group, in turn, demonstrates how the platform's network logics invoke poetic strategies.

Chirasha made a name for himself as a highly active dissident poet in the early 2010s, when he published two volumes of poetry and began organizing a series of literature competitions, foundations, and blogs. In 2016, a series of threats and violent altercations forced Chirasha into exile. After leaving Zimbabwe, he regularly posted political poems on Facebook, until early 2021, when, following a series of increasingly urgent posts suggesting he was in danger, he stopped posting altogether. He now lives in South Africa, where his work focuses on organizing activist poets to promote human rights efforts.

For those five years in which he was most active on Facebook, Chirasha's rapid and regular publication of poems marked a departure from his earlier published work. Unlike that poetry, which features similar political themes but follows conventional typographic practice, his poems on Facebook skip lines and letters, default to phonetic abbreviations, and play with punctuation placement and lineation in ways that suggest the fast, often careless, typing typical of real-time interactions online.

Publication on Facebook provides Chirasha with a veneer of privacy: his posts are public only to his personal friends, granting him limited control over who has access to his writing. Despite this seeming control, Chirasha's poems nonetheless use allusion and indirection to skirt surveillance. Risk-aversion, Eldred Masunungure argues, is common in Zimbabwe, the result of "a process of conditioning over time."[44] Chirasha's use of allusion works as a form self-protection by implicating the audience in the poem's message: understanding the allusion requires shared context; fully grasping its meaning requires the audience actively work to help create that meaning. On 12

October 2017, a month before a military coup removed Mugabe from power, he published a poem titled "In solidarity with those evicted from Arnold Farm we all know by who." The piece's title recalls the eviction of an entire village in early April 2017 by Grace Mugabe, the president's wife, who then took control of the area. A day before Chirasha posted his poem, villagers who had planned to protest the eviction suddenly backed down from the demonstration. In the poem, Chirasha writes:

> I was born along with this country
> , listening to the afro beat of politics
> Fist of slogans smashing into mothers faces
> Sisters raped in the reggae of propaganda
> Sons dancing to the funk music of violence, bathing villages in blood
> I was born along with country, listening to the afro beat of political music.[45]

Written in the first person, Chirasha's poem highlights the speaker's individual experience as the warrant behind his claims. It situates the violence of the eviction within the broader context of Mugabe's regime, reminding the audience of the oft-claimed family structure of the nation—one upended through political violence and reinscribed in music. His linking of the birth of his consciousness to that of the nation produces an image of the poet as herald and citizen. His voice, the soundtrack he writes for himself and his country, then shifts the question of voice to one of song, and participation to violence.

This is not, however, the sort of voice Facebook will amplify. The posts are short, which means app users can scroll through them quickly. And they are abstract, making them hard to comprehend and engage with in the short duration of the scroll. Chirasha's poetry, in many ways, rejects the form of participation Facebook recognizes—and, as such, it often goes without direct recognition. His poetry's circulation relies on the listeners he can engage and on the platform that enables and constrains that engagement. In refusing to be among what Pierre Bourdieu has called "the industrialists of writing," who "follow public taste and manufacture written words [. . .] of popular appearance, but not excluding either the 'literary' cliché or the search for stylistic effect," Chirasha ceded the battle for a consistent, personal audience on Facebook.[46] Although his works—which are urgent, brief, and allusive—follow many of the logics of social media, they do not to adhere to Facebook's algorithmic aesthetics and so are rendered mute to the broader aesthetic network.

Though powerful standing on its own, as it does here, the poem disappears amid relentless scrolling and constant output on Facebook.

Unlike WhatsApp, which lists all messages sent to the group chronologically and unequivocally, Facebook disappears the posts that fall outside its norms, making even small-scale normative shifts difficult. Chirasha's posts rarely appear on my personal newsfeed, even though we are friends and have several friends in common. At best they appear in nested clumps: "Mbizo has posted three times today," followed by three clustered posts. The newsfeed does not reward the sort of rapid posting at which Chirasha excels, and his audience rarely responds directly to his pieces. Perhaps they never see them.

Facebook rewards works that solicit engagement: image macros that require their viewer to linger; easily digestible pith that acquires ready likes. The poetry that does fit Facebook's style reappears, over and over. Young poets seeking to build their networks fit their work to that style: multimodal, clear, generalizable. Building digital networks is especially important for young poets in Zimbabwe. In a region with limited publishing opportunities and a tight-knit literary network, digital connections are often the best way to begin. Digital platforms allow young artists to build their own networks as they develop their work. This pattern is modeled in the work of poet Morset Billie, whose social media presence stands in startling contrast to Chirasha's. When we met in December 2016, Billie had recently moved to Harare from the much smaller city of Mutare to work for Pamberi Trust and develop professionalization workshops for young poets.[47] Billie was a young poet working within the system to build a name for himself, and his Facebook presence reflects that, establishing personal links between posts while hashtagging each post to mark his authorship. His poems and their frequency suit Facebook's aesthetics, enabling him to develop a network within its framework.

Using hashtags and shares to interact with his collaborators' profiles, Billie approaches Facebook's aesthetic networks through a linking strategy that directly positions him in a broader framework of digital logics, working within Facebook's constraints to promote his work. And he uses Facebook's emphasis on images and short messages to his advantage. He posts poems as image macros, the text grafted on top of an image which may or may not totally fit the verse: in figure 4, for instance, he has overlaid the text of a brief poem on a section of his profile's banner image. The cropped image shows clouds set off against a blue sky, with low-lying mountains rising in the background. At the center of the image, the poem reads:

> In a morally dying society,
> I refuse to be associated with
> faked reality and staged actuality.

The image macro poetry would not make sense in most traditional forms of publication, but on Facebook, it gives textual poetry digital traction.

FIGURE 4. Zimbabwean poet Morset Billie uses image macros to capture audience attention on social media. Image courtesy of Morset Billie.

Facebook's streams, which have no beginning nor end and place only the barest divides between media objects, make poetry part of everyday life, as it butts up against status updates, photo memories, and news articles. As poets accede to the demands of audience and algorithm to make their post legible to a broader aesthetic network, multimodal pieces like the image macro are popular for their ability to interrupt Facebook's endless white scroll. Whereas WhatsApp allows users to share images, recordings, and texts at their leisure, Facebook renders each interaction opaque within its broader networks. It codifies platform-specific models of production and interaction, defining its users' needs and desires for them. In that sense, poetry—as an aesthetic and yet networked form—bends to the shape of its platform, reproduced in social media's gaze.

In 2017, at twenty-four years old, Morset Billie had not yet published in traditional print outlets, so he mobilized digital networks to develop his career. Doing so provided him the means to build up a broader aesthetic network and create new connections: he partnered with friends met online to found digital literary platforms and poetry workshops. And, as the COVID-19 pandemic led to lockdowns in 2020–21, he was well prepared to continue digital work and build digital open mics for artists across Africa.

As poets like Billie develop work in conversation with digital algorithms, new aesthetic networks appear, stitched together out of the platform's algorithms, local social norms, and rapidly changing poetic standards. Like WhatsApp, Facebook connects users in two ways: through one-to-one connections and within broader groups. It creates two parallel types of networks. The first—solicited by direct, public postings like Billie's—is the loose network of the scroll. It is made up of ubiquitous interactions that render in-person networks visible but do little to produce direct connections or collaborations. The second—established through shared allusions like Chirasha's—are the deliberate networks of closed Facebook groups. These groups open local poetics onto transnational media landscapes, so that poets might establish aesthetic networks for an increasingly diasporic nation.

For digital aesthetic networks to form, the platform must support users' expectations of mutuality—expectations that are incompatible with Facebook's noncollaborative interactions. In that sense, Facebook's open and searchable networks ironically discourage the formation of fully fledged poetic art worlds. Within these networks, Becker notes, "Knowing the conventions of the form, serious audience members can collaborate more fully with artists in the joint effort which produces the work each time it is experienced."⁴⁸ Innovation within aesthetic networks relies on the regular interactions of a smaller group of people. Within Facebook's vast networks, closed groups foster artists' connections to a broader cultural network equipped to authorize and value their productions. Dissident poets benefit from groups with established protocol for allowing dissidence, which are nonetheless open enough to permit growth while limiting the potential for exposure. Their voices, in other words, require the proper platform to be audible, as well as an audience that can understand them. It is here that Facebook's capacity to connect poets across regions and to establish aesthetic networks shines, even as its potential for exposure remains largely ignored.

One such group, 100 Thousand Poets for Peace-Zimbabwe, was founded in August 2015 and is now run by Mbizo Chirasha. The group is part of a global network connected through 100 Thousand Poets for Change (100TPC), an organization founded in 2011 by American poets Michael Rothenberg and Terri Carlton. 100TPC coordinates global events, from poetry readings to literacy initiatives, through satellite organizations across thirty-four countries. 100 Thousand Poets for Peace-Zimbabwe shares Zimbabwean concerns with poets across Africa to further this goal.

Over its first five years, 100 Thousand Poets for Peace-Zimbabwe grew to 1,179 members, including both Chirasha and Billie, as well as poets from Malawi and South Africa, and others living in the United States, the United Kingdom, Australia, and beyond. The particular settings of the group—private but viewable—means that although any Facebook user can find the group, only those approved by the group's administrator can join it or see its members. Chirasha thus maintains default control over the organization. This control helps ensure that group members share a commitment to dissident art, thus limiting the risk posed to individual artists.

The administrative control also lets the group establish clear protocols for interaction, despite its large size. Chirasha posts much of the page's content, including pieces by other poets who have requested their work be shared in this manner.⁴⁹ No matter their poster, most poems receive at least two responses, often including comments as poetic as the piece itself. The comments turn the Facebook page into something like a living poetry anthology. Because of the closed, nation-specific nature of the group, poets assume shared cultural and contextual knowledge with their audience—an assumption beyond what can typically be made in print. For example, on 10 November 2017, a poet writing under the pseudonym "Sydney Saize" posted:

> They need cyber security in a nation that guarantee safety
> Hero of yester-bushwar
> Are hiding word guerrillas
> Emulating to suppress speech free voice Masenga
> But who said Chirasha shall not speak
> Who dare shun Jambiya pen to streak
> The list is endless
> Meaninglessly endless
> Miombo shall publish
> Tuck will embellish
> The Zimbabwe We Want for peace[50]

The poem assumes its audience knows Zimbabwe's political history and the rhetoric of its leaders; that they understand its political situation and constant threats of censorship; and that they are familiar with its poets, including Chirasha and Jambiya Kai, and a broader Pan-African publication history, of which Chirasha's engagement with *Tuck* magazine forms a key part.

These allusions do not obscure the poem's meaning but instead mark a shared knowledge system, a presumption about group membership, and possibly an understanding that this poem and its meaning are unlikely to leave that reception context. In Zimbabwe's censorial political atmosphere, closed groups on Facebook provide a sense of safety and confidence akin to that of WhatsApp groups, allowing moderated publication to a large but theoretically knowable community whose commitment to political change may be presumed. Closed groups allow poets to post their work for a wide audience who, through links to the group, are presumed to share the poets' political convictions. Though not every member must live in Zimbabwean territory to grasp the poem's meaning or the group's investment, they must all be invested in Zimbabwe as a nation, a political entity with shared cultural histories and institutions. The endless allusions point to the value and importance of audience-specific publication—a form that gains strength in the closed, semiprivate publication enabled by Facebook. Together, the poems posted and the comments, likes, and shares they accrue transform an affective network into an aesthetic one.

Facebook publication draws on and heightens the networked character of poetry, integrating audiences directly into poetic production and forcing poets to preemptively consider their reception. The platform's poetic networks—which are, ultimately, interactive rather than collaborative and provide publication but no indexing or contextualization—encourage and enforce a performative, networked poetics through which poets negotiate larger questions of identity, community, and national investments. The communities that emerge through these spaces link local organizations internationally. They offer alternative publication and promotion opportunities for poets who lack governmental support or corporate viability. In capitalizing on structures established by global corporations so as to expand the scale of African literary production, they engage in the critical work that Bwesigye Bwa Mwesigire refers to as "gate-opening" literary activism.[51]

Beginning in 2020, the organization of Facebook group pages shifted radically: their organization moved from chronological to feed based. As groups grew larger, and their content more profuse, the pages were reorganized to mirror primary feeds. Even small, closed groups are now subjected to the sorting mechanisms that prioritize engagement over novelty. Machine learning algorithms now manage the aesthetic networks that produce literary norms at nearly every level. How does this affect the activist capacities of literary groups on social media? How will it affect their capacity to organize?

Picturing Pandemic Poetry in South Africa

Digital aesthetic networks entwine individuals in a system of cultural production structured by platform affordances. And the more artistic activity happens online, the stronger the effects of algorithmic curation. In March 2020, when the COVID-19 crisis required lockdowns and social distancing across Africa, digital platforms became the singular means of maintaining community and advertising poetry around the world. Pandemic-era lockdowns intensified ongoing changes to aesthetic networks, bringing creative energies online while also deepening artists' structural insecurity. Live streams replaced live events; video-chat happy hours replaced poetry readings; Instagram TV (IGTV) workshops proliferated.[52] In response, artists both shifted their form to accommodate new platform demands and deepened their engagement with digital networks. The transitions to digital-first networks in 2020–21 elucidates the global interplay between individual agency and material limitations in the production of novel literary forms: forced into digital spaces to rebuild devastated careers, artists found new possibility in

FIGURE 5. impepho press's "Virtual World Poetry Day" brought poets together to provide relief during COVID. Image by impepho press.

transnational collaborations and multimodal productions. At the same time, the concentrated pressures of digital environments transformed their work: demands to be constantly available and legible as an authentic, individual creator coincided with algorithmic emphases on multimodal, reproducible works. Tracking poets' adaptations to these new circumstances, both in literary form and community engagement, illustrates how the demands of digital platforms—for novelty, engagement, iterability—transform literary form in the digital age.

The pandemic deepened artists' structural insecurity. Without bookstore sales, commissioned performances, or school events, their few avenues of material support were suddenly cut off. In South Africa, where books are not considered essential products, book sales were prohibited. For poets with limited internet access, the transition forestalled promising careers. Without a strong safety net for already poorly remunerated artists, commercial platforms became crucial infrastructures for both supporting individuals' labor and enabling community organization. Without their usual community-building work, poets and artists throughout South Africa and around the world became increasingly active on social media platforms. The sudden and intense increase in digital engagement helped poets reach new audiences, coordinating events and sharing information at unprecedented speed.

During that time, artists built on already-popular social media platforms to extend their outreach. Poetry on Facebook and WhatsApp allows writers to collaborate or at least interact, yet the closed network structure of those two platforms is at odds with many poets' desires to archive their works and continually reach public audiences. In contrast, platforms focused on open publication and loose networks enable artists to build virtual connections quickly, well beyond that encouraged by the tighter networks of WhatsApp and Facebook. Many poets responded by turning to Instagram, which was already one of the most popular platforms for digital poetry globally.

Because it is linked to users' Facebook profiles, Instagram typically presumes an identity between a user's profile and their artistic persona. This melding of poetic speaker and poster supported the growing popularity of confessional poetry—a style popularized especially by best-selling Instagram poet Rupi Kaur. The connection between the personal and the political online is redoubled for writers of color, for whom—as Urayoán Noel notes in his analysis of queer Latinx poetry on Instagram—"there is still often the expectation of autobiography, that their work must stay in its lane and more or less clearly reflect their social identities and struggles."[53] As artistic energies focused online, Instagram's power intensified. In South Africa, where digital engagement is priced by the kilobyte, Instagram's focus on image and video makes it prohibitively expensive. But it also promises artists the possibility of monetizing creative work through the performance of individual identity. Rather than expand equity, then, the digital turn forced artists to choose between living and livelihood: as poet and publisher vangile gantsho said, "Even for something as simple as making a video, the cost is data, which is expensive. So if you have to choose between data and bread, you're not going to choose data. But if you don't choose data, you'll be isolated from the world."[54]

Unlike Facebook or WhatsApp, the community of Instagram is largely atomistic: no mechanisms exist to create direct connections between users, and individual posts stand alone, with little contextualization. Instead, Instagram organizes feeds based on user interactions: the more a follower interacts with a user's photos, the more likely they are to see that user's photos in the future.[55] Unlike Facebook, posting more frequently on Instagram is always better: higher posting frequencies expand opportunities for engagement, which in turn makes future interaction more likely. Moreover, unlike many similar platforms, Instagram displays only original posts in the feed: to view secondary commentary, users have to open the post, which means the platform expands engagement while consistently prioritizing the primary post in each user's feed. Both Instagram feeds and live streams isolate participants within the paradigmatic squares and rectangles of the era, subordinating connection to aesthetics.

Isolation within spaces of connection proved especially powerful during periods of lockdown. The always-on default of the lockdown era created new opportunities and demand for one-to-one connection, bringing individual artists and events directly into living rooms. These changes led many individual artists to dramatically shift their engagement with digital platforms after lockdowns began. Those changes had long-term ramifications for their artistic production, even after the most severe restrictions were lifted later in the year.

Before lockdowns began, poet and performer Siphokazi Jonas had mostly used Instagram to promote her personal and literary brands, cross-posting extensively to Facebook and Twitter. The vast majority of these posts advertised her ongoing work, the dramatic production *#WeAreDyingHere*. Jonas is a highly active and successful poet and playwright: her poetry won the

Cape Town Ultimate Slam Championship in 2015 and was recognized by the 2016 Sol Plaatje European Union Poetry Award in both 2016 and 2017; she has performed at Poetry Africa, the continent's oldest poetry festival; and her theater company Wrestling Dawn Arts was recognized as "Best Project in the Western Cape" in 2019. Prior to lockdown, her work focused on live performances; digital posts served to advertise that work. In early March 2020, for instance, Jonas published one photograph or video a day from her recent play, *#WeAreDyingHere*, a one-woman show that examines the effects of rape culture and widespread gender-based violence on women's lives in South Africa. Audience reactions to the live performance had been deep and widespread: film actress Chantal Stanfield declared on Twitter, "It's a work that is so desperately needed in our country."[56]

The play was set to tour the country beginning in late March 2020—a plan derailed by the national state of emergency declared on 15 March 2020. The next day, Jonas's posts changed, as the country went into lockdown (see figure 6). Jonas's poetry typically includes layered references to South African cultural and floral landscapes, with deep concern for the historical shape of national politics. Her pandemic poetry, in contrast, responded to an immediate need, with no time for reflection or nuance. In a post dated 15 March 2020, Jonas offered a poem reflecting on the moment:

> This is the time here, when
> minds and heart are sick with fear:
> Be love.
> Be kindness.
> Make good ground for seeds of healing.

The simple sentiment is expressed in a plain sans serif font against a pink-tinted background. The poem was followed by four hashtags, linking it to a global conversation of crisis: "#coronavirus, #CoronaVirusSA, #Shutdownsa, #LOCKSOUTHAFRICADOWN." The short, prescriptive phrases offer a sense of certainty and closure amid the open-ended panic of that early phase.

The pandemic poems offer a form of what Urayoán Noel calls "poemics": a poetic polemic specifically suited to social media.[57] The recirculation of common generic phrases is a hallmark of social media poetry and a cause of both its popularity and its widespread scorn.[58] Yet, as Mike Chasar suggests, it is precisely this generic language that marks popular digital literature's

> **Siphokazi Jonas**
> @Siphokazi_J
>
> This is the time right here, when minds and heart are sick with fear:
> Be love.
> Be kindness.
> Make good ground for seeds of healing.
>
> #coronavirus
> #CoronaVirusSA
> #ShutDownsa
> #LOCKSOUTHAFRICADOWN

FIGURE 6. Siphokazi Jonas first posted her poem to Twitter before posting a screenshot of the Tweet on Instagram. Image courtesy of Siphokazi Jonas.

resistance to appropriation: "Instapoetry deals in cliche, a type of language so old as to be original and 'authentic' and so commonly owned that it bears no identifiable origin or mark of authorship and thus cannot be appropriated because it belongs to no one or to everyone."[59] These phrases create a sort of literary commons, marking an incipient turn away from the individual genius model of authorship. But the cliché is, simultaneously, a hallmark of the digital because of its ready digestibility: we move through it at the speed of the scroll, with little need to interpret. In lieu of an aesthetics of difficulty, it offers an ease and comfort in times of strife.

Instagram funnels publicly broadcast posts into individually curated feeds, in a distribution pattern determined by its machine learning algorithms. According to a 2019 "FAQ" post on its official page, individual user's feeds are customized according to their choices and behavior: active choices, such as unfollowing or following another user or commenting on a post, will have predictable results. But, even in 2019, relatively passive behavior, like letting a video autoplay or lingering on a post, will also affect the feed. Two users following identical accounts would therefore likely see different posts. And because the algorithms rely on machine learning, human actors can only influence its principles, not its behaviors. Rather, the most important tool for poets seeking new audiences on Instagram is engagement. The platform's algorithm promotes not only posts that have more "likes" and comments but also artists whose posts typically see higher rates of engagement. Getting users to comment on and like early work increases the chance that they will see later work. This structure encourages regular posting of complex, visually striking videos and images that encourage users to linger or, better still, click through to engage with the whole post.

Jonas took advantage of Instagram's combination of cross-posted newsfeed and curated profile page to craft a not-quite-live rollout of performance experiences. Over the subsequent months, she continued to use Instagram to publish poetry and advertise her work, but over time, she abandoned the Instapoetry cliché to reformat work she had produced on other platforms prior to lockdown. That work appears in multiple media, changed to alternately fit and disrupt Instagram's aesthetic defaults.

For a week, from 11 to 16 May 2020, Jonas posted brief two-minute clips from her 2018 play *Around the Fire*. The play is a one-woman show that envisions fire as a contrasting symbol of both gathering place and destructive force to investigate women's social role. Isolated into clips, the characters' stories lose their symbolic connections and become stand-ins for a much wider range of stories about gender-based violence and female experiences in South Africa. The first video clip posted—shared several times across Instagram and Twitter over the course of the week—begins in a distant shot. Jonas sits on a milk crate, wearing a hooded flannel sweatshirt over a long white gown, surrounded by objects that represent the various women she plays. She reaches out to her mother and sister, her voice quaking as she recalls her past responses to abuse: "I've done it before [. . .] set myself on fire just to set something that I love free." Jonas's voice, which takes on the range of accents necessary to convey the women's broad experiences, carries with it the physical experience of live performance. In the play, the desire to "hold onto my anger" appears late, contextualized by a vast array of women's experiences. Online, each sequence stands alone; stripped of context, her performance becomes devastated, righteous anger. These videos cut through the #PoemsofComfort that Jonas also solicited and collected, reminding her audience of the human cost of lockdowns, including the fear of increased domestic violence. Her body echoed across time, in sound and movement, even as it was frozen into a loop on-screen.

Over the five days that she posted videos from *Around the Fire*, her video view counts slowly climbed: from 100 for the first video to 135 for the second,

198 for the third, and leveling out around 200 views per video. Although these numbers are not huge, the quick surge speaks to Jonas's ability to use IG algorithms to promote her work. These videos work differently from the live events—readings, workshops, and panels—that many poets organized and attended during the lockdown. Those tend to sit alone, advertised in "Facebook Stories" and "IGTV" circles that float above the primary feeds. Jonas's poetry, in contrast, flows seamlessly with selfies and text posts. Within the flow of followers' lives, they stand apart as carefully edited video recordings of artistic events.

During this time of dispersed sociality, Jonas deployed the distributed temporality of social media to evoke the temporal unfolding of theater itself. By posting regularly, Jonas gained increased attention, taking advantage of Instagram's structure to develop a coeval audience. She thus acceded to the engagement-driven logics of Instagram while resisting its aesthetics to herald a community bound by their shared engagement with South Africa's artistic landscape.

Instagram's algorithms seem to reward nothing so much as high-quantity posts. It agglomerates the disparate work independent artists do to survive. Its default public account settings open posts to a broad audience. Those circuits connect a dispersed art world. And, most important, its connections to Facebook and other social media platforms ask that artists collapse their art into their identity. Where WhatsApp allows poets to experiment with their work and Facebook encourages a sense of the relationship between art and identity, Instagram demands that artists like Jonas—that is, artists who built Instagram accounts first as individuals who make art, rather than as art brands like Rupi Kaur's—remain individuals first. Jonas has largely resisted this expectation, transforming her professional presence instead through collaborations and political affirmations.

Those connections are enabled, in part, by the cross-posting that is key to Instagram's use. Where Facebook emphasizes video and Twitter prioritizes text, Instagram creates links broadly across platforms. Instagram offers a means of curating one's profile, establishing connections between users through tags that do not require other users' approval (which Facebook requires) while reaching out, in a limited way, through hashtags. During the pandemic, poets and arts organizations alike used this capacity to extend their aesthetic networks, building connections across spaces and squares, videos and image captures, oceans and nations.

Shortly after lockdowns began, for instance, the Johannesburg-based poetry organization Word N Sound transformed the poetry slams through which it had first gained attention into a "digital slam." On 21 March 2020—one week into South Africa's lockdown—it posted an image of a pair of black headphones over a yellow background, with the words, "In extraordinary times . . . Exceptional voices must be heard! #WNSDigitalSlam" and the caption, "Shutdown but not silenced. Get your poems ready! #WNSDigitalSlam." Three weeks later, the organization offered directions about how to participate in its first-ever digital slam, which would be reprised every month for the following year. Initially, these events drew together groups of poets who had been frequent performers at the in-person events. The same poet, Xabiso Vili, won the first three slams. But, as lockdown continued and the organization's digital presence grew, Word N Sound gradually drew in a wider range of participants. The final digital slam, in February 2021, featured poets from around the world, with winners from Barbados, Germany, Sweden, and South Africa.

These poems mirror the slam poetry form described in the next chapter: they are between two and five minutes long, with a confessional tone that marks the poet's intimate persona and a heightened rhythm that underscores the otherwise conversational diction. Slam's emphasis on individual performance and audience participation made its transition into digital spaces relatively straightforward. Although the poetry itself remained relatively consistent, the video performances became increasingly elaborate as the event continued. Vili's first poem video, for instance, is a single shot of him, straight on, in front of a white wall and lit by bright sunlight from a nearby window. Intentional glitches—a wavering face or stuttering screen—mark the performance's technologization and nod to the poem's theme. Vili's work titled "The 4th Industrial Revolution" reflects on the nature of sociality "reaching across fiber optics," as "video calls make me look almost human / Zoom in"—a near rhyme that ironically underscores the inhumanity of the Zoom era. The piece's power, though, comes first from Vili's performance: arms outstretched to evoke network cables, vocal tics that mirror the visual glitches. Matching theme to scene, he offers a performance that uses mediatization as thematic intensification, rather than for its own sake.

In a poem about depression and fatalism in the face of inevitable death, Vili's video takes on its own meaning above that of the words. Vili's poem is layered with instruments above a video of him moving between two chairs. He speaks, but the mouth moves out of alignment with the words. The fluidly chaotic movements—leaning forward and back, in and out of chairs, on and off the ground—turn the speech into a narration of a multimodal performance, rather than a poem for its own sake. Audio and visual entwine, as the speaker brings his drinking into our bar, his conversation into our living room. His speech—urgent, conversational, allusive—takes on the norms of digital conversation and connection.

But the key component of the video is its cross-platform, multimodal production. It was shared with the curators through email; posted to its audience via IGTV and Facebook Live; voted on via text message; and published, finally, in Word N Sound's curated Instagram feed. Instagram allows users to repost one another's work and then link directly back to the original post. The platform's emphasis on frequent posting, hashtags, and audience engagement highlights the value of such open, direct, and wide-ranging publication. Hashtags and search functions broaden the potential audience for each work, encouraging experimentation, even as the digital presumptions of multimodality and personal authenticity create new pressures for literary production.

Structurally, Instagram prioritizes the individual content creator. Connections are one-sided; networks are open and loose; posts default to public; images and videos encourage commentary over collaboration. These norms make it a powerful publishing platform for poetry but not necessarily for the production of a literary community. Positioned within digital aesthetic networks, though, it opens new possibilities for poets' self-production. Such commingled publication platforms carry the logic of social media with and through them. They privilege interactivity and direct address, multimodal signification, and urgency, creating an imagined collaboration between writer and receiver that is mediated only by the algorithms of the platform itself. They also facilitate the formation of novel literary communities and aesthetic networks—networks that may, in turn, influence broader behavioral patterns. As producer and consumer merge and mingle online, poetry takes center stage, producing multiauthored, multimodal literary forms and communities. Poetry is now networked.

Contemporary Poetry as Social Network

Poetry's online life yields an alternative, more diffuse structure of engagement that empowers the individual viewer to produce her own poetic community. The audience of the online text is simultaneously everywhere and nowhere, a networked public whom the poet must address at every turn. Poetry's networked address, its ability to create connections across spaces, comes to the fore when we consider the influence of publication platforms on the forms poetry takes. For poets in southern Africa, social media platforms provide alternative methods of publication, allowing writers to speak directly to local audiences and forging alternative aesthetic models. Author-audience networks and feedback loops catalyze transnational poetic networks, which operate at the periphery of the state's gaze.

Digital aesthetic networks inaugurate new discursive modes and speech genres, fostering collaborative genres that reflect digital-first communicative norms. As social media platforms dominate the publication of poetry from Africa, poetry that crosses media channels opens new configurations of poetry-audience relationships. The publication of performance poetry on Instagram creates new forms of audience engagement, even as it places additional pressures on poets to sustain their own work through self-publication. On Facebook, publication options and the problem of in-person networks permits poets to solicit sympathetic eyes while, potentially, disengaging from suspicious readers. These networks entwine with and reshape the immediate, face-to-face interactions of local poetry workshops, festivals, and readings—connections most directly enabled by poetry sharing and critique on WhatsApp, which joins together dispersed poetry communities, such that they may debate and shape new genres.

These platforms and the algorithms that structure them shift poetry's networked forms, blurring the line between poet and audience and informing the development of novel literary products. Through allusion, repetition, and address, social media platforms integrate audience expectations and network aesthetics into the work prior to its production, further blurring the divide between creator and receiver. Algorithmic aesthetics leap from platform to stage, as the networked public sphere demands a networked poetry. But what does the expansion of digital aesthetic networks mean for poetry's offline lives? If poets modulate their pieces for an imagined audience across digital platforms, I argue in the next chapter that the aesthetic norms of social media platforms manifest in the spread of specific poetic genres. I trace the spread of slam poetry through institutional, individual, and digital networks to argue that social media's aesthetic norms—which emphasize urgency, populism, and interactivity—are shaping live performance norms across the region.

CHAPTER 3

Institutionalizing Algorithmic Aesthetics
SLAM POETRY'S REGIONAL NETWORKS

S OCIAL MEDIA PLATFORMS enable the rapid distribution of new ideas and rhetoric. The publics they draw together form new communities, cemented by a poetic rhetoric that marks collective concerns. If, as I argue in chapter 1, the hashtag exemplifies the logic of digital communication—the use of language to create literal links between statements and imaginative links across platforms—then the rise of spoken word poetry in southern Africa exemplifies the structure of algorithmic aesthetics, as paravirtual networks transport literary form across digital and grounded spaces. Over the past twenty years, spoken word poetry has spread rapidly across southern Africa. The form appears to jump, unbidden, across place and space, as poets embrace the vernacular style and organizers found poetry slams. But these forms rely on institutional channels shaped by global funding networks, structured in response to global media paradigms. In this chapter, I ask: How does the logic of the digital screen emerge on the physical stage? And how do the popular spaces of poetry production intersect with shifting models of cultural funding?

In late 2016, nineteen-year-old Zimbabwean-born South African poet Vusumuzi Mpofu posted the text of a slam poem entitled "Foreign Searching for Rain" to his personal Facebook page (see figure 7). The poem uses Mpofu's personal story of economic displacement to trace the joint history of Zimbabwe's failing economy and South Africa's growing xenophobia. His post drew dozens of likes, comments, and shares in its first day. Two weeks later, when Mpofu performed the poem at an open mic in a Cape Town café, many in the audience knew it so well that they responded in anticipation of upcoming lines.

FIGURE 7. Vusumuzi Mpofu shared his poetry on Facebook before performing it live a few days later. Image courtesy of Vusumuzi Mpofu.

Several people audibly inhaled after the simple setup, "I leave Johannesburg, traveling further south, to Cape Town," anticipating the emotional follow-up: "My mother's presence calms the storm in me. She is a home in motion, housing the broken boy."[1] Together with many of Mpofu's friends and fans that night, I experienced the performance—otherwise comparable to the work performed at Cape Town open mics—as a digital piece come to life, and our shared knowledge of it drew us together in sympathy with the performer. The poem's digital life had molded its meaning prior to its performance, shaping its audience into a community linked through Mpofu's words.

Mpofu's performance style, characterized by conversational rhythms and dramatic imagery, exemplifies one of the many styles of slam poetry that developed in Africa through the first decade of the 2000s.[2] Although the poetry slam predates social media, the competition form's rapid spread over the past two decades derives in part from the expectations it shares with social media: poetry slams are competitive; the poetry performed at them solicits audience participation; and it is a youth-dominated field. Its spread, then, parallels the way algorithmic aesthetics shape a broader literary landscape. Slam poets and their institutions bring spoken word styles from the Global North into conversation with locally conventional attitudes toward poetry to negotiate a place for poetry performance in contemporary urban landscapes. In the process, they use available technologies and familiar genres to shift the structure of the form itself.

Slam poetry is transmitted both digitally and in performance. In each case, it responds to the norms of individual platforms and aesthetic communities. For instance, where local events may require cohesive twenty-minute sets, the disjointed structure of a YouTube feed encourages briefer, stand-alone sound bites. New media standards have influenced slam poetry's form, cementing its three-to-five-minute standard. The production, circulation, and reception of Mpofu's poem—inspired by slam poets on YouTube, developed in local workshops, performed at small open mics, and now itself published on YouTube—demonstrates how cross-platform encounters produce the ever-growing global genre of slam poetry. In each case, audience interactions and expectations shape the form's meaning and reception both prior to and within the moment of performance, producing a networked poem that builds on the globally popular genre.

Slam poetry shows how algorithmic aesthetics jump from digital platforms to live stages and back again. Aesthetic networks, which form online, bring poetry slams into urban areas around the world. If, as I argued in the previous chapter, social media algorithms shape how communities engage with poetry, slam poetry's global spread indicates the significance of these changes. Slam competitions' emphasis on participation produced new poetic communities, organized around urban youth groups that take advantage of the form's openness to develop a wide range of poetry and to center themselves firmly in what they see as a globally salient, culturally valuable form. These are the communities in which Mpofu's poem first gained traction. Social media circulations shape live performance venues and genres, transforming poetic form through both the direct action of institutions and the indirect influence of internet platforms. Even as institutional networks establish new poetry slams, slam poetry's publication online constrains its form to the works most readily rewarded by digital audiences: brief, highly emotional pieces that deal with contemporary problems in everyday language.

The institutionalization of these poetry competitions rewards—and thus implicitly standardizes—those works that receive accolades, reproducing norms established by digital aesthetic networks and international funding bodies. I therefore evaluate the joint influence of digital aesthetics and institutional norms on slam poetry's spread through Zimbabwe, Malawi, and South Africa. To understand the decades-long rise of slam poetry in southern Africa, I situate it at the crossroads of literary culture, media structures, and the ascent of what Doreen Strauhs calls "literary NGOs [nongovernmental organizations]" (LiNGOs).[3] In doing so, I ask: How does a literary form move? What institutional and infrastructural support facilitates the geographic spread of a particular literary form? I argue that the digital and the institutional work in tandem to standardize a hybrid literary form, promoting those artists who innovate within its limits to mark their investment in a world literary order. In southern Africa in particular, young poets work within and against formal boundaries, both highlighting the institutionalization of a seemingly democratic form and illustrating how artists from the Global South mobilize that institutionalized globalized form to new ends.

To map the spread and influence of slam poetry in southern Africa, I begin with a brief outline of slam poetry's history and its primary formal characteristics. From there, I trace four characteristics of slam's proliferation: its joint virtual and social circulation; its rapid institutional spread; its local adaptations; and its influence on the broader cultural category of "poetry." These characteristics are epitomized in my examination of "tribute night" at Blantyre's KwaHaraba Poetry Nights, where poets read their favorite poems by other writers, demonstrating how slam's digital spread shapes the local communities that form around its performance. Next, I lay out its institutional history in the region, beginning with the Zimbabwe-based House of Hunger poetry slam. House of Hunger's institutional spread reveals the intricate networks of international cultural organizations that have facilitated the global diffusion of slam. However, slam's insistence on performance gives the individual producer an unusual level of power, as evidenced by Qabaniso "Q" Malewezi's influence on Malawi's poetry scene. The rapid changes and generational shifts in poetry production have engendered anxieties about the role of poetry that are tied to broader concerns about the preservation of culture against foreign influences, as evidenced by conversations spanning print and digital media. Yet slam's performance aesthetics can, in conjunction with local forms, imagine new possibilities for the relationship between performer and audience. The chapter therefore closes with a discussion of Cape Town's Lingua Franca Spoken Word Collective, whose participants use slam aesthetics, traditional forms, and multimedia performance modes to revivify Afrophone performance standards.

The relationships that slam poetry enacts between form and meaning, artist and audience, offer a glimpse into the ways contemporary literary forms, more broadly, are shaped in the crucible of digital production and dispersed art worlds. Slam poetry bridges local spaces with transnational networks, digital norms with grounded performance. These are the conditions of literary production in the twenty-first century, concentrated into a literary form. In these encounters between platform and form, each element of poetic meaning-making is transformed, creating a globally recognizable form that nonetheless varies in its aesthetics and production: consistent length and tone mark a poem's exposure to audience judgment, while the forms of the poems allow variation in rhythm, rhyme scheme, and message that mark the poems' different influences.

Slam Poetry's Global Networks

The competition format of the poetry slam facilitated its rapid global spread, from its starting point in 1980s Chicago through universities and cities around the world.[4] Most poetry slams today follow rules established by the US-based organization Poetry Slam, Inc. (PSI), which requires that each poet perform a work of their own creation in three to five minutes, with winners decided by audience members. Beyond the competition format, though, slam poetry varies greatly: in the words of former PSI president Scott Woods, "Poetry slams are not an art form. Poetry slams are a device, a trick to convince people that poetry is cooler. [. . .] By dressing up poetry in the raiment of a fight or a contest, it appeals to the modern taste for sensationalism in art."[5] Woods goes on to suggest that the contest format draws attention to the work itself, a "gimmick" that serves the production of socially conscious poetry. But the competition format can overshadow the production of poetry, blurring the line between gimmick and goal.

Slam competitions are judged by audience members, who are encouraged to shout out to the poets if they feel moved. Eliciting audience interactions can be key to winning. Poets engage their audiences directly, making them co-performers in a communal poetic experience. The conversational style of most slam poems invokes this personal relationship, while the emphasis on wordplay and jokes keeps a potentially fickle audience attentive. Woods maintains that this interactivity enables one "to experience that work in a way that no book or computer can capture."[6] This personal connection fosters slam's popularity online. Social media platforms have trained audiences to respond and interact directly with published works, an expectation that slam fulfills. Across media, slam poems tend to be highly emotive, often evincing exaggerated anger, heightened enthusiasm, or solemn sadness. The poem relies on the inflection and bodily presence of the performer for its meaning, with dramatic gestures helping render it immediately legible to an audience who must fathom its entire world in just a few minutes.

The capsule quality of many slam poems—what performance poet and scholar Javon Johnson calls "our witty and often heartbreaking three-minute lectures"[7]—has proven well suited to digital circulation: slam poems are brief and easily digestible, they address common concerns, and they rely on strong rhythms and sonic devices that make them relatively repeatable. Moreover, slam's general requirement that poets perform their own work reassures viewers of performers' authenticity—which is especially powerful in the face of digital anonymity. Slam's fit with digital publication has brought widespread popularity to videos like Neil Hilborn's "OCD," which was viewed over fourteen million times between 2014 and 2019. As Kila van der Starre argues: "Through a combination of the oldest form of poetry (oral) and the newest (digital) [. . .] poetry in the twenty-first century is a widespread, actively experienced and annotated, transmedia genre. [. . .] Messages in different media are 'leaping across' all over the place: live stage performance to YouTube, from YouTube to social media, personal blogs and close reading websites, from the Internet to a printed book, from a printed book to television and back to the YouTube video."[8] Digital video publication retains the embodied urgency of slam poetry, which print publication often loses. The popularity of this work—itself largely from the United States—gives emerging poets models on which to build in their own work, standardizing a hybrid form. Many slam poets I spoke with explicitly identified the documentary *Louder than a Bomb* and videos published on YouTube as among their early inspirations.[9]

Poets in southern Africa often draw on the structure of United States–based poetry slams even as they explore Afrocentric poetics. Mbongeni Buthulezi, Christopher Ouma, and Katleho Shoro argue that "the contemporary spoken words forms in the [African] continent . . . draw from the evolved versions of slam poetry popularized by Russell Simmons," even as they build on the "transgressive spirit" of oral traditions.[10] Slam, like other performance poetry in Africa, carries an ethos of community engagement. Jules Banda, who won the University of Malawi's annual slam in 2016 with a poem entitled "My Story," explained that he writes primarily about social issues because "I believe that when I'm doing my poetry, I'm both a missionary, an activist, and also more like a brother to somebody. So I share some of the most painful experiences I've endured, just to inspire the next man."[11]

In each place the form has spread, slam poets work to fulfill the social role they ascribe to poetry. Moses Serubiri, for instance, echoes a common trend in scholarship on spoken word in Africa when he analyzes Ugandan slammers in terms of their continuity with oral traditions and the country's "rich history of performance poetry."[12] South African poet Siphokazi Jonas, similarly, connects slam to Xhosa and Zulu praise poetry traditions in that "it has a very social function. It brought people together. But it was also used to critique leadership, to tell the chief, these are our grievances, and obviously to praise them and so on. [. . .] So that for me, when I write poetry that is around rallying a community, that's the poetry that I'm drawing from."[13] For Jonas, slam poetry fosters connections between poet, audience, and broader cultural landscape. It is thus a modern and largely urban response to poetic tradition. Attention to the social function of poetry ties slam poets to the communities they address, while constraining their critique to recognizable forms.

Although many poets and scholars argue that slam allows a frank discussion of socially urgent topics pertaining to marginalized communities, each performance succeeds or fails based on its ability to convince its audience of its formal and thematic merit. The poets' topics are therefore tempered by their social position and their audience's willingness or intention to listen, which can divide poet and audience.[14] A slam poem's themes must remain within a carefully moderated range, which the author judges relative to its audience. In Malawi, where debates around the legal oppression of minoritized sexual identities have been fueled by anger about international interventions, a poem arguing that homosexuality should be condemned became a popular sensation, where it would be almost unthinkable in most American and South African slam communities.[15] Thus, despite the common claim that slam opens up new venues for unspeakable stories and the wider range of voices it stages, the competition format constrains the work it promotes.

Community desires shape slam's topics, leading many poets and scholars to contend that slam in Africa represents a populist and anticolonial impulse. In Kenya, critic Mwaura Samora lauded the "new poetry" as "unlike the classical poems of yesteryears promoted by former colonial powers in Africa, where conformity controlled creativity," adding that "slams promote spoken word, a relatively new style of performance poetry that gives the artist a license for unprecedented wordplay ... either to extol virtues or to condemn vices."[16] Samora's sense of slam poetry's utopic power reflects commonly held notions that youth poetry offers an expressive outlet for marginalized communities, from queer teenagers in the United States to anonymous YouTube viewers across the Global North. Slam's investment in authenticity, its romantic imaginings of a democratic future, and its association with youth politics all mark its engagement with a digitally mediated cultural shift under which the audience becomes paramount.

This engagement is both metaphoric and literal: for many poets, digital platforms provide key avenues to engage their community. Johnson argues, "It is impossible to think about slam and spoken word poetry communities without considering how [poets] make use of virtual space."[17] In Malawi, as discussed in the previous chapter, WhatsApp's customizable data options allow poets to share recordings of poetry at relatively low cost, whereas open mic nights tap into aesthetic networks through hashtag channels on Facebook and Twitter. Digital platforms support youth-led communities in places where infrastructure otherwise limits travel and communication. At the same time, algorithms beyond the user's control mediate the poetry they access: digital gatekeepers shape contemporary poetry forms. These algorithmic aesthetics reverberate, on the ground, in the popularity of this multimodal, allusive, politically engaged form. This paradox—that corporate-controlled digital media platforms structure a liberatory form enacted in local spaces—encapsulates the contradictions of contemporary slam poetry in southern Africa: made by and for independent youth who operate outside traditional cultural institutions, it nonetheless relies on institutional structures for its success.

Over the past decade, slam poetry's spread has been managed by institutions like PSI in the United States and by international cultural outlets as the Goethe-Institut in Africa. The dominance of such institutional platforms complicates the form's claims to democratize poetry. In the United States, for instance, the "poetry slam" nominatively begins with Marc Smith's appropriation and institutionalization of poetry boxing matches. Moradewun Adejunmobi describes a typical instance in Mali, where "slam poetry was introduced formally [. . .] during the Etonnant[s] Voyageur[s] book festival."[18] These institutions ensure that slam poetry retains its essential form and theme, relying on audience adjudications that reward high emotion and surprising wordplay.[19]

Nonetheless, slam poets regularly suggest that the competition format and the egalitarian publication opportunities of digital platforms can democratize poetry. Urayoán Noel reflects this promise when he writes, "It is not that slam is inherently counterpublic in any interesting sense; it is that it opens up a space for (diasporic, feminist) counterpublic articulation."[20] In other words, the form itself is less important than the spaces it produces and the publics that gather there. In part because of its attachment to digital youth culture, slam poetry seems to spread virally, appearing unbidden in universities, urban community centers, and arts organizations. The form's conventional identifiability, together with its circulation through digital media, facilitates its proliferation in emerging cultural institutions. Yet the goals of slam poetry—popularizing literature, engaging communities, and supporting marginalized voices—are seemingly at odds with the institutional mechanisms that support its spread, including universities and cultural NGOs. So how do institutions manage those connections, offering or denying platforms to particular artists or groups? How do social media platforms and literary institutions interact in the production of local poetic norms?

The Digital Spread of the Slam Poem: KwaHaraba Open No-Mic Nights

Slam poetry's rapid proliferation illustrates the influence of digital aesthetic networks on contemporary literary form. Slam poems published online inform the poetry performed on the ground, producing consistent forms and structures across a range of local cultural contexts. The Blantyre-based KwaHaraba Open No-Mic Night showcases the hybrid superdigital and hyperlocal pattern by which slam poetry spread. It also illustrates how nascent institutions shape the regional spread of poetic forms. Every Wednesday night in 2015–16, a small group of poets and friends gathered to share and celebrate poetry at the KwaHaraba Art Gallery and Café. The evening's MC, poet Yankho Seunda, uses his bass voice, honed to a deep boom through his radio training, to draw the audience's attention to poetry without the benefit of a microphone—an absence he turns into a joke as he welcomes us to this "open no-mic night." The power often goes out during the winter droughts, and the poets and MC must shout over the hum of the venue's generator. But the audience makes up for this lack of power by recording the performances to their cell phones, marking a potential future audience—if one that is inevitably unknowable. As each poet performs, then, she addresses a global imaginary of poetry's audiences for an immediate community of fellow poets.

At each session, poets recited their poems to one another. When they had no new poems to perform, though, they took inspiration from their favorite poets. Often, this meant reading poems by US and UK poets directly from their cell phones. On 21 September 2016, for instance, the theme was "appreciation." All eleven poets performed a poem composed by one of their favorite poets. Though thematically unusual, the tribute night reveals the networks of Malawian poetry worlds. In performing others' work, poets bring it into a new space and context and thus introduce its formal standards into that space. Many poets spoke about the difficulty of choosing a single favorite poet or poem, but five of the eleven performed work by US or South African singers and slam poets, including Tupac, Coldplay, and slam poet Kurt Schroder, while six performed poems by Malawian poets. Five of those chose poems by friends or other younger poets; only one performed a "classic" work, by poet Steve Chimombo. Nine of the eleven artists performed poems they read from their mobile phones. Even in performance, poetry was mediated through mobile technology. Such constant connectivity points to artists' outward-looking, internationalist spirit, eager to engage a broad range of influences.

That night, the poet Muyanga performed a cover of American poet Jackie Hill Perry's "Suffering Servant," which he read from his phone. As Muyanga read, his vocal rhythm evoked Hill Perry's, drawing out the pauses between lines to teach his audience how to respond to the poem's emotional content. The poem begins:

> Some people make me sad
> They walk past me
> With the rattle of buried bodies in their skeletons
> And I am interested in why they haven't // dropped them off yet.

In his performance, Muyanga drew out the intermedial pause, heightening the emotional payoff. In doing so, he also taught his audience how to interpret his rhythms, so that by the time he got to the third stanza, when he paused in a similar moment, they could anticipate upcoming payoffs. The stanza reads:

> I wish I could wake them up,
> Untuck them from the comfort of lonely,
> And remind them that some dreams do come true,
> That a heart with chameleon like pain // Won't always be that color

The pause in the first stanza had clued the audience to his vocal rhythms, so that several audience members snapped after "chameleon like pain"—before they even got to the hopeful resolution of the final clause.

Of course, there is more at play here than a single moment of interaction. Hill Perry's rhythms evoke the heightened rhythms of slam poetry, which

FIGURE 8. Malawian poet Muyanga performing at the KwaHaraba Open Mic. Photo by Susanna Sacks.

circulate widely online. Before hearing Muyanga's rendition, then, the audience may have broadly known how the rhythms aligned with specific emotional responses and were thus primed to respond appropriately. They would have been familiar with the rhythmic signals of the genre, prepared to respond to the poem before they ever heard it. The poem's form and circulation taught Muyanga's audience how to respond to his performance. Such circulation transforms the relationship between poet and audience in live venues like KwaHaraba, as poets engage an audience that is simultaneously local and global.

The circulation of poetry through digital spaces has changed the poetry performed at live venues, bringing outside voices and styles into local spaces and facilitating the spread of new forms. Slam's aesthetics go viral as poets share the poems—published on YouTube and shared through direct links, Bluetooth connections, and personal hard drives—moving the poem beyond its original context and bringing the aesthetics of the original poem into the new context. Even reading others' words, the poets performed their authentic engagement with and attachment to the text, provoking the audience's laughter and sympathy, an emotional response that affirmed broader group affinities. More than the poetry itself, though, the act of sharing a space and sharing attention produced a community ethos that could, in turn, foster poetic attention. The poetry that had been published and initially encountered digitally took on new life in its grounded performance, its recontextualization allowing the production of a locally specific, aesthetically attentive community attuned to global poetic trends.

The viral spread of individual poems often belies the significance of global institutions in producing regional poetry networks. Hyperlocal spaces like KwaHaraba—which serves only a portion of a larger city's poetry community—reflect aesthetic norms that circulate through global networks. Moreover, they rely on material support from transnational cultural and development organizations. Their spread must therefore be situated within global economic structures, which help determine who has access to funding for what kinds of projects. In the next section, I turn to examine how a single institution—the Harare-based House of Hunger poetry slam—can, in conjunction with global funds aimed at cultural development, reconstruct regional literary forms.

Slam's Institutions: House of Hunger, Linda Gabriel, and Zimbabwean Poetry Networks

House of Hunger, as the first local slam in southern Africa to receive consistent funding, would go on to influence the form's circulation and character throughout the region. Between 2003 and 2015, the program attracted about a hundred regular attendees to its monthly slams in Harare. The slams culminated in annual competitions, the winners of which received funding to compete in broader regional competitions. The monthly slams introduced younger poets to mentors who performed at the community arts center the Book Café; winning the annual competitions allowed poets to travel; and franchising the slams began a regional network of competitions. The venue acted as an arts incubator for emerging voices, and its spread would reshape the performance poetry landscape in southern Africa: even as the competition format emphasizes the labor of individual poets, the institution structured poetic accomplishment through the selection of venues and the instruction of judges.

The structure of the House of Hunger Poetry Slams captures both the complex funding arrangements that support slam poetry in southern Africa and the role of digital media in its spread. House of Hunger was sponsored first by Book Café and later by Pamberi Trust. Originally founded as part of the Zimbabwe African National Union–Patriotic Front's push for cultural nationalism, Pamberi is now funded primarily through international cultural funds like Africalia, the Collinson Trust, and Alliance Française. It redistributes funds from organizations rooted in the Global North, reflecting Madhu Krishnan's suggestion that, for many literary producers in Africa, "to accept funding from a Ford Foundation, Goethe Institute, or Miles Moreland Foundation is less a capitulation to the hegemonic norms of an asymmetrically-loaded system of capital and valuation and more a radical act of reparation and resistance."[21] Redistributing funds enables Pamberi to support the arts in a struggling economy. For many Zimbabwean artists, Pamberi represents a light through a tunnel: poet and singer Vera Chisvo told me she felt that, no matter what else the country went through, "as long as Pamberi's there, it will be okay."[22] As simultaneously a funding, organizing, and production company, Pamberi symbolizes the country's cultural heritage and future.

Originally founded in 1993 and operating regularly until 2015, the Book Café was unique because, along with poetry, it offered a safe space for political and cultural discussion that would otherwise be impossible in public. The venue's regular open mics, its renowned featured artists, and its consistent location made it a central gathering point for the city's cultural producers and consumers. Its 2005 launch of the House of Hunger poetry slams opened a space for young performance-oriented poets influenced by the spreading form, as was its founder, Zimbabwean writer and activist Paul Brickhill's United Kingdom–educated son Tomas Brickhill. The slam poem's local manifestation was carried through British-educated practitioners with a wide regional network, offering young poets an accessible, globally salient form in which to center their work.

These networks drove poetic production for nearly a decade. Between 2005 and 2015, the House of Hunger Poetry Slam was an annual event, beginning with a series of small monthly mini-slams to whittle the contenders down to a set of finalists prior to the major competition each May.[23] Its stages helped launch many of Harare's young poets, including poet/comedian Comrade Fatso, international slam champion Madzitatiguru, and poet/entrepreneur Linda Gabriel. According to Gabriel, the insularity of the small slam poetry community could be energizing: because they were performing for the same audience over and over, poets had to bring in new work each month or risk disqualification. Gabriel reflected an attitude common among poets who had once performed routinely in the slam circuit when she told me that, while it did not necessarily lead to her best work, the slam forced her to produce new material regularly.[24] The monthly competitions took on a workshop-like quality, encouraging rapid, highly topical productions and helping amateur poets expand their skills.

For a poetry slam to work, the audience must know its language, its terms of engagement, and its expectations. Their attention is the currency of the evening, determining each poet's success or failure. The MC must therefore manage and focus audience attention. At House of Hunger, like many slams around the world, the MC opens every slam by calling everyone to attention to refamiliarize them with the expectations of the slam: she explains, "We're here for the poetry slam," before going on to describe the event on its own terms. The audience cheers at prescribed moments, which call their attention into question: "Can you all hear me?" "Are you excited?" These call-and-response traditions symbolize the slam's political orientations: audience-driven and adjudicated, the slam is imagined as a utopian, democratic format, where poets are free to present their personal experiences and be judged purely on their merit. The MC thus creates the conditions in which a slam poem can succeed or fail, offering normative aesthetic judgments against which audience and poet negotiate what constitutes a successful performance.

The success or failure of an individual performance will rely on the poet's ability to capture the audience's emotions and fulfill their expectations of what a poem should do. As each poet takes the stage, the audience starts off silent, waiting for the performer to earn their reactions. Gabriel's poem "Sins of Our Mothers" won the 2010 House of Hunger slam championship thanks to its direct audience engagement. The poem lists the exploitations women endure to care for their family, from prostitution to outsourced labor. It typifies the slam form in its humanization of a taboo subject, its complex audience engagement, and its rhythm and wordplay. As the performance opens, Gabriel stares down her audience and asks them to consider:

> Sins of our mothers
> That are never told to us
> That are written in silence, on their hearts
> Printed on their palms and repeated in their footsteps[25]

The opening metaphor of writing evokes the problem of poetry, inscribing the invisible "*A*'s to *Z*'s of life." From there, the poem runs through a series of anecdotes about gender-based exploitation, each one relying on wordplay to deepen its impact. The ambiguous plurality of "us" and "our" anonymizes the poem's speaker to tell a story of cultural trends rather than of individual pain and suffering. The poem's story, with details too numerous and contradictory to belong to any one person, becomes a story of collectivity. It gains momentum beyond its immediate performance, drawing the audience into the accusatory gaze of gender-based exploitation and suffering.

The sociopolitical force of "Sins of Our Mothers" relies on Gabriel's performance, an embodied experience complicated in digital remediations. Gabriel explained, "When I'm [live] on stage, my emotion, my voice, my body, everything is to do with the poem."[26] The relationship between embodiment and poetic meaning is preserved in digital recording. Yet the immediacy of digital publication—whose audiences can theoretically access the work from anywhere, at any time—comes at the cost of context, addressing a local poem to an unknowably broad audience. As Johnson argues, YouTube publication presents a tension for poets: "Easily circulated videos [on YouTube] allow us to feature the body not just in poetry but also as poetry," honoring the relationship between text and performance. Yet YouTube also fundamentally changes the poem, because "what was once a specific physical venue in which people shared their most difficult thoughts is now open to millions."[27] The relative abstraction of digital performances, which lack specifiable reception contexts, flattens the generalized critique that allowed Gabriel's live performance to avoid censure into a rehearsal of stereotype and taboo. Uprooted online, the message loses its grounding in local politics to produce a globalizing narrative of women's experiences.

The circulation of Gabriel's poetry highlights the tension of digital publication, which flattens a work by removing context-specific nuance, even as it builds connections across contexts. Gabriel capitalized on this connective possibility in 2015, when she collaborated with the Goethe-Institut Südafrika to organize the Spoken Word Project, a digitally facilitated slam competition and collaboration meant to render visible the networks of spoken word artists spanning the continent. The event began with a slam in South Africa. From there, a series of competitions in Madagascar, Angola, Kenya, Uganda, Cameroon, Mali, Côte d'Ivoire, and Germany asked poets to integrate elements from the previous country's winning selections, dramatizing the networks of poetic influence in Africa. The project became a digital anthology of "traveling stories" that culminated in a series of collective performances by the winning poets in Germany, when the memorial website was launched with recordings of the winning performances.[28] Gabriel intended the site to become a central organizing platform for poets and networkers to announce events and festivals, collaborate on ideas, and share inspiration. But shifts in funding structures led Gabriel's primary collaborator to leave the Goethe-Institut before these goals could be realized. The site remained primarily a memorial to the live event until late 2020, when it was quietly removed.

The site presents the project—and slam poetry more generally—spatially, with poets' biographies and videos linked to the city in which they performed, while swirling orange lines and arrows indicate lines of influence and engagement (figure 8). Pale grey lines imply a universe of interactions and influences beyond those mapped and created by the project. The image testifies to the expanse and limitations of slam poetry on the continent: it imagines, literally, an aesthetic network spanning capital cities across Africa. The seventy-four winners and runners-up dress in suits, t-shirts, and colorful dresses. They are all young, between eighteen and twenty-five, and live in cities. They all perform in Europhone languages, and their poems replicate the rhythms of slam poetry. Their topics include colonial traumas, contemporary inequalities, love and childhood, God and family. Their work thus typifies the global state of spoken word poetry, a memeplex that has launched an international project.

With its networked focus and hybrid online/offline form, the Spoken Word Project is perhaps the clearest realization of Gabriel's goals: to heighten

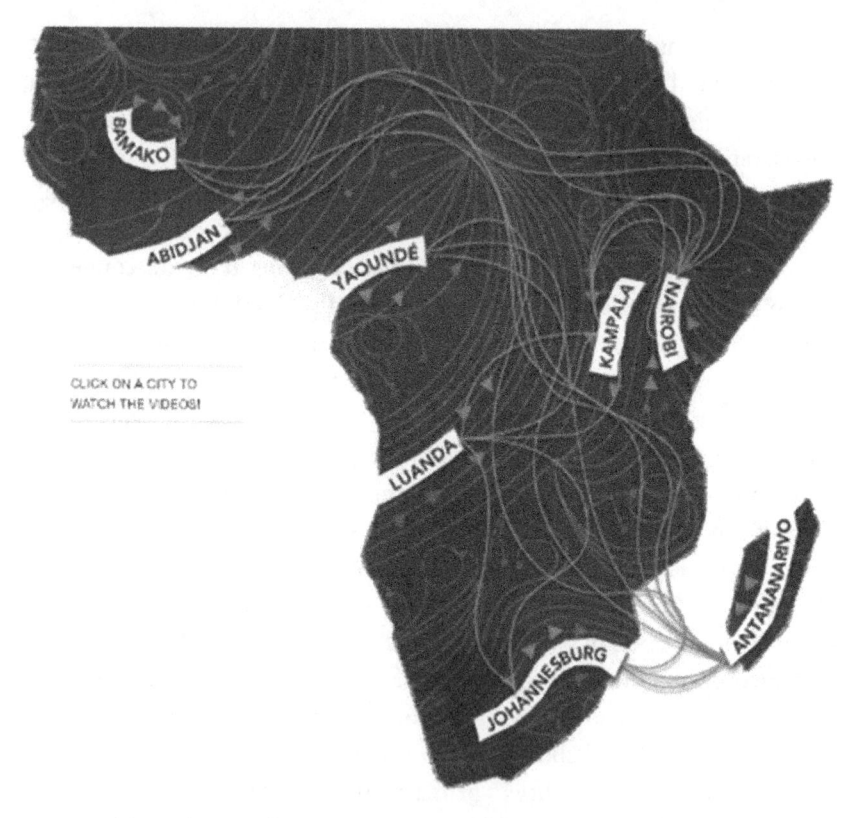

FIGURE 9. *The Spoken Word Project*. Image courtesy of the Goethe Institute Sub-Saharan Africa.

awareness of Africa's place in global literary production, to connect poets and performers across the continent, and to offer examples to inspire young poets. Gabriel's goals were largely shared by the spoken word artists I interviewed, who see digital networks as a key opportunity to connect communities in areas with limited or unreliable infrastructure. The digital, in these paravirtual frameworks, exists to facilitate grounded connections: beyond an artistic marketplace, digital distribution primarily offers a means to community development.[29] The Spoken Word Project made use of digital networks to spread a prejudged poetry form, encouraging the development of a global, performative poetics. By the end, it had created a canon of its own, honoring its twenty-four winners with prizes and critical essays. At the same time, the project's abrupt end highlighted the limits of digital connections that promise lasting collaboration but produce static recordings. The active engagement that sustains networks requires a large community of occasional contributors. International grants, though, favor short-term productions with quick payoffs, at the expense of ongoing networks and programs. This "fast policy" aimed at injecting immediate cash and addressing current needs creates enduring institutional insecurity, leaving artists reliant on external platforms with their own goals.[30]

Establishing local poetry networks instead requires identifying locally specific spaces with committed organizers. Gabriel's experience organizing poetry networks began with House of Hunger. In 2008, she worked in South Africa on behalf of the Book Café to found a satellite branch of House of Hunger in Johannesburg. While there, Gabriel collaborated with the Goethe Institute, which funded the development of a House of Hunger poetry slam, and the Alliance Française, which hosted it. The regular slam was a near-immediate success and remained so for nearly nine years, holding annual slams and workshops. House of Hunger's success has inspired the launch of other themed slams, including Word N Sound, which features musical- and rap-inspired poetry; the network-focused Poetry dot Slam, organized by Joburg Theatre Youth Development and Current State of Poetry; and the team-based Open Slam. Gabriel effectively mobilized German and French cultural NGOs to catalyze Johannesburg's poetry communities.

House of Hunger's institutional ties facilitated the development of depersonalized projects, venues, and performances. The institutional support tapped into extant networks in each city to bolster the audience that the events could reach. At the same time, it rendered the project more fragile, since the loss of any one sponsor could mean failure. In contrast, individual passion endures: as Krishnan finds, "Literary entrepreneurs and activists note that their own initiatives only survive because of the time, capital, and effort they are willing to bring to their projects, motivated by a wish to open up the space for new stories, new debates, and new modes of citationality to proliferate."[31] The stability of passion faced with unstable funding has created what Weinstein calls a "permanent instability" that is "not unusual in youth spoken word poetry."[32] For Gabriel, the motivation to support poetry networks across the continent exceeded the support any one organization might provide: it was a push to move away from one-off, grant-based funding models into broader capacity development.

Because most organizations rooted in the Global North are committed to cultural diplomacy generally rather than to a specific country, any given project within a given country is inevitably at risk. The Goethe-Institut Südafrika, for instance, seeks to "encourage intercultural dialogue and enable cultural involvement" as part of broader efforts to "convey a comprehensive image of Germany by providing information about cultural, social and political life in our nation."[33] Individual projects may falter and fail if individual actors within the organization pursue alternative routes to these goals. This structure mirrors the organization of digital communities, where artists largely rely on platforms built by programmers based in the Global North for audiences largely based in the Global North. Building platforms often requires direct, and significant, intervention. Gabriel thus acted as a mediator, working to impose what she saw as a way forward for youth poetry onto the goals of these NGOs. However, the structural constraints of these organizations—which reflect their responsibility to funders in the former imperial seat—limit the possibility for forward-looking projects. Gabriel's passion enabled her to foster new connections, but the same institutional networks that facilitated those connections ultimately reduced their durability.

The Personal Poetics of Slam Networks: Q Malewezi and the Malawian Slam Scene

Aesthetic networks like Gabriel's require that individual artists, entrenched in local networks, mobilize NGO funding to broaden aesthetic expression. However, in countries where NGOs are predominantly focused on issues of health and economic development, artists must establish funding opportunities of their own. Artists in Malawi, facing limited arts funding, make use of digital media to expand contemporary poetry performances. Digital media allow Anglophone poets to reach a broader audience internationally; they enable arts organizers to maintain connections across national space; and they maintain poetry's position as part of daily life.

Poetry is embedded in Malawian national culture: histories depict the country as a land of poets and singers, and communities define themselves by cultural memories preserved in song and by discourses perpetuated in song composition and dissemination.[34] Since 2000, the country has seen a surge of popular performance poetry in concerts, radio shows, and commercial jingles. Slam poetry—as a form committed to urgent sociopolitical concerns—emerges in this context as an urban and youth-based response to poetic tradition, one of the few spaces where political critique is encouraged. Nonetheless, the form has faced an uphill battle for institutional support: at the 2013 Lake of Stars festival, Malawi's largest arts event, MC/poet Q

Malewezi made his exit by declaring, "Finally, poetry is on the main stage—poetry wins!"[35] Sponsored by Scottish and Malawian NGOs as well as several major international companies, the festival offers artists exposure to a larger audience than they could have drawn on their own, granting those genres and media it acknowledges privileged status.

Malewezi's work has been instrumental to slam poetry's growth in Malawi. Between 2008 and 2018, Malewezi established a series of organizations, educational programs, and festivals through his media company Project Project. His work harnesses Malawi's cultural infrastructures to support a slam-oriented poetry community and audience. Malewezi's performances of slam-style poetry bring his background as a hip-hop artist into a poetry form addressing Malawian themes, using pronounced rhythms, wordplay, and call-and-response interludes to directly engage his audience as coproducers of his poetry. Their engagement connects them to the form's political stakes: as Lupenga Mphande argues, orality "provides a forum for participation in the political discourse by ordinary members of the community."[36] Malewezi's poetic form and style build on oral participation patterns, ultimately permeating youth poetry scenes across regional and linguistic divides through both the artistic force of his work and the organizations he created.

Thanks to his popularity as well as his prolific program management and mentorship relationships, Malewezi's poetry has influenced the broader national poetry community. In June 2015, for instance, he began performing a new poem, and released it as a radio single. The poem, entitled "People," has a simple structure, linking together subject and object to plea for empathy. It begins:

> People—like people.
> People—know people.
> People—love people.
> People—make—people—happy.

From this pleasantly saccharine opening, it develops into a hurried, restless, redoubling refrain by complicating the premise: "People like people people like / People want people people have," before turning violent, reminding us that "People burn people / People bomb people," and concluding with the rejoinder:

> We are more than just people.
> We
> Are a just people.[37]

The simplicity of "People" makes it easy to follow, and its structure invited substantial adaptations. These poems use repetition and a single word's many valences to carry their message—moves that were typical of "People" and that have become increasingly popular in its wake. In one such poem, which she performed during the 2016 launch tour of Malewezi's album, poet and singer Lily Banda contextualized its address, calling instead to the "Fire People" in reference to Malawi's name, which means "land of fire."[38] Her poem, composed separately from and yet echoing the structure of "People," changes Malewezi's "people" into "we the people," thus transforming the humanistic piece into an explicitly nationalist one. Lily Banda is not alone in her use of the structure: Robert Chiwamba's popular poem "Flames Sidzamva" (Flames Won't Learn), a reference to Malawi's failing national football team), repeats "Flames sidzamva, Flames sidzamva, Flames sidzamva" to frame the team's failures. The anaphoric form quickly became a recognizable poetic subgenre linking poems about the state of the nation.

Such poems spread through live performances, through WhatsApp groups, and through publication on digital platforms like YouTube and the Malawian poetry site SapitwaPoetry.com.[39] These platforms open up apparently global—or at least broadly regional—audiences and acclaim, but only after poets gain recognition among highly local communities. Malewezi's poetry workshops have helped establish communities for emerging artists since 2008. In 2012, he founded Project Project, which encouraged Malawian youth to use poetry to "project" their voices. The "Project," whose nominal repetition echoes Malewezi's poetic style, transformed his informal mentoring efforts into a professionalizing endeavor to help young poets earn money from their passion. His collaborators have in turn established their own poetry programs. Jules Banda, for instance, launched an education initiative in 2016 to provide school fees and tutoring for secondary school students. Phindu Banda set up a poetry workshop at Dzaleka Refugee Camp to encourage refugees to explore their experiences through poetry. And Robert Chiwamba worked with UNESCO to bring poetry programs into schools and community centers as part of broader literacy efforts. Together, through a series of small organizations, Malewezi and his mentees are building a youth-oriented poetry infrastructure in Malawi.

For each of these program organizers, poetry is a communal good realized in performance: each season of Chiwamba's program concludes with a series of performance competitions, and Phindu Banda's work at Dzaleka Refugee Camp culminated in a festival performance. Their work corroborates Weinstein's observation that "[a]rt, justice, and cultural consciousness are core concepts for youth spoken word poetry. Each is centrally about communication, about claiming voice and being heard."[40] But, unlike most United States–based spoken word organizations, many of these performances are commissioned by international agencies. Poets commonly rely on commissions from NGOs and commercial organizations to supplement their income, performing jingle-like poems in support of the group's message or programming—even as they wish for the freedom to critique them.

As in Zimbabwe, the primary funders of poetry in Malawi are foreign NGOs with their own goals: in 2014, for instance, the World Bank ran a poetry competition on the theme "What will Malawi look like in 50 years." The winning poems, by and large, emphasized personal responsibility as key to the struggling country's economic future. These institutions gate what poetry is heard and promoted: the World Bank winners converged on issues of personal responsibility and anti-corruption, aligning with the World Bank's policy initiatives at a moment when the organization's involvement in Malawian policy was under question.[41] By promoting certain works, these organizations implicitly draw attention away from others, often filtering out critical poems in favor of flattering ones. Local organizers like Malewezi play key roles in helping poets make a name for themselves based on less purely ideological evaluations.

Emerging poets rely on local recognition and validation before their work can gain traction in the transregional spaces of YouTube and Facebook. This traction can develop surprisingly fast. In late 2015, just after he had recorded "People," Malewezi posted to Facebook requesting names of promising young poets to join him on his album launch tour. The tour would culminate in a performance at Lake of Stars, the country's largest arts festival. Open calls for collaboration allowed Malewezi to reach a diverse cross section of youth poets. Fans of Phindu Banda, who was then a student and had just begun performing, suggested her name. Through their contact on social media, she went on to work and perform with Malewezi, launching a national presence from a few local successes. The digital thus opened opportunities and networks well beyond that provided by traditional, geographically bounded writing workshops.

Interactions online shape the poetry performed in person, even as live performances create new communities to interact online, highlighting the interpenetration of these seemingly incompatible spaces. The poem Phindu Banda presented at that year's Lake of Stars evoked the repetitive trend popularized by Malewezi's "People." Her poem begins quietly, but as it progresses, her volume and tempo rise in the crescendo of slam poetry:

> This is a nothing poem
> Written by
> A nothing poet
> For a nothing nation with nothing to show the next generation
> These / are nothing letters
> Molded into nothing words
> Joined together to form nothing sentences
> To highlight your nothing prison sentences.[42]

The wordplay, rhythm, and repetition are common features of slam poetry, but the clear political message sets this poem apart. It indicts the largely international audience's perceptions of Malawi as an impoverished, "nothing" nation populated by uneducated, "nothing" people. Because of the circulation of this form across languages and media, audiences could recognize the poem when they heard it. They learned from Banda's cues how to respond to her poem: by the end, they sighed in time with her rhythm, creating a collective performance.

Spoken word requires cultural legibility to take hold, a specificity that ironically translates more readily across national spaces than within them. The standardization of literary forms, through both algorithmic management and international travel, has created cosmopolitan networks that stretch across nations but do not necessarily engage local communities outside urban centers. In Malawi, popular poetry radio programs help poets gain exposure, but such programming has also standardized poetic production, with most poets falling into a few distinct stylistic camps, whether serious or comic, intensely rhythmic or lightly conversational. Digital publication enables poets to share work for an international audience on their own terms but lacks the built-in audience of the radio show. It opens gates for those poetic works that suit its publication and aesthetic norms: ones that are multimodal, interactive, and emotional. In other words, this digital institution—absent intervention by individual gatekeepers like Malewezi—implicitly promotes slam-influenced poetry styles, in both its local production and its transnational reproduction.

Troubling Slam's Conscience

The self-publishing impulses of social media have encouraged a growing number of poets and commentators to describe, film, and photograph their experiences, producing narratives of what poetry is—or might be. But it has also provoked debates about the nature of "poetry," as a form, reflecting broader concerns about who can claim the prestige that comes with the title "poet" or "poetry." Stanley Kenani, one of Malawi's foremost living writers, wrote in an interview with the *Nation* that young Malawian poets should instead be called "jokers: writers who write jokes and try to pass them out as poetry. They show no interest to learn more about the art and are more interested in quick fame."[43] For Kenani, the speed of slam poetry production reflects a shallow engagement with literary tradition, leading him to reject spoken word artists' claims to the label of "poetry."

Responding directly to these debates, Chiwamba contends that the term *poetry*, and its attendant anxieties, are essentially colonial holdovers. For Chiwamba, "poetry" as an elevated verbal form with specific aesthetic standards refers to "traditional English poetry," which has no place in a decolonized Malawi. Chiwamba argued that gatekeepers want poetry to engage deeply with idioms and proverbs—"things no one understands anymore." For Chiwamba, the job of the contemporary Malawian poet is to make poetry relevant to current issues, embracing the engaging rhythms and wordplay typical of slam poetry. He said: "The current generation hardly speaks proverbs, hardly speaks idioms, hardly speaks any language. They just speak plain language, and it is an instant in society where they don't have to go to a poem and start getting the proverbs to start understanding. They just want something that is plain, something they can understand. And the poets have responded to that and shifted from the traditional poetry to other one." Instead, the future of poetry in Malawi lies in rejecting the term *poetry* altogether: "What the current crop of poets is doing is vernacular spoken word, whilst what the older group of poets is doing is traditional English poetry [in Chichewa]." Many Anglophone poets have responded by calling themselves "spoken word artists," abandoning the term *poet* altogether and carving out an alternative niche for themselves in the process. Nonetheless, Chiwamba, who writes only in Chichewa, holds onto the position of *alakatuli* (poet) because "poetry can have a huge impact on Malawi, because I am saying many people are now following poetry, and the poetry artists that are well known are very few in this country."[44]

But, as detailed in the introduction to this volume, "poetry" has deep political stakes, tied in the sixteenth century to the development of a literate class; in the eighteen and nineteenth centuries to the rise of national identities; in colonial practices to the division of civilized and savage peoples; and to the fetishization of folk practices and political investments in the avant-garde. In Malawi, Hastings Kamuzu Banda founded and commissioned the Chichewa department at the University of Malawi to begin writing poetry in Chichewa as a way, first, to demonstrate the language's ability to carry culture and, second, to promote it as a national language.[45] And, as Harri Englund notes, Chiwamba's prescriptions are far from universal: Benedicto Malunga, for instance, emphasizes the presence of traditional literary motifs in political and religious speech.[46] "Poetry," and its Chichewa near-synonym *ndakatulo*, thus remains a culturally potent term, one that carries the weight of history with it—a history that makes the stakes of the current artistic debate remarkably high. Poetry's cultural prestige constrains the forms of literary production that may claim its label. The debates that rage over its future will further shape the poetry that emerges.

To no small degree, this debate is generational, as the digital circulation of slam's form and its insistence on competition produces an eternally young set of practitioners. Several of the poets I spoke to—both current and retired slam poets—suggested that poetry competitions are for young poets and that established or older poets will inevitably turn to longer-form and more meditative performance forms. Linda Gabriel, for instance, told me that at thirty-one, she had stopped slamming because "slam is more like a spring board. [...] Slam for me is about energy, because I only have three minutes and have to give it my all. So that energy is different than when I'm storytelling," as she does in her long-form performance pieces.[47]

Although a few older poets take part in the slam poetics of the younger generation, younger poets are acutely aware of the insecurity of their position. Mbongeni Nomkonwana, cofounder with Lwanda Sindaphi of Cape Town–based Lingua Franca Spoken Word Movement, disclaimed the poetics of his own work before performing at a book launch at Cape Town's Book Lounge in May 2016. The launch featured two poets, both of whom came from a slam background: Nomkonwana, who performs in English and isiXhosa, and Blaq Perl, an Afrikaaps and English poet from the Cape Flats.[48] Together, their performances showcased the range of poetic languages and performance styles currently popular in the city. Before beginning, though, Nomkonwana told the audience, "I am a spoken word artist. Notice I don't use the word poet, because that word carries all sort of problems."[49]

Nomkonwana later clarified that, for him, the primary "problems" with the word "poet" lay in the formal expectations it carried. Abandoning the "lyric, haiku, blank verse" forms that failed to reflect "the state of our country," "we write mostly about what happens in our daily lives, so most of the time, you don't think form, you think, I want to say something," and to do that, the simplest and most direct way is often best. Moreover, those imported forms will often fail in local languages: as he points out, "In isiXhosa [as in most

Bantu languages], one word can have seventeen syllables"—making syllabic forms like the haiku or blank verse inappropriate at best.[50] Instead, the key is to write a poetry of life, evoking feeling rather than explaining it, producing a sympathetic experience between performer and audience. The shared experience of the spoken word poem allows highly local experiences to travel broadly through a recognized format, crossing media in order to cross cultural experiences while retaining its form.

Even as he rejects the term *poetry*, Nomkonwana embraces the cultural engagement it presumes. He writes primarily in isiXhosa to encourage literary expression in his home language. When we first met, the Fees Must Fall protests were at their height, and student protesters had been tear-gassed the day before. Considering the political and historical circumstances in which he found himself, Nomkonwana told me: "Amidst all this fighting, there's one thing that we might lose and forget, it is our tongues, it is our culture, it is where we come from. If you look at it, we fight in English, we have to speak in English every day, we are fighting a system that is mostly colonial so you have to keep the culture, so that by the time that's done, you still have a home to come back to." Nomkonwana's perspective echoes that of many younger spoken word artists. For them, poetry tells the story of everyday struggles and triumph, and it does so through "minimum words" and the immediate emotionality of images.

In September 2014, Lingua Franca was asked to organize the "Poetica" portion of the Open Book Festival, Cape Town's largest annual literary festival. Guided by Lingua Franca, the festival brought together young poets from across South Africa, culminating in a debate about whether the current slam-centric state of performance poetry in the country was sustainable. The debate focused on what it would mean—politically and aesthetically—to make slam poetry indigenous. Could, and should, slam poetry draw on indigenous poetry performance traditions? Reflect local poetic norms? Or do its roots in United States institutions, and its practitioners' education in Western-style universities, preclude such adaptations? Lingua Franca brought its concerns to the attention of poets based in Johannesburg, where the country's slam scene is largest and most cohesive. The goal, according to Nomkonwana, was to open a conversation about the cultural politics of slam poetry, broadening its generic forms to include a more diverse array of aesthetics. Although slam's sound has traveled with the format, bringing the recognition that comes with competition to a younger and wider array of poets, the contentiousness of this debate—with many poets feeling attacked or silenced—suggests that the form carries a political and cultural cost that has yet to be fully confronted. Lingua Franca recognized that poetry moves as a cohesive cultural unit which transforms as it spreads while maintaining its essential form and ethos. Framing the debate in terms of indigeneity, the group challenged the poetic community to transform the spoken word form, to make it meaningful to local audiences.

Localizing the Spoken Word: Lingua Franca's South African Slam Poetry

Led by Nomkonwana and Lwanda Sindaphi, Lingua Franca mobilizes the popular formulas of spoken word in service of local poetic productions that honor Cape Town's layered, multicentric cultural history. The collective embraces the goals of slam poetry but uses Xhosa instruments, a wide range of genres and languages, and collective poetics to produce a hybrid poetry that addresses the city's past and its people's history. The work as a collective thus reflects the hybridity Jahan Ramazani has identified in postcolonial literature writ large: "The aesthetic complexity of literary texts [...] invites the exegete to attend to the intercultural tensions and fusions at the level of language, style, concept, and genre," in part because the diversity of the collective enacts these very fusions.[51] Lingua Franca's most recent production, *Umzila ka Moya* ("Spirit's Path"), uses participatory poetics to confront the legacies of colonialism and urbanization. The production features a series of poets performing pieces about their heritage and their home lives in their home languages, with music and dance incorporated to mark sonic continuities across the poets' experiences. During the performance, each speaker moves fluidly between center and periphery, as easily claiming as yielding the speaking stage through a choreographed event that mirrors the structure of an open mic but abandons its atomizing effects in favor of a clear, cohesive whole.

Umzila ka Moya asks its poets and its audience to announce their heritage, their home place and tribe, or else to confront the absence of a past, the deracination and displacement that is the legacy of colonialism and apartheid. Nomkonwana's "Dying Tongues," as incorporated into *Umzila ka Moya*, dramatizes his linguistically mixed background. The piece begins as he claims his identity in isiXhosa, sePedi, and seTswana, before spitting out:

> We now write in English, we speak in English, we dream in English
> I think my spoken word sounds better in English.
> Even computers don't recognize our tongues:
> They underline every word red as if we degrade our language

INSTITUTIONALIZING ALGORITHMIC AESTHETICS

> I am sick up to the neck with spelling check
> I do not loathe the English language
> I am suffocating from the stench it has left on my people's brains because
> It has rotted underneath our languages, forgotten
> And our government is slumbering while indigenous languages are dying[52]

Audiences laugh along with Nomkonwana's criticism of Microsoft Word but are often stopped short by his outrage at having to abandon his mother tongue for the sake of technological globalization. Nomkonwana dramatizes the impossibility of finding roots in a neocolonial state while indicting the South African government for its Anglocentrism. The poem blends personal history with political acumen to insist on the relevance of artistic expression to social progress.

But Nomkonwana does not take the stage alone. *Umzila ka Moya* is structured around audience engagement: the audience enters the venue through the stage, joining the poets in dance, song, and clapping, before they take their seats. Eventually, the performance itself takes over the space of the audience: one poem, performed during the group's 2018 residency at Northwestern University in Illinois, speaks of funerals, homesickness, and the eternal feeling of rootlessness. It begins in silence as the performer, Katleho Kano Shoro, kneels on the ground to light the herb *impepho*. The cleansing smoke

FIGURE 10. Lingua Franca perform *Umzila ka Moya* at the Poetry Foundation, Chicago, IL on 4 April 2017.

diffuses over the audience, entering their bodies as they inhale, and Shoro begins her poem in an incantation:

> Funerals
> Sound
> Like wailing.[53]

The lighting of impepho, Shoro's resonating voice, and the rest of the performers standing behind her bring the audience physically into the performance, even those who remain seated. The interactivity of the poetry slam is transformed by the rituals of the impepho into a shared, embodied experience of the breath. Simultaneously a poetry performance and a ritual, the performance is a reminder of the spoken word's many guises and powers: multiple audience members and poets reported feeling a "spiritual calling" during the work. At any given performance, audience members cry, wail, and weep. They come away speaking of catharsis and healing.

After the success of *Umzila ka Moya*, Lingua Franca developed the production into a workshop for its youth mentorship program, the Cape Youth Poetry Hub for Expression and Rhythm (CYPHER). The workshop provides "a pedagogic approach that helps individuals who are longing for a place to belong. [. . .] Through songs, rituals, and indigenous/mother-tongue idioms, each poet goes through a cleansing ceremony by unlearning what was imposed by colonial forces."[54] The workshop offers what Lingua Franca calls "naked storytelling": stripping away clichés and generalities to get at the personal specificities of each participant's experiences. Through weekly meetings and occasional retreats over the past four years, CYPHER has fostered a community of young poets from across Cape Town's suburbs and townships, moving beyond the institutional bases of poetry slam competitions—often focused on universities and cultural NGOs like the Goethe-Institut—to instead draw on forms circulated in township theater, orature, and popular music.

These workshops honor the host of cultural influences shaping young poets' lives. Participants develop works that use personal experience to express political critique—including Vusumuzi Mpofu's "Foreign Searching for Rain." In the poem, whose multimedia circulations opened this chapter, national difference is expressed through Mpofu's body, forced to reckon with a new place and a new language. The poem opens:

> Zimbabwe was burning
> We were burning along with it

> These charcoaled skins we are mocked for are not by accident
> We come from burning homes
> Clouds have burnt to ashes
> My people are thirsty
> Migrating to the southern side of the border in search for rain, becoming
> Foreign back home
> We spoke of South Africa as the blessed land where anyone could quench their thirst from the plentiful pouring rain[55]

Throughout Mpofu's piece, Zimbabwe and South Africa stand at odds with each other, each framed through the speaker's imagined understanding of the other and of his own lost home. As Mpofu enters South African life, the border recedes, and his story comes into focus as one of migration, displacement, and personal longing.

Umzila ka Moya and Lingua Franca's pedagogical work imagine an alternative poetic structure that expands the potential of the slam poem itself. It animates poems like Mpofu's, which use personal exigencies to address global experiences. The form encourages the type of international critique that Mpofu levies, challenging nationalist ideas that center cultural power in economically powerful countries like South Africa or the United States. Responding to slam poetry's emphasis on the political elements of personal experience, on a performative collaborative format, and on the direct participation of audience members, Lingua Franca has produced a multicentric performance form that incorporates a range of poetic and musical attitudes. Their minimalist performance style—relying on acoustic instruments, simple costuming, the flow of individual bodies, and attentive listening—allows the audience to directly enter the scene, expanding the stage to incorporate the entire performance venue and resist dichotomies of audience/performer inscribed in slam poetry and theatrical performance forms. The production becomes a collaborative, populist endeavor, producing a local poetics of engagement through the global logic of slam.

Regional Networks, Local Poetics

Lingua Franca's work in *Umzila ka Moya* combines the interactivist ethos of slam, the social role of performance poetry in southern Africa, and the hybrid aesthetics of Cape Town's contemporary cultural landscape. Poetry slams brought Lingua Franca's members together—and into the poetry scene—by offering a hybrid, anticolonial image of what poetry can do. The slam moved the poem from the classroom into a social space where it addressed current issues in everyday language and in an exciting form. By maintaining slam's participatory culture but rejecting the competition "gimmick," Lingua Franca offers a model of performative poetics that evokes both House of Hunger's slams and Malewezi's mentorship programs.

Slam's rise has empowered young artists. Major arts institutions incorporated the work of young slam poets as a means of engaging popular audiences. Spoken word poetry brings together the popular and the elite in a sometimes uneasy alliance in such spaces as university classrooms and literary festivals. Slam poetry's emphasis on current events and social relevance reflects culturally potent models of poetry as producing social affiliations and critiquing social action. Its competitive format and youth-oriented aesthetics have shifted its audience, producing urban communities of young poets who are making new stages for themselves. Its regional rise testifies to the importance of digital circulation and social mediation in contemporary poetic production and communities. The relative consistency of slam poetry's aesthetic form and thematic concerns speak to the ongoing cultural influence of institutions rooted in the Global North, including Button Poetry and Def Jam, but its variations illuminate processes by which artists reclaim their own cultural heritage. Although the form may be bound by global power structures, its practitioners sustain its liberating potential.

At the same time, however, the ongoing role of cultural NGOs in establishing and maintaining poetry slams should encourage skepticism: How is cultural power negotiated in these spaces? What is the relationship between transnational funding organizations, digital aesthetic networks, and shifting poetic forms? These questions come to the fore in the international arts festival, the focus of my next chapter. Drawing together questions of performance, audience expectations, nationalism, and digital virality, I interrogate international poetry performance events in South Africa and Zimbabwe, treating them as sites through which poetic agency may be negotiated apart from, yet in conversation with, digital sites of production and digital aesthetic norms. I argue that the imagined cosmopolitanism of the contemporary poet comes into tension with the international audience's expectations of an "authentic" performance, staging anew the poet's conscription into the collective logics of the nation.

CHAPTER 4

Migrating Movements
POETRY FESTIVALS AND THE LIMITS OF DIGITAL COSMOPOLITANISM

DIGITAL NETWORKS POSITION poets in a vexed relationship to both popular audiences and broader institutions. In a digital world, all poets implicitly perform for a vast, unknown, unknowable, and ultimately foreign audience. Their poetry is always already on display for a broader audience, implicitly made to represent their identity and community to an outside gaze. Digital poetry thus repositions the poet as cultural ambassador—a role that comes to the fore in the national arts festival. Online, the emphasis on authenticity has facilitated a rise in confessional literary forms, including many of the slam poems discussed in the previous chapter. But it can have paradoxical effects on African literature, recapitulating colonialist and neocolonial fetishizations of "authentic" Africanness. If, as James Yékú argues, "the dialectical tensions between popular culture and public spaces in Africa today cannot be adequately understood without critical attention to social media and its performative and theatrical possibilities," then the tensions emerge most strongly in spaces where poets are compelled to perform national identity and culture for an international audience—such as the national arts festival.[1] National arts festivals compel poets to perform their local, particular identities to transnational, cosmopolitan audiences, recapitulating the structures of digital publication. They simultaneously reprise poetry's historic role in defining national culture while opening new questions about the position of the poet in public life.

The contemporary arts festival stages the tension between poetry's role as sacred and profane and the poet's position as local and transcendent. Since

FIGURE 11. *"But actually, they are people just like us."* Malawian musician Faith Mussa performing at Tumaini Festival in 2016. Image from Tumaini Letu's Kickstarter campaign, 1 November 2021, courtesy of the Tumaini Festival.

2014, the Tumaini Festival in Dowa, Malawi, has hosted the world's first arts festival within a refugee camp. In Malawi, where there is only one refugee camp and where refugees lack freedom of movement or employment, the experiences of the nearly thirty thousand people living in Dzaleka Refugee Camp—most of them from Rwanda, Uganda, the Democratic Republic of Congo, and Mozambique—remain largely invisible to the national public.[2] But for one day each year, nearly two thousand people come to the camp, not to engage in "voluntourism" but to see art. During the festival, Dzaleka's daily routines shift, as artists set up tents to sell their work and performances appear on stages around the camp. Videos from the event testify to the audience's engagement: interviewees describe the camp's bustle and vibrance, so unlike the impoverished environment they had envisioned (figure 11). Artists from Dzaleka perform alongside popular Malawian acts, reminding the visitors that their work stands together in a shared artistic world. The performances reflect the artists' diverse national and cultural backgrounds, with renditions of Rwandan dance and Congolese music. The arts festival, simultaneously a space of national celebration and cosmopolitan interactions, highlights the role of the international audience in affirming national identities. Ironically, this role is heightened for the stateless artist, for whom the festival becomes a space of individual agency in a cosmopolitical community.

Where Tumaini offers refugee poets—otherwise stateless subjects—cosmopolitical agency, other festivals produce a more vexed response to poetry's cosmopolitan imaginary. The poetry festival simultaneously enables the performance of cosmopolitan engagements and consecrates poets' attachment to inalienable national identities. Poets at arts festivals navigate what Eileen Julien has called an "extroverted" gaze, at once universalizing and particular. If, as Julien has argued, the "extroverted novel" was the means by which African identities were constructed and reified for a simultaneously national and transnational audience, then the poetry festival is a space to experience those identities, staging "'global' practices and institutions [that] become the means of expressing local identities and values on a world stage."[3] Poetry performances stage embodied national identities for both conationals and the rest of the world.[4] If the canon of African literature has been constructed through "border crossing" works, rather than through the work of literature in situ, arts festivals construct a uniquely material space of cultural reception, one in which to perform and realize an Afrocentric cosmopolitanism. They bring to the ground interactions happening online. Contemporary poetry festivals demand the artists perform their national identity to an audience that is simultaneously highly local and (imagined to be) entirely cosmopolitan. Publishing for international audiences requires that poets offer relatively universalist poems, while the audience's "cosmopolitan" tastes demand a "native" authenticity. Such cosmopolitanism situates contemporary imaginaries of the national subject within transnational frameworks.

In this chapter, I situate Tumaini alongside the South African literature festival Poetry Africa and the Malawian arts festival Lake of Stars to illustrate how poets navigate between the cosmopolitan imaginaries of digital publication and the fetishizing demands for "authentic" performances—not merely of the poet's individual brand identity but also tied specifically to their national identity. Poetry Africa, the oldest and largest poetry festival on the continent, brings together a range of poets from around the world to perform for South African audiences. Lake of Stars, a music festival founded in 2003, stages Malawian acts to attract international tourists. In each case, performance festivals become sites of poetic community formation in which the particular anxieties of digital interactions—anxieties about identity and authenticity, about urgency and reactivity, and about community and connection—are worked out. After providing a history of poetry and arts festivals in the twentieth and twenty-first centuries, this chapter analyzes audience-poet interactions at Poetry Africa and Lake of Stars to demonstrate how poets navigate audience expectations and broader structural constraints at festivals. The paradoxical demand for "authenticity" across online and offline spaces emerges from the cosmopolitan imaginaries staged at arts festivals—a paradox I explore further in the vexed presentation of marginalized identities at Poetry Africa and Tumaini.

Like the poetry slam and social media platforms, the poetry festival is invariably a commercial entity—if one that purports to exceed commercial valuation, offering cultural value, community, and historical connections. But unlike the protest poem, the poetry slam, or the digital poem, each of which penetrates everyday life, the poetry festival is a time set apart from everyday life, sanctifying and authorizing poetic distinction. Nonetheless, arts festivals increasingly accede to the norms developed online in their own curation, inviting slam poets and encouraging audience interactions. Attending to the vectors of power and influence in this space demonstrates the tension between contemporary cosmopolitical ideals and consumerist demands for local specificity in the production of cultural capital.

The Poetry Festival and the New Nation

In many ways, poetry festivals evoke an imagined origin point for poetic production by bringing a community together to hear poetry from its source. The contemporary festival tradition developed from nineteenth-century arts festivals in Europe as a middle-class attempt to reimagine and reclaim nationalist folk identities. Poetry in particular offered a language for the expanding European and Euro-American nation to identify itself and claim its history during this time.[5] Pascale Casanova's *World Republic of Letters* traces this rapid rise of national literatures to "these dominated areas within Europe," which had suffered under internal empires, because "already by the time the first nationalist claims began to be asserted in the nineteenth century they had accumulated sufficient assets of their own to cause upheavals that were registered in the centers, upsetting the old hierarchies of the established literary order." Thanks to such Herderian nationalisms, "literary institutions, academies, school syllabuses, the canon—all these things now having become instruments of national identity, the idea of dividing up national literatures on the exact model of political units began to acquire a sort of natural appeal and, indeed, inevitability."[6] The literature festival, in turn, models national identity and culture for an extranational audience.

The contemporary festival was necessarily preceded by the advent of twentieth-century liberal cosmopolitanism, which espouses the virtue of intercultural exchange in and across urban centers. The international arts festival specifically emerged after World War II, during a moment of troubled nationalism, as failing empires and emerging anti-colonial movements sought to define themselves both for their own people and for a broader, international world. They often did so through poetry and epics: forms that have historically been pressed into service as prototypically national expressions. Many poets embraced this role, writing nationalist poems of admiration, but many more found themselves read in nationalist terms despite ambivalent personal attachments to the nation.[7] Matthew Hart contends that, beginning among the high modernist poets of the early twentieth century, print poetry moved from being implicitly or contentiously nationalist to being explicitly, deliberately, and often confrontationally national. What Hart calls "synthetic vernaculars"—a printed, reified version of vernacular speech—allowed poets to claim and reframe national identities, creating nations from their poetic projects.[8] This was especially important for poets who worked across national contexts: the writers Hart describes, such as Kamau Brathwaite and Melvin Tolson, move internationally, contending with their position as speakers of either "minor" or "major" vernaculars within implicit power structures but from a physical and social position outside their nation of birth, citizenship, or education.

These movements, staged in the poetry festival, establish a cosmopolitan ideal of literature: eminently translatable, poetry would bring together artists and audiences from across national spaces to create a form of global community. As anti-colonial movements mounted in the Global South and European countries strove to redefine themselves following World War II, arts festivals brought together these contrasting ideals in a tenuous binding of corporate sponsorship and radical idealism, a partnership that persists today. The prototypical festival of this period was the Edinburgh International Festival, founded in 1947 to showcase the range of Scottish artistic and cultural products to the broader European and Anglophone worlds.[9] The festival was marked by a tension between artistic radicalism and commercial authorization from the beginning, though: within two years, avant-garde and popular artists excluded from the official festival began a "fringe" festival which has since eclipsed the original international festival. This tension has remained a hallmark of national arts festivals.

In southern Africa, poetry festivals evoke an imagined connection between poetry and cultural norms. This connection comes from both internal and external cultural forces. Poetry was central to nationalist endeavors in the colonial and independence eras.[10] Praise poetry, in particular, was empowered to tell communal histories and thus establish a national collectivity bound by that history. Independence leaders turned to praise poetry to suggest popular support for their cause.[11] Poetry was thus connected to popular performances and political claims. Across the British Empire, meanwhile, colonial administrators deployed literature in general, and poetry in particular, to spread English culture and teach colonial behavior, promoting what Kwame Dawes describes as "the colonial genius" for "constructing a myth of greatness."[12] Anti-colonial agitators turned these impulses against their oppressors by mobilizing poetry to prove their cultural worth and well-being. In South Africa, in particular, students and teachers at missionary schools brought English and Indigenous literary traditions to the broader cultural and political fight against colonial impositions.[13] These poetic uses became popular at political rallies and strikes, where they entertained protesters as days dragged on, before consolidating into formal festivals by the mid-1980s.[14]

Today, arts festivals proliferate across the continent. They exhibit tensions between artistic experimentation and institutional consolidation, presenting a wide range of artistic forms that promote diverse and sometimes-contradictory political norms.[15] The expansion of these nationalist events in the twenty-first century reflects anxieties about the nation's exceptionalism in the face of global cosmopolitanism and transnational digital networks. Contemporary arts festivals serve diplomatic ends, highlighting the nation's position relative to its neighbors. They show off the host community's best artists, as well as its ability to draw together and support great poets from across the world or target region. Performing a national self for an international audience, the poet at the arts festival offers a cosmopolitan vision of poetry's translatability—even as she invariably flags her own poetry as in need of translation. Emphasis on authenticity has grown in the confrontation with digital media, the distance and accessibility of which provokes anxiety about the content producer's identity.[16] In an African context, though, this digital emphasis on "authenticity" recapitulates colonialist fetishizations of the "authentic" African.

By staging transnational audience-poet interactions, the poetry festival places the poet at the center of a cultural "contact zone," where, Mary Louise Pratt writes, "disparate cultures meet, clash, and grapple with each other, often in highly asymmetrical relations of domination and subordination."[17] The festival implicitly establishes norms for political and cultural engagement. It confers on the invited artists what Heather Inwood has labeled "cultural citizenship": "Being a poet-citizen [. . .] involves declaring membership in a broader poetry community through participation across multiple media spaces, adherence to specific interpretive strategies for reading and writing poems, and being recognized as a poet-citizen by other poets, critics, and academics."[18] And, at contemporary festivals, poets simultaneously become "cultural netizens," declaring their participation in a broader landscape of cultural diplomacy that bridges print, performance, and digital spheres.[19] By deciding who to let in, the festival implicitly determines what sorts of poetry, or art, merit attention in the first place. But festivals also require that poets appeal to an unknowably broad audience—one immediately present at the festival itself and one reaching into futurity, in the festival's archives.

Arts festivals thus promote twentieth-century ideals of cosmopolitanism even as they confront twenty-first century anxieties about authenticity, exoticism, and cultural tourism. Whether local visitors in search of the best their community can attract or tourists looking for the best the community has produced, attendees turn to festivals for snapshots of the local cultural scene. As communal spaces for poetic reception, these festivals implicitly legitimate certain cultural producers, establishing norms for political and cultural engagement. But to retain that power, they must remain current, demonstrating their ability to sanction even trendy cultural productions. Leaping across media platforms, poetry draws in new audiences, demonstrating a piece's widespread relevance. They create connections across local and regional, digital and grounded, networks. If, as I argued in the previous chapter, the poetry slam models the movement of literary production across platforms, the festival space represents a unique opportunity to investigate how forms of *reception* leap across media technologies and poetic genres.

Much like social media engagement, the poetry festival makes reception primary, embedding the audience in the space and network of the festival itself. At festivals, canonicity, pedagogic practice, and the hard-won realities of artistic life butt up against each other as artists, organizers, policymakers, and everyday literary audiences enter one another's circles. Poets are expected to communicate their unique, individual experience yet reflect some essential poetic nationhood, while simultaneously representing a universal subjectivity. They are expected, in sum, to create a synthetic nation that reads as universal. Festivals contextualize poets relative to one another, the audience, and the location. Where digital poetry is framed by the implicit possibility of connection, the poetry festival isolates individual performers in order to recontextualize them and thus forge novel connections. Festivals transform individual poets into cosmopolitical subjects, at the mercy simultaneously of their own state and of judgment by a global, metropolitan audience. As Neil Lazarus declares: "To be at home in the world is not only to be travelled and 'worldly,' it is to be capable of retaining one's centre of gravity, one's ability to be oneself, wherever in the world one might be. One is not born, but *made* cosmopolitan. To inhabit cosmopolitanism as a structure of feeling, one has to develop a critical faculty and to assume command of the affective and institutional means of using it."[20] Festival performances implicitly empower poets to perform their cosmopolitanism through their inhabitance of a specific, locally grounded, national subjecthood.

Contemporary festivals project themselves forward into a past they are busy creating. As communal spaces for poetic reception, festivals are events of and for history and therefore inevitably concerned with their own archive. Contemporary festivals project themselves forward into a past they are busy creating through the obsessive archives of social media. Social media publication allows poetry festivals' advertisements and archives to blend seamlessly with a wider array of cultural products, potentially even removing them from their national contexts. In the obsessive archives of social media, which are both indelible and yet functionally illegible, festivals continue to archive themselves. As reading cultures evolve, poets' popularity on social media itself marks cultural currency for festival organizers. Social media popularity can further enhance a viral poet's cultural cachet by getting them invited to the festival itself. Festivals' digital engagement is thus cyclic: poetic virality influences which poets take the stage, and the digital archives they manage in turn influence who goes viral.

Arts festivals stage the negotiated nature of national and networked identities: historical frameworks and top-down hierarchies structure expectations, but they succeed only insofar as they align with popular demands. Shifting poet-audience interactions at literature festivals illuminate the processes by which digital norms shape literary form: changing audience's expectations, creating new curatorial pressures, and even restructuring the broader social environment. How do these poems position their national authority? And how do the contexts of their publication, performance, and reception interpolate them relative to the nation's possibilities? At Poetry Africa, the largest and longest-running poetry festival on the continent, the institution of the host university takes precedence over the performance, compelling poets and audience members to adhere to its norms in their communication. But audiences, trained through poetry slams and social media to enter into conversation with the performers, find ways to shape the event for themselves.

Creating Poetry's Audiences at Poetry Africa 2016

Poetry Africa is the largest and oldest poetry festival on the continent. Each year since 1997, the organizers—who are based at the University of KwaZulu Natal (UKZN) Centre for the Creative Arts (CCA)—invite poets from around the world to a weeklong residency in Durban. While there, the poets perform each night to an audience of students and local enthusiasts at the university's Elizabeth Sneddon Theatre. During the day, poets hold workshops, give performances, and attend events at schools, community centers, and prisons around the city. The festival brings poets together with both national arts audiences and local community organizations. Each year, too, different poets are invited to the festival, reflecting shifting trends in poetry style and popularity. The participating poets are, by and large, well-established writers and performers who attend international festivals regularly. Nonetheless, in interviews and during performances, many participants remarked that Poetry Africa stood out among its peers by embracing poetry's ability to transform social relationships.

Poetry Africa grows out of a moment, and a space, when poetry was newly empowered to confront oppressive circumstances and seek alternative structures. Late apartheid structures denied spaces for Black performance arts. In 1994, as South Africa negotiated new political formations, Bhekizizwe Peterson wrote: "The paucity of performance venues is the result of the state's policy that black cultural practices had to be catered for by their respective racial or ethnic administrations. Since urban Africans were regarded, in accordance with Verweordian ideology, as temporary sojourners en route, hopefully, to their respective ethnic homelands, no encouragement was to be given that would contradict this eventuality."[21] Although certain urban performance venues highlighted Black artists' work, including the Market

Theatre and the Windybrow Theatre in Johannesburg, these had operated for decades under the strict threat of censorship, and no state-sponsored theaters operated anywhere in townships.[22] As new spaces and possibilities opened up in the early moments of democracy, poet, organizer, and sociologist Ari Sitas wrote: "We have been facing a 'brilliant chaos' of words, for the last few years have been tremendous for poetry in Natal. But we have also been reeling from collisions between two poetic traditions, a scripted and an oral one. And both traditions have been colliding in the context of political and labour initiatives in the area."[23] Amid the optimistic flourishing of the mid-1990s, Poetry Africa offered a new space to bring together a range of performance styles and histories onto a single stage reflecting the postapartheid "rainbow nation."

Poetry Africa began, in part, as a national venue for poets of African descent to highlight South Africa's linguistic and cultural diversity after apartheid. It retains a nationalist orientation common across arts festivals: the hosting institution, as synecdoche for the hosting country, is always the primary focus of the festival, of the artists who perform at it, and of the audience members who attend. Festival participation allows audiences and artists alike to mark their cultural expertise and connections. This is especially tangible in the case of arts festivals hosted in South Africa, because South Africa's economy and cultural institutions dominate the region: it is home to the second largest economy on the continent and six of the ten best-ranked universities in Africa. Poetry Africa's connection to UKZN, and to South Africa's arts industries more broadly, make it a particularly appealing venue for both emerging and established poets because it offers entry into South Africa's literary networks. Despite the festival's international focus, though, more than half of invited poets come from South Africa. In part, this is to be expected: artists work within relatively tightly bound networks; festivals extend organizers' networks only a few steps. The 2016 festival, for instance, featured thirteen poets from within South Africa, six from other African nations, and four from beyond the continent. Yet it also speaks to the broader purpose of the festival itself: to map South African identities and ideals within and against international conversations.

In South Africa, arts festivals must also contend with a tension between poetry's place in everyday life and the festival's position as a space of cultural sanctification. This structural imbalance emerged powerfully on the opening night of the 2016 festival. The kickoff performance, which was hosted at the university's large Elizabeth Sneddon Theatre, was held on a Monday evening—not poetry's prime time. Nonetheless, the 413-seat auditorium was nearly two-thirds full. The event had been heavily advertised throughout Durban and was highly anticipated as one of the CCA's three large annual festivals. That night, though, poetry did not hold center stage for long: after a short performance by King Goodwill Zwelethini kaBhekuzulu's praise singer in honor of the Zulu nation's bicentennial, the event was turned over to festival organizers and university bureaucrats. The evening became an opportunity for the twenty people on stage—royalty, organizers, and university administrators—to celebrate one another's efforts, to declaim honors, and to defend the university itself. In the fraught moment of the Fallist movement, these speeches and prizes sought to establish the festival's credentialing capacity: its power to gatekeep, define tastes, and legitimize certain performance forms. But that credentialization only succeeds if the audience accepts it. In this case, the audience sat uncomfortably silent through the many honors, shifting nervously as their colleagues' efforts at academic decolonization were attacked, and finally beginning to filter out as the prizes dragged on.

Poetry Africa positions itself as a celebration of Pan-African cosmopolitanism, yet in doing so, it principally celebrates the host country's own exceptionalism. At the 2016 festival, which ran just as the second round of Fallist protests shut down universities, the festival's constraints chafed. On opening night, Poetry Africa's audience sit quietly in auditorium seats. Neatly separated into rows and columns by chair backs and armrests, over two hundred people laughed in time with the poet who joked about his experiences traveling between Zimbabwe and South Africa. We gasped in response to the poet Mata-Uiroa Manuel Atan, who took the stage wearing a loincloth, chanting in Rapa Nui, a language largely unfamiliar to the audience. Yet it was in our silence that we experienced the poetry, with bodies and voices constrained by the rows of auditorium seating. Even though Poetry Africa includes a wide range of poetry and performance styles, and is a rare festival dedicated purely to poetry, the audience who had come for an evening's entertainment behaved as the auditorium venue compelled them to behave.

Auditorium seating directs attention strictly forward, restricting movement and resisting interaction. It presumes and attempts to enforce a model of theatrical sociality that grows out of nineteenth-century Europe. And it is in direct opposition with popular performance practices in South Africa, where theater is a participatory experience more commonly performed in the round. The tension between venue and audience bespeaks broader cultural and generational shifts—a reflection of the festival's more broadly contingent position in the national space.

Even at a formal event such as Poetry Africa, the audience's own goals will invariably shape the event beyond organizers' intentions: as Jill Dolan writes, "live performance provides a place where people come, embodied and passionate, to share experiences of meaning-making and imagination"[24] Audience members can silently speed along unpopular speeches or extend popular ones through cheers and applause. Even though poetry was put on a back burner on opening night, the crowd had come prepared to receive poetry, and they responded accordingly. One audience member, a professor of political science at the university, called out in isiZulu to reinforce speakers' excitement about the twenty years of success for Poetry Africa. She embraced poetry as a participatory form, starting cheers and ululations that spread throughout the crowd. The cheers divided the crowd between those who could understand isiZulu and those who could not, audibly affirming the province's enduring cultural and linguistic split. But even with these divides, the excitement spread through the crowd, and more and more people called out their support or derision of the speechmakers as the evening progressed. Bringing populist feedback mechanisms into the sphere of high culture, the audience's behavior can either reinforce or negate the festival's capacity to authorize certain forms of performance and to confer cultural capital.

Audience interactions directly shape the performance, affecting its length and meaning. These responses highlight the audience's role as what Richard Bauman and Charles Briggs call "co-performers," who play an "the active role [. . .] in performances": "In conversational narratives, audience members are often accorded turns at talk, thus rendering narration coperformance. [. . .] Performance, the enactment of poetic function, is a highly reflexive mode of communication."[25] Verbal interactions are invariably shaped in the interface between producer and consumer or artist and audience—an interaction that organizes a piece's poetic endeavors. The fact that performance, like all verbal modes, is inherently interactive enables the audience to curate their festivals. Such participatory structures foster connections. Nonetheless, many contemporary poetry performances separate poem and audience: maintaining the style of twentieth-century poetry readings, poets interact with the audience only when introducing or explaining the poem. When reciting the poem itself, they maintain a relatively flat affect and leave no space for audience response.[26]

Poetry Africa, in contrast, embraces its history as a space for diverse and popular forms, presenting a wide range of contemporary poetry performance styles: performances typically included several musicians, poets reading from published books, a handful of slam poets, *iimbongi*, and experimental performers. Audiences responded to the cues of the poets whose style they could recognize—and learned from those they do not recognize. When Zulu praise poet Jessica Mbangeni performed during the opening night, a few audience members called out isiZulu responses to her formulated questions and ululated in recognition of her emotions. The next time she performed, in a thirty-minute set days later, many more joined in, prepared by what they had heard before. Similarly, during the first musical performance—Lucky Tembo's playful mbira songs—it took several beats for the audience to abandon their interpretive silence and engage the sounds on their own terms. Each specific genre cued audience behavior, as did careful signaling in the poets' postures, their tone, and their gestures.

On opening night in 2016, after nearly two hours of speeches and introductions, the event was turned over to the poets, each of whom would perform for five minutes. The organizer explained that each poet would give a "taste" of their work, which he contextualized by summarizing the poets' backgrounds. By that point in the evening, the audience was depleted, their energy expended on lectures about the history of the program, the honor of the amaZulu, the troubles of the younger generation, and the university crisis. But as the poets took the stage in sequence, each one reading or performing their highest-energy, most engaging poem, the audience's enthusiasm gradually returned. More people cheered for each subsequent poet, gaining energy from one another's emotional output and coalescing into an affective public.

Halfway through the introductory performances, when a slight woman with a calm demeanor took the stage to talk about a taboo topic—female sexuality—the audience was keyed in, leaning forward, ready for her performance. Roché Kester, an award-winning spoken word artist and poetry organizer, had first made a name for herself as a slam poet in Cape Town. The poem she performed that night, together with her composed bearing, blends shock and outrage into empathy and excitement to produce a personal poem with political implications. Every time Kester introduces the poem, its title, "Premium Poes," draws giggles of discomfort and excitement from her audience. The poem is about "reclaiming the P word," as Kester puts it, and defining personal boundaries. In it, Kester addresses her audience directly, implicating them simultaneously as coconspirators and as part of a broader oppressive social apparatus. She begins with a question:

> Give it up?
> What do you mean—give it up?
> Give [*points to her pelvis*] her up? Just like that?
> Disregard her, as if she deserves no respect?
> Just to inform you, the only giving up will occur when I'm secure that the language is pure
> And even more so, that every part of me is sure.
> Now—don't get me wrong.
> I'm not—prissy or—pompous
> But my pussy needs fluent talk
> Passionate, poetic, articulate conversation, soulful words, powerful chatter,
> an art of rhetoric consisting of intellect
> And mutual respect, because these lips
> Don't speak to just anyone.[27]

Like many slam poems, "Premium Poes" relies on an exaggerated performance of self, an identity between speaker and performer which promises the audience that the stories they hear are genuine, part of a broader constellation of experiences with which they can empathize. The poem's focus on sounds and bodily performance flattens the distinction between speaker and poet, an indistinction that Kester's direct address to the audience further encourages. This identity creates a sense of intimacy and connection between poet and audience.

Throughout Kester's performance at Poetry Africa, the audience responded enthusiastically—especially female audience members, whose cheers drowned out any murmurs of discomfort. The poem becomes increasingly explicit as it continues, asserting a woman's right to choose her sexual comfort with unusual forthrightness:

> I'm talking about preem-yum poes
> Top of the range, not to be exchanged with vulgar laughter
> To satisfy him and his thing [*pointing to her pelvis*]
> No profanities when speaking to her
> No jab-bing con-ver-sation that is [*thrusting hips*]
> Short lived and lacking in content

Kester's expressive movements keep time with the accelerating rhythm, directing the audience's laughter and cheers with orchestral precision. Her audience is so carefully managed and emotionally in sync with her that, by the end, Kester turns to them for a call-and-response, allowing them to fill in the blank of her pun:

> It's a choice
> A choice of quality
> Because not any Tom—
> [*she pauses as the audience laughs, cheers, and shouts:*]
> Dick!
> Or Harry is gonna infiltrate the sanctity of my punani.[28]

The pause interrupts the rhythm of the sequence, disrupting its aesthetic coherence and enhancing its performative impact. By integrating the audience's voice into the sequence, Kester both showcases her skill as a performer and animates their agreement. "Premium Poes" reclaims a word, a series of gestures, and, ultimately, a choice, all while carefully managing audience responses through identity performance and puns. Kester uses humor and shared cultural references to carry the audience through an often-contentious subject, until they even shout along with her, bringing their own voices into the poem.

Kester's poetry represents a relatively trendy and youthful performance style, showcasing how slam poetry and digital aesthetic networks have transformed gatekeeping structures.[29] Over the past decade, Poetry Africa has included an increasing number of young poets who gained acclaim in popular spaces first. The official introductions to each poet provide insight into the curatorial process: print poets are introduced in terms of their publications, whether in the number of volumes published or in the relative prestige of journals; musicians in terms of performance style and accolades; and spoken word poets by their championship titles or YouTube followers. In 2016, three poets—Roché Kester, Maya Wegerif, and Bassey Ikpi—were introduced through their novel digital and social engagements: Wegerif as a "viral poet," whose popularity developed on YouTube; Kester for her work developing and marketing a poetry open mic in Cape Town; and Ikpi as a "slam poet," famous for her performances on the HBO show *Def Jam Poetry*.[30]

Audiences, before they molded the reception at the festival itself, helped decide who got to the festival in the first place: for instance, Wegerif's viral poem "Why You Talk So White," which she published as a YouTube video, helped bring the young poet to the attention of a wide array of events organizers in the United States and Africa, including the organizers at Poetry Africa. The change in Poetry Africa's programming over the past decade reflects the country's broader move toward digital aesthetic networks—and the generational and national changes that move has heralded. It is therefore, always, a space of contradictory identifications. The rise of popular poetry online exacerbates tensions between poetic traditions: bridging the imagined divide between written and performed poetry (or elite and popular cultures) ironically highlights that divide. As poetry gains popularity online, festivals—under pressure to prove their relevance and significance as governments embrace austerity measures—court popular audiences. Gatekeeping, then, increasingly reflects quantitative metrics over prior forms of cultural legitimation. The curatorial changes, in turn, shift the nature of the performance space: like music fans, these poets' audiences know how to respond to them, and what to expect from their work, because they have heard it before.

And as poetry gains popularity online, its audiences shift too. In their responses, the audience gives new life to a poem, allowing it to echo into longer and deeper afterlives—a legacy embedded in the festival's archives. Those archives, in turn, mark the festival's ambivalent relationship to its own social media presence. Every Poetry Africa performance since 2011 is archived on its YouTube channel, managed by the CCA. The digital archive creates a poetic past of empty homogeneous cosmopolitanism, onto which an internationalist future can be projected. As of 2018, Poetry Africa's YouTube channel is among the largest archives of African poetry performance anywhere. Due to its size and accessibility, such YouTube archives are helping shape the poetry's aesthetic norms, integrating text, video, and sound recordings and inviting direct audience feedback in forms immediately familiar to social media users. In many ways, Poetry Africa's YouTube presence takes the place of the sort of print anthologies that have historically emerged from annual literary festivals. Where other major poetry festivals, such as Poetry International in Rotterdam, mark their progression by creating biographical pages in ever-expanding websites for each of the poets who performs on their stages, Poetry Africa creates an ever-expanding documentary experience for the viewers who follow its publication. By publishing on YouTube, Poetry Africa engages the networked logics of contemporary literary production. It acknowledges its own position in a moment when poetry is increasingly driven by multimedia communication and, thus, by multimedia performance.

Yet audiences are practically inaudible in the videos: the festival's imagined future, its sense of its own history, allows no space for the live audience. And, alone among events I have attended, Poetry Africa discourages audiences from recording the events themselves: in addition to widely posted signs stating these prohibitions, ushers actively reprimanded audience members on phones. Nonetheless, social media–trained audiences look through their phones to experience and engage with the events. Each year, Twitter buzzes with audiences mentioning poets, tweeting at the event organizers, or both. More noticeable, the poets themselves use social media platforms to build their own brands. The public or semipublic connections they make to other poets—tagging themselves in photos together, following one another on Twitter, becoming friends on Facebook—bring their names and faces onto the feeds of one another's followers. The festival invitation itself legitimates their names, but social media networks amplify them, giving them the direct support of a single individual trusted by their followers. Their attendance at Poetry Africa lent the festival credibility, showing that it could represent and attract a full range of the moment's most influential poets. It also legitimized them as artists, demonstrating their resonance across national and cultural positions—their weight on an international stage. Hence the reason for revisiting the poetry festival in the twenty-first century: the problem of creating authenticity, and of curating identity, in an increasingly connected world.

The vectors of power and influence are multidirectional. Official arts events are increasingly bound to the popular taste of social media audiences. That taste is informed at least in part by norms established through social media corporations. We must therefore attend, as Bronwyn Williams has suggested, to the fissures within the production of global cultural capital. For the international film festivals Williams studies, "The growth of multinational corporations, the rapid movement of economic capital, and advanced technologies of communication and transportation have facilitated the expansion of mass popular culture in the same way they have facilitated the expansion of global financial and manufacturing systems." Therefore, she reminds us, "the workings of globalization, in regard to popular culture, are not homogenous or smooth, but are instead marked by connections and gaps, understanding and confusion, acting both in concert with local culture and in opposition to the same culture."[31] The large-scale music and arts festivals that have become increasingly popular in the twenty-first century illustrate the tension between local celebrations and global culture. The inclusion of poetry at these festivals speaks simultaneously to the poetry's increasing popularity and to the festivals' desire to tap into poetry's cultural capital.

Directing Poetry's Audiences at Lake of Stars 2016

At Malawi's Lake of Stars Festival, music organizes the audience's responses to poetry—and poetry's position in the national cultural imaginary it constructs. A thousand miles from Poetry Africa, by a platform stage a hundred meters from Lake Malawi's glittering waters, the crowd thrums with expectation, as two hundred people shuffle against one another to hear poetry. Framed between the stage's sunset orange platform and a woven roof, poet, singer, and actress Lily Banda answers the cheering audience with her own effervescent alto. Her poem opens with a gospel-style tune, as she sings, "Created in the image of the *most* high," before considering women's struggles with body image, entering a venue wearing too-small red high heels, "Squeezed my being for that moment I walk in. [. . .] The shoe/nothing like this red soil I walk on."[32] The poem is new, but by the third refrain, a few people pick up on the theme and shout along. Lily Banda's exaggerated vocal cadences and physical gestures emphasize the poet's physical presence and encourage the audience to respond directly to the performer: they can predict the next beat and the next poetic move, so that the poet becomes a conductor, and the audience, her orchestra. As the audience shouts out their reactions, the poem grows in meaning, its varied references and allusions expanded by each listener's responses. The crowd—a diverse mix of people who have traveled to the festival from across Africa, Europe, and America—coalesces into a single audience through the poem.

Poetry's inclusion at arts festivals heralds its shifting cultural position, bringing the form's cultural capital to the popular arts scene. Unlike Poetry Africa, Malawi's annual Lake of Stars is a three-day concert series, without the talks, readings, or awards typical of the literature festival. Music festivals, which generally draw audiences and musical acts from around the world, are more numerous and more profitable than literature festivals. But Lake of Star's inclusion of poetry alongside music is not unprecedented. Instead, it reflects poetry's increasing prominence in digital spaces, as Instagram poets and YouTube channels bring poetry into conversation with comic strips, memes, and pop songs. As poetry becomes popular online, as slam poetry's performance styles influence the performances of print poets, and as spoken word artists integrate music and movement into their performances, poetry shares the stage with musicians, encouraging further intergeneric innovations.

These changes signal the influence of digital aesthetic networks on artistic curation. If, as Jahan Ramazani argues, "intergeneric dialogue has been an especially pronounced feature of poetry in the late twentieth and early twenty-first centuries, when media spectacle and mass-reproduced or digitally circulated texts, sounds, and images have increasingly permeated the private spaces once thought to be poetry's preserve," then poetry's interface with music reflects the interpenetration of public and private spaces facilitated by digital media.[33] Digital aesthetic networks continually open up new contact zones, decontextualizing and exoticizing the very same cosmopolitan poetry that they enable. The arts festival, in turn, stages the connections poetry forges between poet and audience. It shows how poetry's emotional impact, its performance, and its form draw viewers together into an audience—one motivated to take part in the poem's message. This can happen because of the message itself, the poem's format, or the medium of publication. The copresence of audience and performer enables poetry to cross media and create publics. Poet, audience, and venue shape one another's identity and experience.

Lake of Stars is Malawi's largest arts festival, an annual event featuring performance and visual arts. Founded in 2003 by Englishman Will Jameson and sponsored by Scottish and Malawian nongovernmental organizations (NGOs) and several major international corporations, the festival offers Malawian artists access to a broader audience than typically attends local performances. According to official festival marketing, Jameson wanted "to raise money for a developing economy, help promote Malawi as a tourist destination and expose Malawian artists to an international audience."[34] Lake of Stars has been hugely successful in international outreach: as of 2015, 34 percent of the 2,350 visitors came from outside Malawi.[35] The festival's official publications highlight this success by quoting from international publications, which situate Lake of Stars primarily relative to other festivals: one describes it as among the "top 20 festivals in the world," another as "one of Africa's most respected music festivals." Otherwise, reviews evaluate the festival through the lens of tourism: "a fascinating opportunity to experience the pulse of this inspiring country." The festival pitches itself as, first, a world-class music venue and, second, a nationalist venue showcasing Malawi's outstanding qualities and "launch[ing] young Malawian talent."[36] Its insistence on "Malawianness" reflects both Lake of Stars's specific debts to Malawi's tourist industry and the broader goals of the arts festival, performing nationalism for international audiences.

All the poets who have performed at Lake of Stars have been Malawian, in keeping with the festival's aims to showcase Malawian art: according to director Hector Macpherson, each year's festival features 50 percent Malawian artists, 30 percent artists from the rest of Africa, and 20 percent artists from outside Africa—largely from the US and Europe.[37] In doing so, they emphasize the strength of Malawian art both on its own merits and in relation to global artistry. Poetry's presence at Lake of Stars is both a confirmation of the form's relevance for a younger audience and a declaration of the value and strength of Malawian poetry for a global audience. Yet the poetry that features at Lake of Stars reflects the festival's audience more than it reflects the Malawian poetry scene: although page poets and performance poets alike are popular across generations in Malawi, only young spoken word artists perform at Lake of Stars. The bombastic, highly dramatic performance style of spoken word makes their work legible in a popular music venue. The combination reminds the world of Malawi's connections to a global arts network that often ignores the small nation, positioning its artists as cosmopolitan subjects who engage across local and global conversations.

In that sense, Lake of Stars reflects the typical logic of arts festivals: claiming national significance in front of, for, and relative to an international audience. Such cultural diplomacy is, in Julien's sense, an extroverted performance, appropriating external genres and discourses to declare the value of the local to the international. Yet this cultural diplomacy risks essentializing national identities, requiring poets to perform their nationhood for an international, othering audience. This is a logic that novelist and publisher Shadreck Chikoti has articulated especially well. Chikoti, whose anthology of African speculative fiction, *Imagine Africa 500*, included Malawian, Ugandan, South African, and Nigerian writers, explained he wanted to show that Malawians could compete on an international stage—that they were good enough and deserved inclusion. And, indeed, Lake of Stars has shown that, in Chikoti's words, "Malawi can compete on the world stage."[38]

As Malawi's largest festival, Lake of Stars grants those genres and media it acknowledges a privileged status. But Lake of Stars is not predominantly a poetry festival, and poets initially struggled for inclusion. In 2012, Q Malewezi worked with event organizers to get poetry integrated into the festival's main program. The plan was a huge success: closing his performance at the 2013 Lake of Stars Festival, Malewezi made his exit by declaring, "Finally, poetry is on the main stage—poetry wins!"[39] Malewezi's excitement that "poetry has made it" to the festival's main stage in 2013 reminds us that poetry has a prominent place in the Malawian art scene. It suggests that poetry could draw international tourists. And it argues that Malawian performance poetry can compete on the world stage. At Lake of Stars, the poets become ambassadors, rendering national traditions legible to an audience who has come to see the best Malawi has to offer. Their words come to speak for, rather than to, the country they would address.

From the very first poetry performance at Lake of Stars, social media enabled audience members to disseminate recordings and evaluate artists. Videos from this first event testify to the audience's eager responses to poetry. Digital repositories brought the events to a much broader audience than would otherwise attend; they also decontextualized the work and the performance. The most widely accessible recordings from these early events were made on audience members' cell phones and posted to YouTube. In these recordings, unlike in Poetry Africa's professional archives, audience voices share the stage with the poet's. The participants shape the production as clearly as the artists themselves do. In 2012, cell phone cameras were not primarily designed for video recording, so the video and audio quality are both compromised. In some ways, ironically, this more directly represents the atmosphere at these events. The sound is flattened: noises from the audience and the speaker come from everywhere and nowhere in particular. The dim lighting leaves the visuals fuzzy. But the performer stands in stark relief, the camera focused solely on him. The audience makes up his atmosphere, but he is the object on which the experience centers. Together, they dramatize the encounter between local and global imagined in cosmopolitan discourse.

In the videos from the event, Malewezi's audience—sometimes with American or British accents—responds to him as if part of the poem. As though intimately familiar with his shifts and turns, they speak along with or call back to him, performing alongside him. Malewezi uses the audience's engagement both to strengthen his poem's message and to implicate them in the creation of that message. The poem, "Wikipedia," is in many ways typical of Malewezi's performance style. It relies on vocal links to tie together disparate ideas, moves rapidly between hard, closed consonants and repetitive, elongated syllables, and is stylistically highly fluid.

After three minutes of fast-paced commentary touching on nearly every aspect of Malawian public life, Malewezi concludes by suddenly slowing down, allowing a lulling repetition to enter the poem:

> The sun is also the central symbol of the Malawi flag
> That has been changed from
> The rising sun
> To the risen sun
>
>   [*audience (synchronous):*] to the risen sun
> And then back to the rising sun
>
>   [*laughter*] rising sun
> And they say this was done,
>
>   [*cheering*]
> To show where we have moved to as a people
> Our sun has risen,
> Malawi's sun has risen
> Yet its sons and daughters remain in a deep sleep,
>
>   [*sleeeeeep*]
> sleep, sleep, sleep
> Sleep is what we do when hunger, greed,
> Poverty, sin and fear blind our eyes
>
>   [*cheering, whistles*]
> From seeing our real risen sun.[40]

The agentless changing of the Malawian flag, the nameless political "they," even the disembodied, free-floating evils of modern life all insinuate an intimacy between performer and audience—one acted out when, as he speaks the words "its sons and daughters remain in a deep sleep," Malewezi raises his hands to shoulder level and moves them in small, rhythmic circles, eliciting the proper response from his audience: a rhythmically ululating "slee-ee-eep." Carefully conducting his audience, Malewezi creates his poem—and his indictment of Malawian governance—through their cooperation, making them complicit in the poem and its message.

Throughout the performance, Malewezi uses his body language, soft shifts in intonation, and even hand gestures like a hypnotist or an orchestral conductor, eliciting emotional responses from his audiences perfectly coordinated with his own vocal and bodily rhythms. Moving between the rising and the risen suns, Malewezi gradually raises and lowers each hand, so that when he proclaims, "Where we have moved to as a people," the sudden upswing and increasingly chaotic hand gestures—mirroring and yet mocking the smooth rising and falling of the sun—reinforce the relationship between poet, audience, and nation his words have created.

The arts festival becomes a training ground for poetry reception even as it transforms individual poems and poets into symbols of poetic and national community. Through his deliberate linking of poem and audience in his performances at Lake of Stars, Malewezi recalls the poet's imagined role to enable political dialogue. In a 2013 interview with *Nyasa Times*, Malewezi admonished his fellow poets, claiming, "We are poets because we've issues. [. . .] And we need to bring these issues up through performances. Poetry can be gainful." The interviewer described Malewezi's work as "power packed pieces . . . clearly rich in both form and content," while "a number of social ills such as economic exploitation, abuse of power and injustice . . . seemed like his flagship theme running through the veins of his poetry."[41] Malewezi's poet-as-crusader persona aims to incite his audience; his poetry requires a connection to the immediate and to the everyday.

Malewezi's poems focus on governmental letdowns and the value of education—two issues common in public discourse and, coincidentally, among the UN Millennium Goals. His presence as a young poet made him a symbol of the future, a core focus for Lake of Stars itself. But his audience was, in the majority, not Malawian. In the context of a festival designed to "raise money for a developing economy, help promote Malawi as a tourist destination and expose Malawian artists to an international audience," his performance was entangled in his Malawianness and with the country's international status—a concern necessitated by the audience of Malawian elites and international travelers.[42]

As poetry became a baked-in part of each subsequent year's festival, the performances expanded to include Malewezi's core performance collective. Poets he had collaborated with in his Project Project and Living Room Poetry Club featured in the festival with him.[43] But such social gatekeeping proved untenable as the event expanded. The successful performances of established poets in 2013 and 2015 gave way, in 2016, to a performance set that included emerging poets. Prior to the event, Malewezi put out a call on Facebook asking his fans which poets inspired them. In turning over the curation to his fans, Malewezi implicitly recognized the audience-driven market created in social media. The list they produced was varied, and Malewezi vetted the poets in turn by asking them to submit recordings of their own pieces. He worked for a year with those he chose, including Phindu Banda, before bringing them to the festival in 2016. These poets were mostly less established, and many had not yet published their own work. Yet their names were now entwined with Malawi's best. By bringing them on stage with him and introducing them to a wider audience, Malewezi suggested that the best Malawi has to offer are not necessarily those at the current height of their careers but those with the potential to grow.

In the context of the contemporary arts festival, poetry has been transformed into a form of cultural representation. It offers a form of nativism that Sarah Nuttall has described as "about the reclaiming of an essential self superseded by an intrusive other. [. . .] Yet it is a form of agency which does not in the end overcome or supersede the victimization of which it overwhelmingly speaks. Nativism relies on the possibility of recognizing an essential self, while elevating the Other in particular ways."[44] Removed from its immediate address and faced with the judgment of a cosmopolitan Other, performance poetry at international arts festivals instead reifies its message for a cosmopolitan audience. It must defend its place in Casanova's "world republic of letters" and yet perform a "local" authenticity unique to the poet. This internationalist demand for poetry-as-cultural-representative reflects a broader shift in cultural consumption in the so-called global age, one that infects all forms of arts. Cindy Wong contends, "Over the years, the definition of 'international' has expanded and most film festivals actively solicit films from all corners of the world to the rapt attention of critics, cinephiles, and scholars. One can then argue that film festivals, at a very minimal level, have normalized the inclusion of films from all over the world as one of their practices. At the same time, in many Western A-list festivals, these favorites, 'negotiated' amid considerations of novelty, localized productions, and competition among festivals, have gained greater exposure and resonance with global political and economic transformations."[45] Brought to a regional center, asked to perform for a global audience, the poet is transformed into a novelty, and their poem is reduced to what Sitas calls "communication trapped in print."[46] Arts festivals reveal the paradox of digital cosmopolitanism, which requires a sense of the local to express itself as other-than-local: a contradiction that inscribes some identities—particularly those of vulnerable groups like refugees—as never-yet universal.

Negotiating Audience Demands: The Festival Poet as Ambassador

Performing at national arts festivals transforms the poet into an ambassador, charged with representing a monolithic nationhood for an international audience.[47] Although the investment in representation predates the digital era, the capacity to instantly access audiences around the world pressures poets to perform their geographically specific identities—summed up in early chat relay demands for "a/s/l."[48] This representational structure simultaneously empowers and limits the poet: her work will be contextualized in relationship to a singularly identified "home nation," no matter how ambiguous that relationship is. The grounded space of audience-poet interaction thus carries as much meaning as the poem itself, structuring relationships between local and foreign. But the spatial relations of poet and audience are never equal. For a poet writing across nation-spaces, an outsider to the audience, the location of a poem's reception is especially important to its meaning. The speaker must occupy the space between two places, a guest in the space of her performance and at risk in the place of home.

Poetry's cultural and political weight makes performance a risk for many poets. These risks are heightened in prominent festivals like Poetry Africa. Performing at Poetry Africa in 2014, Zimbabwean poet Wadzanai Chirirui, who writes under the pen name Black Pearl, enacted the migrant poet's experience, made to represent her own country across ambivalent borders. She had been visiting Durban with fourteen other poets, who asked her to speak to Zimbabwe's political situation. The poem she performed in response cedes to their desires only halfway, protecting herself and her position between countries throughout. Before beginning to read, she looks around, and asks: "What do you do with the footage that you take here?"[49] Laughing away this moment of estrangement, she notes that she had composed the poem only that week, while sick with the flu, and it is the flu that shapes the poem she reads, making her body metaphor for her country. The poem starts simply, reminding the audience of her discomfort even as she projects her address far beyond them:

> A lot of people want me to say something about you, my Zimbabwe,
> And particularly you, my president.
> But I never got around to laying you down on my canvases
> Perhaps I have a debt to our culture of silence and adaptation.
> I do think about you and desperately want to tell our story,
> The story of the gallant sons and daughters of the resilient nation.

Black Pearl's speaking voice echoes across national boundaries, drawing in an absent audience—"you, my Zimbabwe"—while absenting the present audience by withdrawing from them physically. As she performs, Black Pearl looks down, speaking softly and drawing into her body, as though separating herself from her audience. Her physical posture and speaking style reproduce the anxieties of poetic address, speaking to Zimbabwe as she shares the space of literary production with her South African audience.

Her voice and body bridge the space between audience and addressee: where Zimbabwe's story appears only in overwrought abstraction, the speaker's own bodily ailments are much more immediately audible. With a sigh, Black Pearl turns from her country back to her own voice to explain why she cannot write or speak of Zimbabwe on this South African stage:

> But today, I am too sick.
> You see, I am down with the flu.
> The doctor gave me cough syrup, antibiotics, and probiotics
> To clear out the disease
> But they haven't quite made me well, yet.
>
> I guess that's how medicine works.
> The syrup makes me drowsy
> The antibiotics give me thrush
> And the pro-antibiotics make the thrush go away
> But they have long-term effects.

As physical ailments take the place of national maladies, cultural abstractions are replaced with the tangible promise of medicine, which can "clear out the disease," erasing all traces of illness so that it might never have happened—even as her exhaustion and literal illness is performed for her audience and captured in a video now preserved on YouTube. Even the body does not heal so readily, and the seeming transparency of medicine—empirically tested and obviously effective—yields to the ironically looping failures and inadequacies.

Black Pearl closes her poem with a direct appeal to the audience, reminding them of their position as critical interpreters—and of her own as vulnerable traveler. Calling attention to the poem's central metaphor and to its primary existence, she closes:

> But eventually, I'll be okay.
> Only then will I write for them
> The story of my Zimbabwe—
> But perhaps I have already written it
> You just need to find it
> In this poem.

By aestheticizing critique, Black Pearl puts the responsibility of interpretation in the audience's hands, freeing the poet from potential rebuke: anyone who could see criticism in her poem must, themselves, participate in that criticism. But this poem's quiet performance, its occasional composition, and its displaced address all signal its attempts to un-speak, to say without saying, the experiences of living and speaking across boundaries. Her silence and misdirection signal her resistance to her audience's voyeurism. By replacing the nation with the body and taking her country's woes into her own illness, Black Pearl brings critique onto herself, as well; by performing critique as aesthetic, she releases her own responsibility onto her audience. The poet's body thus figures literally and metaphorically as a container for and protector of the performance, enacting distance even when the speaker is copresent with her audience.

The performance of self, and of self-as-citizen, is particularly fraught for the Zimbabwean poet in South Africa, where—at the time of Black Pearl's performance in 2014—implicit state support for the autocratic government was accompanied by increasing Afrophobia within South Africa. Anita Howarth argues that South African and Zimbabwean national identities are mutually constituted, creating "a dialectical interaction between processes of identity construction and foreign-policy construction."[50] The two countries' parallel history of minority rule followed by democratization split at the turn of the millennium, when Mandela pursued a policy of reconciliation in contrast to Mugabe's policy of land restitution. Since that time, Zimbabwean migration into South Africa has created an ambivalent relationship between the neighboring nations. The performance and construction of a poet's individual identity in the context of the international arts festival may be understood as, first, part of the construction of a state identity and, second, the negotiation of foreign policy. It is thus the South African audience and context that defines the performance and its reception as an implicit risk to poet, audience, and nation alike.

In moving between countries, migrant poets speak beyond the boundaries of national interest to develop a shared world of concern. Their performances refigure the migrant poet as an exile and thus as part of a nation that extends beyond its own borders. The position of migration and alienation becomes, in Black Pearl's performance, an opportunity for national self-construction, a chance to acknowledge the place of exiles and of refugees within the nation—while risking rearticulating the very national structures that have created its condition. In performance, the poet's bodily presence and the possibility of audience interactions produce transnational spaces through which the positions of migrant, refugee, and poet blur.

Black Pearl's initial anxieties, and her performative erasure of distance, indicate a problem unique to the contemporary poetry festival and particular to the migrant poet at that festival, that is, representation within the lingering archives of social media. Pointing to the festival's cameras, she articulates a real problem of agency for the performing poets: "What do *you* do with *your* footage of *my* performance?" Digitization threatens to make a local and temporally specific performance accessible to an unknowably broad audience. Sponsorship by foreign organizations, governmental bodies, and the festival itself transforms the poet's performance into a commodity, pressuring performers to present their "true" selves to the audience.[51] The festival setting rebirths authorial authority. Poets are expected to present themselves as unique individuals, providing works and performances that make them vulnerable to the audience. They also become representatives of their particular cultural origins, as reference points in the discursive sea of digital publication.

Just as Poetry Africa's audiences asked Black Pearl to perform a poem about her Zimbabweanness for their gratification, so the structure of the poetry festival compels each poet to perform their world for an unfamiliar audience. Their performances allow alienated audiences to imagine themselves in the poet's position and see, through her body, the experiences of another. Black Pearl's performance appears to be highly critical of expectations that force the poet to perform an authentic self for a voyeuristic audience. Yet for many poets, the opportunity to perform their experiences for an attentive audience represents an opportunity to be made whole through the recognition of their performative self. Tyler Hoffman explains that, in the case of young American slam poets at the turn of the century, performing an authentic identity was itself an act of resistance: "These poets wear their identities on their sleeves: they embody their resistance to the dominant culture on stage and page and through the transmissions of new media, even as they look to undercut, or at least complicate, the ideological effects typically associated with those media and their spectacles."⁵² The poets Hoffman describes find liberation in the opportunity to perform their selves, in a context where their identities were rarely represented in public and were frequently the object of scorn and resentment. Though slam can fetishize the authentic performance of marginal identities, for some poets in positions of oppression, the opportunity to perform their selves remains a liberatory one.⁵³ This is especially the case for refugee poets in Malawi, who remain marginalized in national politics and largely invisible to the national public.⁵⁴

As part of its efforts to support Malawian artists, Lake of Stars has partnered since 2014 with the Dzaleka Refugee Camp to sponsor the annual Tumaini Arts Festival. Dzaleka is the only permanent refugee camp in Malawi, home to nearly thirty thousand refugees from across central and east Africa. These large numbers, combined with a generally poor perception of refugees, has made Dzaleka an ongoing political question in Malawi. The festival works, in a small way, to address these questions, aiming to "empower" refugees, who gain skills in expression and entrepreneurship, and to foster "cultural exchange" both among refugees within the camp and with the national population. These two goals seek to bridge divisions and to improve public perceptions of refugees. At Tumaini, then, authenticity may recover its potential to provide authority to the speaker, instead of having it imposed by cosmopolitan others.

Even if, as Neil Lazarus asserts, "one is not born, but made cosmopolitan," certain subjects have readier access to cosmopolitanism than do others. "Cosmopolitan discourse is not always authoritative. [. . .] But inasmuch as it appeals to experience, comparativism, and worldly wisdom, the cosmopolitan judgment often looks suspiciously like an edict."⁵⁵ In performing authenticity for a cosmopolitan audience, the artist-refugees appeal to an ideal cosmopolitan imaginary, which dissociates subjecthood from national belonging. These appeals are fraught with questions of judgment and authority, of authenticity and sufficiency, and of individual agency. Unexpectedly, Tumaini courts this judgment, perhaps to then position its artists' own agency as cosmopolitical subjects, and—in Paul Gilroy's terms—renew "the cosmopolitan mentalities nurtured by the tri-continental network of anti-colonial struggle."⁵⁶

The Tumaini Festival features refugee artists and storytellers who work simultaneously as artist, audience, and organizer to bring their work to a Malawian and international audience. In addition to tapping into skills and work already present at Dzaleka, Tumaini highlights poetry developed in arts workshops and poetry classes sponsored by NGOs and run by many of the poets involved in Lake of Stars and other organizing efforts. This art is thus implicitly transnational. It blends cultural norms and political experiences from elsewhere under the guidance of Malawian artists, for a broadly international audience. But Tumaini invites its audiences to treat the space of performance as, also, a space of habitation: the context from which the poetry speaks and that it is then made to represent. Poets are expected to speak to, in some way or another, the experience of that space—even if this experience does not exist outside the time-space of the festival itself.

But, of course, it does. According to a fundraising video featuring founder Menes La Plume, "The festival was founded to foster pride for the refugees, by giving them a platform to display their talents. Also, I thought that it was very important to open the doors of Dzaleka Refugee Camp to the world, to the Malawian community and to the international community, so that people could travel and see what is going on there and change the negative perception people do have towards refugees."[57] La Plume worked with local artists and arts facilitators, including Robert Chiwamba, Phindu Banda, and Jules Banda, to bring workshops to artists within the camp and to spread the word beyond the camp. La Plume himself also traveled to poetry events around the country, including KwaHaraba Open Mic Nights and Lake of Stars itself, to promote the event and highlight the artists' talents. In this sense, Tumaini enabled an unusual level of direct contact between Malawians and the residents of the Dzaleka Refugee Camp.

In founding the Tumaini Festival, La Plume's goals were akin to those of Lake of Stars founder Will Jameson: to remind outsiders, who casually derided or ignored Dzaleka's residents, that refugees are capable of great and moving art—capable of opening up and creating worlds for an audience of outsiders. The promotional video for the event includes an interview with an attendee, who says, "When you mention the camp [. . .] people expect it is a place where people are just being kept and there is no real life. [. . .] I didn't have much of an awareness about what happens in Dzaleka. [. . .] So being here, and seeing the sharing of different cultures and music, it's very impressive." As one artist interviewed for the video tells the viewer: "They see that, actually, they [refugees] are people like anyone."[58] At Tumaini, artistic expression is imagined to confer cosmopolitan agency. Yet it is, at the same time, a performance for outsiders, asserting the value of these nonstate subjects, who are identified in the video by their country of origin. The video itself was posted to GivingWay, a social media–style fundraising platform that imagines a global redistribution of wealth based predominantly on individual values. It thus implicitly targets individuals from relatively well-resourced countries, who would then use their resources to support artists perceived as structurally marginalized. Global media and international festivals thus reinforce, rather than break down, the tie between artist and national identity.

In moving between nation-spaces and communities, migrant poets speak across bounds and beyond the particular limitations of national interest to develop a shared world of concern. Their performances refigure the refugee as an exile and thus as part of a nation extending beyond its own borders. Performing as a Zimbabwean for a South African audience, Black Pearl suggests that the position of the poet—whether migrant, refugee, or exile—must always be carefully negotiated relative to her audience. Performing their humanity for a Malawian and international audience, in turn, the poets and artists of Tumaini make a claim for their own legitimacy and for legal recognition and freedoms.

The poet-refugee holds a unique position in contemporary discourse, transforming disindividuated masses of humanity unable to live in or return to their native spaces into exiles who, as Edward Said argues, "compensate for disorienting loss by creating a new world to rule." Writing at the end of the millennium, Said contends, "Our age—with its modern warfare, imperialism, and the quasi-theological ambitions of totalitarian rulers—is indeed the age of the refugee, the displaced person, mass immigration"—an era-defining characterization that intensified in the twenty-first century.[59] In the production and conquest of new worlds, the migrant poet enacts the work of the exile, making a mark on lands to which she will never fully belong. The refugee poet-as-exile produces a world bridging and reimagining the space between her home and host states. Said's insistence on the romanticization and spirituality of the exile grants them an agency and an individuality denied to the refugee—attributes sought in the performance of poetry for international audiences.

The poets at Tumaini share their life stories with a rapt audience who, in an ideal world, carry that message out to a broader political sphere. The affective sharing between audience and poet creates a collective event, a common experience that carries forward into and inflects the audience's and poets' everyday experiences. The poem's connection to everyday life remains an open question, but poetry's connection to the other verbal arts, and to language's everyday uses, is not. As Jahan Ramazani writes, "Poetry draws on and intensifies features of language in other oral and written uses, from which it can never be conclusively separated."[60] Poetry's connections to language in all its uses allow the form to reverberate from its point of origin to draw together performer and audience in a shared presentation of cultural meaning.

Troubling Digital Poetry's Cosmopolitanism

In the poetry festival, poetry shines as spectacle, singular events set apart from the mundane world. Yet the spectacle of poetry in the digital age insists on poetry's connection to the everyday, even as the festival context pulls literature into the realm of the sacred. National festivals are among the most consistently publicized poetry events, clearly indexed in digital searches in a way that smaller regional events often are not. Bringing together the most highly regarded and influential poets from across a region or within a community, festivals confer prestige on those poets, providing models for attendees. And they are large, drawing in a bigger crowd than local events. Yet they implicitly integrate the outside world in their production. The festival setting offers individual artists a chance to spread their names and their work, gaining acclaim through the attention international crowds and marketing carry. The poetry, then, is part of a broader performance, a performance that unites poets' words, actions, body, and charisma into a coherent, legible brand. The poetry festival performs and makes real the intimate connections between the "digitally circulated texts, sounds, and images" and "the private spaces once thought to be poetry's preserve" that they now penetrate.[61] In the face of digitization, poetry has become simultaneously extroverted and popular, blurring divides between cultural fields and decentering the academy in the process of cultural curation.

The digital cosmopolitanism of contemporary poetry registers the changing shapes of poetic reception and of cultural diffusion. For audiences, the live performance of poems primarily encountered through digital or printed mediation can be a powerfully orienting experience. The previous chapters have demonstrated the influence of social media on poetic community structure and aesthetic form. But what about the communities that coalesced through poetry? What happens when the digital interfaces with the material? Poetry at arts festivals highlights the interplay between digital cosmopolitanism and local performance cultures. More than that, festivals normalize the shifts wrought through digital aesthetics, establishing a new set of literary norms and expectations. As I argue further in the next chapter, this change signals a transformation in how cultural capital is established and distributed: not in opposition to material capital but in a quest for it.

CHAPTER 5

But Canons Continue

KOLEKA PUTUMA'S *COLLECTIVE AMNESIA* AND THE DIGITAL
FIGHT OVER CULTURAL CAPITAL

THE POPULARITY OF poetry on social media has both broadened its audience and brought a new, populist form of gatekeeping to the fore—one that predicates cultural value on virality. It has shifted the flow of cultural capital, as traditional processes of cultural validation, marked by professional training and institutional investments, now contend with the force of algorithmic recommendation systems.[1] Elite cultural institutions are now legitimized, in part, by their appeal to popular sources: traditional cultural authorities displaced by personalized recommendations, seemingly individual but organized by algorithms that reflect cultural norms and presumptions from the Global North.[2] These shifting structures of recommendation and authority transform the process of cultural capital accumulation as well: where, following Pierre Bourdieu's canonical model, cultural capital was marked by a removal from material concerns and elite taste by a distance from the popular, elite success today proceeds from market success, and cultural capital from a familiarity with the popular.[3] In southern Africa, where cultural capital has been associated with a formal schooling that reproduces colonialist cultural norms, this change reflects a broader tension for literature in the digital age: even as access promises revolution, digital curation threatens to reinforce bias.

The blurring of elite and popular spheres creates a surprising entanglement of poetry and business.[4] In June 2018, when *Forbes Africa* posted its first annual list of thirty "Under 30" top creatives to watch, the list included supermodels and fashion designers alongside three rappers, two songwriters,

FIGURE 12. Koleka Putuma launched *Collective Amnesia* in popular poetry spaces that spanned digital and live events. Courtesy of Roché Kester, Grounding Sessions.

and two poets: Sudanese American Safia Elhillo and South African Koleka Putuma. This was the first time any similar *Forbes* ranking list had included a poet, and its description of Putuma's career is especially telling. The article reads: "Putuma grabbed the world's attention with her poem "Water," a thought-provoking piece of writing and challenging performance on issues of race and religion. She's a poet, director, playwright and author. Her bestselling book, *Collective Amnesia*, is a powerful, intersectional text that tackles race, sexuality, class, politics, and poetry. [. . .] *Collective Amnesia* has been prescribed at tertiary level and made part of the curriculum. [. . .] Her work has traveled around the world, with her poetry winning prizes such as the 2014 National Poetry Slam Championship and the 2016 PEN South Africa Student Writing Prize."[5] Where singers are described in terms of commercial success—as "best-selling artists" (Kwesta, ranked twenty-ninth) who are "currently running the world of Africa[n] music" (Wizkid at seventeenth)—poets' success is measured through the institutions they've conquered: prizes won, audiences attracted, classrooms entered.

The *Forbes* listing highlights traditional markers of cultural authority:

educational and prizing-granting institutions. But what remains implicit is that while Elhillo accrued prominence primarily through local collaborations and international prizes for print poetry, the classic springs of elite valuation, Putuma's "Water" first "grabbed the world's attention" through the digital and live performance platforms that staged her work—and, in fact, by rejecting typical institutional springs. Putuma performed the poem in September 2015 at TEDxStellenbosch, a platform specifically designed to launch young voices. But that night, Putuma reported, the poem alienated the largely white audience, who approached her later to express their distress at the poem's explicit racial politics.[6] The venue decided not to publish her performance as a result. In response to their dismissal, Putuma published her own recording of the performance, bringing further attention to the event. Her piece was adapted into a video-poem directed by José Cardoso and published on YouTube by InZync Poetries, who also host monthly poetry readings in Stellenbosch. The video went viral. Its success laid the foundation for Putuma's debut collection, *Collective Amnesia*, which quadrupled average poetry sales figures by selling thousands of copies within months of its release and was soon integrated into tertiary curricula across the country.

Although the National Poetry Slam Championship and PEN Student Writing Prize legitimated Putuma's work, it was her popularity in digital spaces that created the cultural capital necessary to penetrate the historically closed canon of the classroom reading list. *Collective Amnesia*'s commercial success—predicated, in part, on its author's ability to promote her work at poetry slams and on YouTube—presages a transformation in the establishment and distribution of literary capital. I therefore want to ask how the rise of digital poetry has influenced the distribution of cultural capital and, with it, the formation of literary canons. Barbara Hernstein-Smith suggests that the twentieth-century Anglophone canon was determined not only by the syllabus but also by the space of the classroom, where literary evaluation is conducted and relayed within "a complex set of social and cultural activities central to the very nature of literature."[7] Literary judgment is a socialized process, modeled in classroom discussions and newspaper review pages. In southern Africa, as in much of the world colonized by England, this socialization was used to produce colonial cultures and reinforce the myth of colonial genius.[8] Still today, in South Africa and Malawi, as in much of Anglophone Africa, English language proficiency and cultural knowledge operates as a marker of both class and intelligence.[9]

Classroom teaching forges new literary frameworks through confrontation with dominant cultural concerns—a confrontation I argue now occurs predominantly online.[10]

Digital publication disrupts the cycle of cultural power distribution. If Bourdieu's nineteenth- and twentieth-century authors marked their cultural capital through a rejection of material capital, in the digital-literary landscape of the early twenty-first century, cultural capital is accrued through a rejection of social capital.[11] Writers who would claim authenticity avoid the traditional networks of academia and art worlds to instead position themselves alongside the everyday audiences to whom they appeal: disaffected youth, frustrated by a received model of poetry, who engage their work on Instagram, YouTube, and Twitter, and for whom all communication is, implicitly, multimodal. Success in these popular markets can then trigger elite recognition. While literary institutions maintain structural power through festivals, prizes, and publications, their claims to authority rely on their increasingly fragile ability to assert cultural relevance and manage the relationship between two competing forms of cultural capital: the increasingly institutionalized popular, and the rapidly fading elite.

Putuma's *Collective Amnesia* has been celebrated for defying odds: its unprecedented sales numbers and tour events broke boundaries and broadened poetry's public. These successes represent the culmination of the longstanding transformations in literary socialization and cultural production catalyzed by the rise of social media. Driven by the quantitative emphasis of digital structures, contemporary performance poetry connects individuals in a crowded cloud. *Collective Amnesia* draws on the popularity of performance poetry, as well as the marketing force of social media, to establish its power in a traditional publishing milieu. The story of *Collective Amnesia* and Putuma's rapid rise to popular canonization reflects larger shifts in literary production and cultural capital distribution—shifts driven by digital norms and supported by emergent literary networks that span digital and grounded communities. It illustrates the growing impact of popular, Afrocentric literary institutions. Their "gateopening" practices contend with traditional gatekeeping structures to establish a literary movement in the interstice between the popular and the elite.[12]

Networked Poetry in the Literary Public Sphere

Collective Amnesia evaluates the social impact of shifting technological epistemes from an African perspective, highlighting under-recognized knowledge communities. The collection is organized in three sections: "Inherited Memory," "Buried Memory," and "Postmemory." The first section focuses on issues of identity and nonconformity in the face of religion and tradition. The second section deals with mourning, grief, and death as metaphor for depression and self-discovery. Each section slowly mutilates poetic form, moving from clearly lineated stanzas in the first section to deformed lines and words in the second and into the radically prosaic forms of dictionary entries and footnotes in the third. Through its progressions, *Collective Amnesia* questions the relationship between received wisdom and literary form.

The collection's most famous poem, "Water" reimagines South African history through the sea, the ships it carries, the bodies that gather around it, and the knowledges that emerge from it. It insists on a relationship between speaker and space that transforms communication into an assemblage of material objects, from "black tights and Shoprite plastic bags" to "history books that do not tell the truth." Knowledge communities form around these objects to re-create meaning in response to shifting communication technologies. Putuma's poetry underscores how preexisting power structures manipulate communication to create new meaning, even as marginalized communities work against those same structures. In so doing, it presents a poetic logic attuned to both the forms and the norms of the network: associative, allusive, connective.

In the video for "Water," Putuma sits on jagged rocks by the sea at the edge of Cape Town and critiques stereotypes of Black South Africans.[13] Much like the video-sharing platform that presents it, the poem juxtaposes the profane and the sacred to offer symbolic reworkings of everyday injustices. Replacing racialized readings with ritualistic rehearsals of history, Putuma sighs:

> I often hear this joke
> about Black people being scared of water
> or not being able to swim [. . .]
> Every time our skin goes under,
> it's as if the reeds remember that they were once chains
> and the water, restless, wishes that it could spew all of the slaves and
> ships onto shore,
> whole as they had boarded, sailed and sunk.

> Their tears are what have turned the ocean salty,
> this is why our irises burn every time we go under. [...]
> We have come to be baptized here.[14]

The poem, which begins and ends at the water's edge, centers the sea as simultaneously a reminder of colonial trauma and a space of spiritual renewal. Isobel Hofmeyr identifies this tendency with *hydrocolonialism*, "signal[ing] a commitment to understanding a world indelibly shaped by imperial uses of water."[15] For Putuma, Hofmeyr argues, the water represents both imperialism's point of departure and an escape from the colonization of the land. Baptism by the sea simultaneously recalls slavery and colonialism—the reeds that "were once chains"—and invites rebirth, away from the shore where colonialism reproduces itself.

"Water" crosses land and sea to reject cultural as well as geographic colonialism, liberating soul and ocean simultaneously. The video establishes a spatial iconography that rejects a Eurocentric vision of artistic merit—one that would be implicitly tied to a settler Christian normativity: Putuma walks through the aisles of the Slave Church Museum and whispers, "For all we know, / the disciples could have been queer," playing on visions of a Black Jesus to reject the colonial heteropatriarchy. As the poem draws to an end, she stands amid passing crowds at the Company's Garden and declares, "Another one (who looks like me) was murdered today, by your kind. / May that be the conversation at the table."[16] The words condemn the systematic violence facing Black women in South Africa.[17] Putuma's direct gaze makes the suffering personal, rendering the digital viewers complicit in violent structures.

The poem draws on stereotypes of Black South Africa, African cosmologies, Christian references, and colonial history to criticize Cape Town's often-unspoken legacies of colonialism and racism. If the language in "Water" ties together contemporary stereotype and colonial history through biblical references, its geographic iconography postulates an alternative relationship to space, one mediated not purely by the Bible or colonialism but instead by the tension between the individual and the collective, which is invoked in images of passing crowds, empty pews, and a lonely beach. The video's spatial references—the Atlantic Ocean in which slaves are buried, the church in which they worshipped, and the gardens that beautify the city's violent past—suggest a broader collectivity further evoked through layered audio and ghostly visuals.

As the range of references in Putuma's work makes clear, poetry by and for African youth—exceptional and ordinary, transcendent and everyday, direct and mediated—frequently operates across cultural frameworks illegible within Western literary studies. Instead of appealing to a broadly imagined "public sphere" incorporated through an agreed-upon canon, it offers narrow allusions that invite a networked audience attuned to its references. It is thus a poetics of the networked public sphere, claiming and directing attention through shared allusion. In this way, it points up the shifting structure of the contemporary public sphere. The Habermasian vision of the Enlightenment public sphere—that third space of the coffee shop, in which public discourse is constructed and contemporary values established—has, of course, never existed.[18] Instead, as Michael Warner argued in 2002, publics are constructed through their investment in a shared rhetorical framework: "The idea of a public [. . .] is text-based—even though publics are increasingly organized around visual or audio texts." Writing at the advent of Web 2.0, Warner identified a rapidly fracturing series of shifting investments, which, he writes, "makes us believe our consciousness to be decisive. The direction of our glance can constitute our social world."[19] But this belief is misleading: instead, it is the "link" between discursive moves that creates our social world. Public discourse and "market reflexivity," for Warner, are entwined by the production of texts as commodity. Lyric poetry creates intimate connections between strangers, situating the speaker and reader alike in relation with imagined others, a discursive intimacy that structures poetry's connection to national identity.

Whereas academic discourse imagines poetry to be being primarily textual, digital media bring other sensory experiences forward: touching the screen or hearing the words creates a tangible connection between audience and text. Putuma's poetry responds to a broader, popular vision of literature as connective tissue, bridging discursive fields in a networked public sphere. Her work fulfills Denise Newfield and Rafael d'Abdon's call for multimodal approaches to literary education in South Africa. Multimodal poetry, Newfield and d'Abdon argue, "is premised upon the synesthetic quality of representation and communication and examines shifts across modes in the making of meaning at different times and in different contexts, as well as the combination and orchestration of modes in multimodal ensembles at particular moments."[20] Such relational approaches to poetry highlight the limits of the literary classroom—which prioritizes print works—as the space of cultural capital formation. This focus is especially inappropriate in an African context, where literary expression emerges in a reciprocal relationship between oral and print media.[21] Networked poetry, unlike that of the classroom, draws its capital from the relationships it builds and the network it supports. It is a poetry of and for its own imagined public.

Newfield and d'Abdon's relational approach to poetry education offers insight into the limitations of prizes and the critique of literary institutions. Newfield and d'Abdon, both practicing poets and teachers, reimagine the literature classroom as a space where works of the Western canon mix with contemporary pieces that speak to local experience, implementing a hybrid critical/creative approach to encourage students to apply those poetic lessons to their own writing. Curricular structures have traditionally been understood to provide students with core training in elite valuation of aesthetic forms, providing the necessary cultural capital to position themselves in the higher classes.[22] At the tertiary level, though, these structures are driven by an interchange between the teacher and their class: Rachel Sagner Buurma and Laura Heffernan, for instance, suggest that student demands can yield a more fluid and responsive curricular structure.[23] This interactive model is especially important in the digital age, when cultural currency relies on fluency in what is new and popular.[24] The drive for pedagogic reform points to shifting attitudes about the role of the literature classroom, as popular processes of valuation displace elite ones. Thus as cultural needs shift, educational models increasingly embrace alternative structures of education in literary valuation, gradually reinforcing contemporary ideas about poetry as a public form.

The success of "Water," in particular, and of *Collective Amnesia* more broadly, lies in the poetry's ability to navigate the interchange between popular reception and elite valuation. As literary production and reception find their place in viral videos and digital forums, literature becomes networked. The collection is, in some ways, merely exemplary of a broader shift, over a decade in the making: the relative openness of digital media spaces linked closely to discrete communities, from WhatsApp to YouTube, fosters experimentation, even as their rapid inventions create new norms at seemingly unprecedented speeds.[25]

Economies of Poetic Prestige

The rise of populist gatekeeping strategies means failure in traditional settings can springboard success in popular ones. An author's self-fashioning often relies on their ability to position themselves in opposition to rivals in a shared cultural field: individual branding requires not just a positive assertion of identity but also a negative relation to an oppositional other within the broader cultural field.[26] And networked connections intensify pressures on individuals to perform their oppositions and create individual spaces. In South Africa, in particular, this can require performing opposition to a white-dominated cultural sphere. The tension that emerged amid the multiple debuts of "Water"—on stage, online, and in print—exemplifies the role of digital gatekeeping in literary production: the poem's early rejection by an elite cultural sphere at TEDxStellenbosch catalyzed popular interest, which primed its later YouTube publication for success. In this context, cultural capital is not opposed to economic capital but formed instead in opposition to the elite cultural sphere.

This conflict between elite and popular forms of cultural prestige mirrors the divide between cultural and economic capital that persists elsewhere, demonstrating the artist's autonomy from an elite literary sphere controlled by prize-granting institutions focused on the Global North. Narrowly, the scandal of Putuma's rejection at Stellenbosch brought further attention to her already-popular work online: her blog post on the topic is one of the most viewed and shared on Word N Sound's site, if, in part, because of the fame she later accrued. Fame begets fame. But although the relationship between popularity and canonization is cyclical, it is uneven. As John Guillory points out, "Canonicity is not a property of the work itself but of its transmission, in relation to other works in a collocation of works—the syllabus in its institutional locus, the school."[27] In southern Africa, the literary syllabus and schoolroom have historically reinscribed the aesthetic values of Western literature.[28] But the rise of digital publication has decentered the school in the production of cultural value, as popular artists like Beyoncé Knowles become cultural touchstones in the extra-pedagogic sphere of the podcast and the live stream. Literary socialization is instead modeled in "BookTok" reviews and digital commentators, as well as short stories monetized through product placement and advertisements.[29] The "cultural authority of recommenders," as Lindsay Thomas writes, has moved from elite to popular spheres—from academically trained book reviewers to "people like you," whose preferences are strategically promoted by curation algorithms.[30]

Populist publication technologies alone will not transform power structures: digital literary texts and audiences interact in a web that drives attention, institutionalization, and the preservation of certain knowledge structures over others. In *New Digital Worlds*, Roopika Risam argues that the humanistic study of digital cultures recapitulates extractive and colonial patterns of knowledge production. Risam therefore calls for practices "that challenge the centrality of Europe in both the cultural record and digital humanities scholarship, to decenter hubs of capital in the production of knowledge, and to engage with the liminal, abject, or subaltern by placing them at the center of inquiry in the digital cultural record."[31] To read poetry without attention to its publication platform, the audiences that form around it, and the cultural institutions that support it, is to neglect the broader cultural framework in which it operates and through reference to which it makes its meaning. Moreover, while digital cultural frameworks may not always be local, they remain geographically specific: as Stephanie Bosch Santana writes, "The fact that distinct digital forms have emerged in different locations tells us that real geographies are still important for understanding their production, circulation, and consumption."[32] The literary form that Santana analyzes—blog fiction from South Africa—varies in both its form and its reception context: audiences engage with the work on mobile phones, bringing literature into transient spaces tied to cultural practices of mobility and migration. Attending to local media histories helps disentangle the regional production of knowledge from its global circulation.

Poetry's impact on community life derives from its engagement with that life, its ability to speak meaningfully to its imagined public and thus draw their gaze. A poet's success relies on the relationships forged in local open mics and WhatsApp groups. Artists therefore engage intercostal spaces between popular and elite spheres to strategically pivot their address, forging a locally oriented canon in contrast to the "extroverted" performance of the arts festival and the YouTube poetry slam. In this way, they offer links to establish a networked literary sphere bound by poetic discourse. By mobilizing popular performance styles, contemporary poets like Putuma put digital media structures to work in favor of decolonial methods of knowledge production.

When uHlanga launched *Collective Amnesia*, the publisher built on Putuma's digital popularity, promoting the book through social media posts like the one at the beginning of this chapter (figure 12). The book tour included readings at galleries, open mic nights, and poetry slams, in addition to events at universities and bookstores. Putuma even crowdsourced additional stops: on 21 April 2016, she posted the preliminary tour dates on Facebook and wrote, "If you organise the venue and marketing, I will put your city on the route," ultimately adding two more tour sites. Though she jokes later, "I can't remember what possessed me to put out this call," the tour was a remarkable success. The literary blog Brittle Paper called the publicity campaign "a lesson in innovation" which could "change how we sell African books."[33] Professor Uhuru Phalafala, who introduced Putuma's reading at Stellenbosch, added the text to her course syllabuses. In doing so, she implicitly placed the text into a broader South African literary tradition, using her position as a cultural authority to mark Putuma's work as worthy of careful conversation and analysis. Popular and formal institutions entered into a dialectic relationship mediated by digital marketing: their negotiations shift the balance of power in the establishment of new aesthetic forms.

Collective Amnesia's marketing heralds a shift from elite (and institutional) to populist (and algorithmic) gatekeeping. This shift reflects the turn from print to digitally mediated forms of literary consumption—a turn that has engendered diverse networks of canon formation. Digital success precedes canonization, a move away from the publication and prizing structures that typified literary institutions in the twentieth century. As Sarah Brouillette, Ariel Bookman, and Nathan Suhr-Sytsma have shown, literary aesthetic networks in the late twentieth century sustained the rise of postcolonial literature—both through university writers' groups and literary festivals such as those Suhr-Sytsma traces or through the more direct marketing schemes of the multinational publishing industry Brouillette reveals.[34] The rise of literary prizes, in particular, has created a Northern market for writers from the Global South and subsequently promoted a self-critical aesthetic that, as Brouillette argues, produces a self-conscious relationship between the writer and their position in the market.

Nonetheless, poets continue to face an ingrained hierarchy of literary production, one that is shaped by cycles of demand and consumption. While small publishers like uHlanga can make outsized marks by taking bigger risks, literary publication across Africa is largely dominated by a few large, multinational publishing houses, which focus on school textbooks and didactic texts for young readers.[35] This imbalance is exacerbated by the structure of the prize economy, which continually reproduces the binary between elite and popular fields of literary production or, in Madhu Krishnan's words, "African literature" and "African literary production." Prizes consecrate African literature but only rarely acknowledge African literary production—that is, "the larger fullness and diversity of literary activity emanating from the continent and its diasporas."[36] But, as Rachel Mennies's work shows, prize competitions are a risky proposition for poets: the cost of submission can be prohibitive, encouraging poets to write strategically to appeal to judges' tastes.[37] Prizes not only limit what sort of work is recognized, then, but also what work is produced.

These prizes reproduce the same institutional structures that limit poetic engagement with the popular sphere. The AKO Caine Prize, for instance, is awarded only to published short stories, effectively dismissing the self-publication spaces where many popular artists find their start. The Commonwealth Prize, in contrast, is open only to unpublished works, but its aesthetic orientations reproduce structures and forms popularized in what Mark McGurl famously called the "program era" of the MFA.[38] While, as Doseline Kiguru demonstrates, the contemporary prize field "has enabled many writers to get published, [. . .] it has also meant that gradually, the international prizes have filtered through to the production level. [. . .] Consequently, the award becomes the producer of value rather than the value of the creative product attracting the prize only for its quality"[39] The prize-granting organizations and their attendant workshop settings operate within a global economy of prestige, "in which the many local cultural markets and local scales of value are bound into ever tighter relations of interdependence."[40] These relations are, themselves, vexed by a tension between the desire for autonomy (or its appearance) and the need for global recognition—the same tensions, in other words, that shape the poetry festivals discussed in the previous chapter.

"Water," published on YouTube, would not have been eligible for most poetry prizes, which require the work either be printed in a recognized publication or be unpublished altogether. Yet that ineligible (illegible) work drove *Collective Amnesia*'s tour and sales numbers—the numbers that drew elite attention to the work. Putuma's digital success constituted a reaction against literary institutions, consecrating a new form of literary merit. As Hernstein-Smith argues, "The value of a literary work is continuously produced and reproduced by the very acts of implicit and explicit evaluation that are frequently invoked as 'rejecting' its value and therefore as being evidence of it. In other words, what are commonly taken to be signs of literary value are, in effect, its *springs*"[41]—in other words, while initial recognition may be somewhat arbitrary, it drives further recognition, or nothing predicts virality so well as prior virality.

Those springs are, still, largely controlled by organizations otherwise uninterested in cultural development. As Graham Huggan writes of the Booker Prize, "As state subsidies of the arts have dwindled [through the late twentieth century], alarmingly in many countries [. . .] corporate sponsorship has largely overtaken the earlier, predominantly hierarchical systems of private and public patronage through which ideas of literature and literary value were upheld."[42] Winning a prize, with or without corporate sponsors, can guarantee market success. Literary prizes—key springs for legitimation—reproduce normative structures of value by encouraging aspiring writers to conform their own work to judges' expectations. This can happen in multiple ways: through modeling, like in slam competitions and prize anthologies; through experimentation in small, enclosed groups; or through formal training in any of a proliferating array of professionalization workshops, sponsored by local writers' organizations and international agencies alike.

In 2017, the popular literary blog Brittle Paper began its own award series, focused on digital literatures and arts organizations that directly engage a broader literary community. Their guidelines imagine a relational poetics built on open-access principles: nominations are open to "works published on *any* platform, literary or pop culture or otherwise," provided that they are "available for free online." Yet even these broad categories neglect the most popular digital platforms by insisting a work be recognized through publication in an established literary editorial like the *Johannesburg Review of Books* or *Granta*. The old economy of prestige persists, displaced onto digital media.

Prize economies reinforce the coincidence of cultural and economic capital in African literature, reflecting the general rule that "the production of cultural value [. . .] is always politicised and leans towards the prevailing social, political, and economic power."[43] But these two frameworks come into tension. As Krishnan writes: "In the making of African literature, these two modes of capital appear to curiously coincide in a mutually reinforcing system in which one mode of capital—the economic—itself functions as a mechanism through which another form—the cultural—is inhered."[44] Of course, these tensions are exacerbated by the fact that in Malawi, Zimbabwe, and South Africa, prizes are often organized and funded, if not always adjudicated, by foundations centered in the Global North. They extend the global redistribution of economic capital to cultural capital: underdeveloping African literature while providing a symbolic framework of plausible deniability.[45] The question then becomes: To whom is this cultural capital meaningful? If culture becomes capital by granting its proprietor access to material resources, then what does that relationship look like in the digital age?

Creating New Networks

The failure of elite literary institutions to recognize popular poetry encourages poets to form their own communities, institutions, and even—in the case of the poetry slam—prizes. Digital platforms built by and for African artists are, themselves, mapping a new landscape of cultural prestige and capital distribution. The largest curated archive of African poetry and performance through much of the 2010s was the Africa Centre's Badilisha Poetry X-Change, based in Cape Town and founded by Wanjiru Koinange and Malika Ndlovu. Badilisha's funding structure is unusual: three of its four funders—the National Lottery, the National Arts Council, UNESCO's International Fund, and the Spier Wine Estate—are domestic, and three are public organizations. This national and regional funding structure supports Badilisha's capacity to emphasize regional, Afrocentric approaches to publication.

The website, podcast, and collective all grow out of a series of large-scale poetry festivals, hosted between 2008 and 2011, much like the Spoken Word Project, discussed in chapter 5. But Badilisha's relationship with the Africa Centre, an independent organization driven to "use Pan-African cultural practice as a tool to [. . .] ensure that people living on this soil can define for themselves what is possible and what their reality looks like," guaranteed a relatively consistent funding stream that such initiatives rarely enjoy.[46] Under this heading, Badilisha sought to make African poetry widely accessible within Africa, through podcasts accompanied by publication and consistent outreach. Its website noted, "Africans have limited access to the vast poetic work of both historical and contemporary African poets. There has never been an archive of these poets' work that is both expansive and easily accessible."[47] That archive disappeared with Badilisha's closure, underscoring the precarity of arts institutions.

The particular reason for this lack of access varies dramatically: in Malawi, for instance, extreme censorship under Banda often drove poets underground or into exile and led to the banning of many local texts that could undermine his singular claims to authority; in South Africa, access to books is limited by government tariffs; and in Zimbabwe, the limited print infrastructure means few can afford to buy them. And, of course, the formal publishing industry established under colonial regimes maintained those colonial perspectives and infrastructures past decolonization. The Heinemann African Writers

Series, perhaps the preeminent global publisher of African literature in the twentieth century, was founded in part as a neocolonial venture for British firms to capture and profit from a growing educational market in emerging nation-states.[48] These firms, as Henry Chakava writes, operated "to collect good manuscripts and forward them to London for vetting and publishing."[49] By the 1970s, "sales for learning readers in Africa backed the rest of the Oxford University Press publishing program," establishing a "neocolonial knowledge industry."[50] While, as Tanzanian publishers Walter Bgoya and Mary Jay detail, independent African publishers established partnerships to expand market reach through the 1990s, lack of international structural support consistently stymied cultural development efforts.[51]

Access to literature of any sort—print or digital, elite or popular—is confined by this underdeveloped publishing industry. Digital media promised affordable access to a wider range of authors: as Shola Adenekan writes, "African writers are not putting their work in cyberspace just for the sake of it; it is because communities—both local and global—are being constituted in this space. [. . .] In the context of Nigeria and Kenya, marginalized groups such as the queer community have found digital space the ideal site for their voices to be heard."[52] Lack of representation in schools and public media led many of the poets I'd met to seek out digital spaces. But online, in the mid-2010s, they mostly found channels like Button Poetry, which prioritize voices from the Global North. And, as recent work on algorithmic mediation has shown, many popular publishing sites—such as YouTube, Facebook, and Wattpad—reproduce racial and geopolitical inequities, implicitly reinscribing their programmers' cultural norms and expectations.

In this context, digital publication platforms provide crucial alternatives for African writers and readers. By publishing poetry online, in multiple formats, Badilisha opened new possibilities for reception and engagement. The site sustained multiple organizational paradigms: the digitally dominant metrics of "Latest" and "Top" are accompanied by the classic print structures of "Language," "Country," and "A–Z" and the editorializing "Theme" and "Emotion." And Badilisha's vision of "African" poetry is expansive: poets from Canada, Cuba, the United Kingdom, Sri Lanka, and Germany figure alongside those from Kenya and Nigeria. These structures, ironically, reproduce the dominance of certain Anglophone African countries in literary production: after South Africa, the most-represented countries are Zimbabwe, the United States, Kenya, and Nigeria. These distributions reflect, in the first case, physical proximity, and in the other three, the relatively robust digital and educational structures that support poetic growth.[53] Yet by subordinating geographic organization to affective and thematic organizing structures, Badilisha allows us to reimagine the default, nation- and period-based, approaches that have so long sustained the study and valuation of African literature. These multiple sorting categories enable Badilisha to become a living, user-driven anthology, creating unexpected connections between poets in Mali and Malawi at the same time as it helps establish an accessible poetic nucleus.

In doing so, the site establishes its own expectations for poetic content and meaning. The submissions section of the website specifies guidelines for both the poet—"African or part of the African diaspora"—and the poetry: "The poem and the vocal delivery must both be of a high standard. The poetry must be submitted as a high-quality recording. [. . .] Poetry backed by music is welcomed, but the poet's voice and poetry content must be the core focus. If the piece is more 'sung' than 'spoken,' it is likely to be more appropriate for a music platform."[54] This focus on background and style marks Badilisha's departure from Eurocentric poetic norms. And although the guidelines reproduce the default Anglocentrism of the web (any non-English poems must be accompanied by translation), the digital platform allows Badilisha to reach well beyond the traditional confines of the poetry anthology, which must so often be marketed either to pedagogues or to the Global North.

The site opened opportunities for professional accreditation and legitimation to both established and emerging poets. Ndlovu's and Koinange's professional reputations, together with the opening festivals, brought in acclaimed poets Kwame Dawes, Keorapetse William Kgositsile, and Warsan Shire, who had recently gained international attention for her collaborations on Beyoncé Knowles's visual album *Lemonade*. These names lent the platform credibility. And, in 2012, Badilisha published early work by a student poet who had just finished second place in her first major poetry slam performance: Koleka Putuma. These juxtapositions legitimize the work of young poets, suggesting—if implicitly—that they might profitably be read alongside those whose work had already achieved acclaim. Without overtly questioning prior processes of canon formation, they open new paths to cultural capital acquisition.

Badilisha joined a rapidly growing array of platforms centered on performance poetry. Where Badilisha sought to foster Pan-African poetry, though, those from beyond the "Big 5" publishing countries have sought to establish nationally specific support projects.[55] In Malawi, Robert Chiwamba's website

Sapitwa Poetry aimed to directly intervene in this process.[56] Founded in 2014 and active until 2021, the website (www.sapitwapoetry.com) was modeled after the highly successful platform MalawiMusic.com. To be published on Sapitwa, individual artists submit their work to the platform, where it was vetted (according to Chiwamba) not for quality but simply for profanity and other risks to the publisher's security.[57] Once uploaded, the poem would appear in a grid, amid hundreds of other works. Viewers could either listen to the poem online or download it for a nominal fee, which is then transferred to the artist.

The front page featured three sections of poems marked "#HOTTEST," "#LATEST," and "VIDEOS." These categories mirror the algorithmic aesthetics of social media: the demand for novelty, and the use of popularity as a singular metric of value. The stylized "#" appended to the first two categories—which does not function as a link on the site itself—marks their cultural and aesthetic connection to social media norms. The videos and artists featured in the first section are largely consistent from week to week: nothing predicts popularity so well as prior popularity.[58] In addition to these categories, users can navigate the poems through direct search and a secondary "Discover" menu, which organizes poems by language and genre. These additional functions bring emerging and student poets into the orbit of well-established ones, like Chiwamba and Malewezi.

At its peak, Sapitwa Poetry got hundreds of hits per day; the most popular pieces received thousands of views and dozens of comments, while even the relatively unsuccessful are guaranteed a few dozen sets of eyes. Without Sapitwa, most young Malawian poets would struggle to achieve this level of exposure (indeed, most poets anywhere struggle for more than a handful of readers). The site connected poets across generational, linguistic, and stylistic lines, opening new opportunities for innovation, engagement, and audience development. As the single largest repository of contemporary Malawian poetry, Sapitwa worked alongside the country's print-focused literature curriculum and performance-focused popular sphere to establish new norms for future generations of Malawian artists. But Sapitwa was also self-funded by Chiwamba and two colleagues. Its demise, partway through the COVID-19 pandemic, speaks to the broader insecurities of publishing in Africa and the ephemerality of digital projects more generally.

The rise of digital poetic forms has been especially important in opening new avenues for performance poetry, furthering efforts to "re-emphasise texts that are not easily detached from their performative context," as Nikitta Adjirakor writes of literary fieldwork.[59] Performance poetry—legitimized by digital metrics and authorized by elite institutions seeking their own relevance—has come of age alongside digital media. The establishment of popular poetry institutions like Sapitwa Poetry, House of Hunger, and Badilisha created new centers of gravity for literary production. At the same time, they often recapitulate forms of judgment inscribed by digital platforms driven by algorithmic curation: Sapitwa Poetry defaults to highlighting poems that are "trending" and "most viewed," whereas Badilisha offers a new-first focus. These organizations offer new models for popular poetry and new methods like the slam and the "Like" and "Share" buttons for evaluating success. The success of these digital institutions, in turn, transformed the traditional springs of literary value by emphasizing quantitative and populist signs of success.

Yet the very platforms that help legitimate emerging artists, as well as offer material support for poetry, themselves faltered on the shaky ground available to arts endeavors more generally. They relied on individual passion, rather than institutional structures; grant-based funding of projects over organizations; and, ultimately, infrastructure that came from outside. As digital platforms, they promised to democratize access to the arts, but the very technology that enabled connection limited durability. The rise of digital publication structures is a promise of change built on fundamentally unstable grounds.

Digital Institutions and New Media Canons

Digital platforms erase divisions between the concerns of everyday life and those of the artist. As poetry collections like *Collective Amnesia* become bestsellers for the first time in a century, market access and cultural capital derive simultaneously from success in popular spaces. Quantifiable metrics of popularity now precede institutional recognition, as mass recommendation systems replace the literary agent as early gatekeeper. This is not unique to poetry by any means: popular food bloggers get cookbook deals; fashion influencers write comic memoirs. But poetry's domain has so long been elite and isolated that the popular embrace of poetry can feel like a betrayal: the term itself is so strongly affiliated with high culture that many commentators and scholars struggle to positively identify popular verse as "poetry."[60]

The transformation of cultural power in changing media landscapes is therefore of particular consequence for poetry, which has long been a staple of the literature classroom. Its value is rehearsed at podiums and in examinations, often to the derision of youth who, as Newfield and d'Abdon detail, feel it is "too difficult, elitist, or remote from the concerns of everyday life." However, "if poetry were reconceptualised as a multimodal genre, it could play a constructive role in the motivation and self-esteem of learners struggling to acquire competence in English."[61] Whether this change enters classrooms themselves, it is showing up in popular media, creating avenues for expression, connection, and evaluation in horizontally structured social spaces. As poetry moves from the literature syllabus onto Instagram pages, digital anthologies, and podcast streams, its references have shifted, embracing a populist discourse in conversation with everyday life.

Poetry like Putuma's flourishes online by building connections between the poet and her public, embracing new referential frames and thus interpellating new audiences. Poetry is centrally defined through its references: "Poems come into being partly by echoing, playing on, reshaping, refining, heightening, deforming, inverting, combating, hybridizing, and compressing extrapoetic forms of language. [. . .] A poem faces both inward and outward: it enriches itself in its play on euphonies and dissonances within itself and across an array of earlier poems, and it feasts on, digests, and metabolizes linguistic forms of other kinds."[62] Poetry's connection to other forms—whether to the news and prayer, as Jahan Ramazani's study of twentieth-century Anglophone poetry details, or to the chants and hashtags for I've discussed—binds rhetorical communities. But what happens when the canon is determined by popular vote, rendering the always-great expanse of literary production suddenly visible?

The rise of Instagram poetry, for instance, encourages renewed attention to the aesthetic and material forms of poetry—not as metatext but as themselves textual.[63] The Zimbabwean South African poet Nomonde Mlotshwa, who writes under the pen name Nomonde Sky, follows this trend when she tweets images of her poems that draw on the aesthetics of typewriters: using a courier font, miniscule lettering, and a cream-colored background to distinguish the image from the stark white, serif, left-justified platform to which it is posted (see figure 13).

By aestheticizing its own mediation, Sky's work implies a long history of print poetic conversations. In a piece published on 20 April 2020—shortly after Zimbabwe had begun its own lockdown, amid deepening economic depression and desperation—Sky wrote, with her own pen name inked below:

> I pray we heal.
> Our amen will have blood
> clots accompanying it so
> our lord knows we chewed
> our tongues as a
> sacrifice for words unspoken-unheard-
> undeserving

While much of Sky's work is more explicitly erotic, this post paired a poem of anguish with an image of Sky herself, seated wearing only a long shirt draped between her open legs, looking directly to camera. Her work—which may be understood both as the individual poem and as the broader, curated feed—juxtaposes text and image, vulnerability and anger, in a sometimes-uncomfortable mélange that reflects the pervasive engagement of always-on technologies. And her work is immensely successful: with over fifty thousand followers on Twitter, she is among the most popular Zimbabwean poets online.

The rise of social media platforms over the past decade, their seeming ubiquity across places and generations, and their influence on a range of communication strategies has obscured but not diminished the role of either distance or difference in assigning value. Poetry especially remains tied to persistent ideas about the nation, about local identities, and about individual authenticity. Sky's regional success draws, in part, on a local community: many of her early posts were video recordings of erotic poetry and love poems, to which fans responded enthusiastically with stories and experiences of their own. Over the course of 2020, though, her themes became increasingly varied as more people turned to digital spaces for emotional sustenance. On 2 August 2020, for instance—as Zimbabwe arrested protesters who spoke out against government corruption—she posted an image of a poem in a courier font that began:

> Help me gag my sorrows.
> Let me praise our God
> with a mouth filled with
> ballooning saliva.

The poem's strong beginning dissolves into enjambed chaos. Its conversational attitude reflects Sky's performance style: direct to camera, intimate, and confessional. But a day later, fed up with poetry's ambiguity, she posted a clear statement of political urgency: "ZIMBABWE IS GOING THROUGH

FIGURE 13. Poets online pair text with image to tie the author's personal brand to their words. Image courtesy of Nomonde_sky.

A MASSIVE HUMAN RIGHTS ISSUE," repeated five times. Poetry quickly jumped registers from personal performance to direct appeal, blurring aesthetics and politics.

Sky's work insists on the connection between the personal and the literary. By inscribing the author's name and image over each post, social media publication emphasizes the author function in all forms, revealing how identity play and community reform poetic production: "The internet has amplified the image of the literary author beyond the confines of literary circles into the digital public domain."[64] It establishes a particular relationship between producer and product in which the author brand, identified by the pairing of name with logo, authorizes the content; the content, in turn, verifies the brand. The rise of social media publication has engendered a rise in celebrity literary brands like Chimamanda Adichie's and Koleka Putuma's, which are tied as often to TEDx talks and Facebook think pieces as to poetry and literary fiction. Adichie's "How to Be a Feminist," which generated attention and controversy on her Facebook page before it was published as a standalone essay, helped make the best-selling novelist into a globally discussed public intellectual. Ainehi Edoro-Glines argues that Adichie "shape[d] the text's formal and rhetorical structures to align with user-generated content on Facebook" to construct a platform-specific form whose digital virality launched public support.[65] Similarly, pioneering South African poet Lebogang Mashile's TEDx talk "Memory Matters" drew together Mashile's poetry with her broader intellectual project to highlight Black women's perspectives in history and politics. These works highlight the continuity between literary production and popular knowledge—a blurring of traditional divides encouraged by the flow structure of the digital landscape.

Edoro-Glines's analysis of "How to Be a Feminist" compels us to read "social media as platform." But, more important, for Edoro-Glines, these shifts are always "also about African literature and digital culture," because "contemporary African literature offers a uniquely rich archive on the impact of social media on literary discourse."[66] The form of social media platforms themselves inflects the content and structure of contemporary poetry. *Collective Amnesia* highlights the networks through which Putuma's work circulates: her acknowledgments thank dozens of South African womxn poets along with "the InZync team," "Word and Sound Live Literature Company," and "Lingua Franca."[67] The poems in the collection engage deeply with issues of mediation and network, using footnotes, bullet points, and lists to demarcate their connection to and rejection of the poet's postcolonial schooling. Many are dialogic, invoking another's voice or suggesting interviews as Putuma questions the power of hegemonic epistemes and their influence on Black women's health and security.

The dialogues that structure the volume reflect the interactivity of digital verse: even though Putuma's work was published first in a print volume, it consistently honors the digital aesthetic networks through which her poetry flows. Her poems reflect shifting attitudes about how poetry moves through the world, as more "under 30s" read poems on their screens, hear them in person, and configure their lives around the short, allusive, ambiguous texts that typify digital communication. The poem "Online," for instance, details the unspoken rules of digital discourse:

> Do not share a meme of your panic attack on social media
> Your 3456 friends do not know of the epilepsy that came before
> ....
> Do not post a selfie of your self-mutilation.

God forbid your status reveals that you are lost or breaking.
No one will comment on how raw or close to healing your tumour is.[68]

This poem betrays the speaker's skepticism of the connections and art supported on social media. The "3456 friends" that make up the subject's social network (nearly the limit of total friends Facebook allows) cannot separate exterior and interior lives—or the personal and the social. The numbered friends interrupt the narrative, delegitimizing qualitative experience. They read their own lives in her posts, and the online speaker becomes identical with the work that she creates and the viewer she addresses. The unshared posts become themselves an absence which structures online life and self-presentation: "No one will comment" on concerns that remain unspoken. In this social landscape, which divides digital self-presentation from lived self-conception, the poem challenges aesthetic norms that otherwise subordinate offline lives.

The collection takes an ambivalent stance on digital media, celebrating the connections it enables even as it questions the commodification of those connections. Putuma's work establishes a South African poetic lineage that confronts colonial and patriarchal social structures in the context of new media technologies. Sometimes that work is imagined as solitary, as in "Online"; at other times, it enacts a conversation with colleagues; in each case, it is informed by a long history of poetic production. Responding to the threats in "Online" of digital self-mutilation and emotional tumors, the poem "Lifeline" opens with a three-page list of Black womxn thinkers, from Kimberlé Crenshaw and Audre Lorde to Malika Ndlovu and Buhlebezwe Siwani. Putuma acknowledges:

> you will say that this is not a poem
> and I will say that you are right:
> it is not
> it is a lifeline.
> every name is a gospel shut up in my bones.
> every name
> chants
> *Black girl—*
> *live!*
> *live!*
> *live!*[69]

The list of names invokes the speaker's personal deities—the artistic ancestors who inspire and inform her work—as the literary canon into which a South African performance poet must write. Unlike the gods, of course, these women can speak for themselves—and, in most cases, published prolifically. Yet on Putuma's stage, their words emerge anew. The un-poem is then an incantation, externalizing the embodied sensation of knowledge and lineage. It is conversation, prayer, list, and chant simultaneously; as such, it performs poetry's density and connectivity, creating a network from within its own novel framework.

By prioritizing a single voice, Putuma's poetry uses a performance-oriented lens to situate speaker and reader together within a networked public sphere. This is not to suggest that print or digital poetics is identical with performance and theater-making. Rather, it indicates that the "real-time" potential of digital publication has pushed print norms toward a network paradigm. The shift in poetry's reception transforms its mechanisms of authorization, driving readership through tweets that precede textbooks. Social media publication, like an anthology, embeds individual poems in larger conversations; unlike an anthology, though, it encourages movement across conversations, building both expected and surprising connections. Poetry's networked form highlights and heightens its dialogic character. The dialogues of contemporary poetry invoke the interactions of historical memory and cultural nuance.

At the Limits of Canon Reform

Putuma's poetry offers a critical commentary on canon formation and the production of cultural capital. Many of her poems cite news stories, prayers, and idioms ("*Before dark* meant *home time*") to critique underlying ideologies, thus naming and replacing cultural touchstones in the South African canon.[70] In their place, she offers a new canon, one learned not in school but through experience. The poem "Teachings," for instance, redefines "*archiving* (v.): a FUCK YOU to the canon."[71] The tension that Putuma identifies between the canon and the archive—the first marked by judgment and selection; the second by expanse and accumulation—reflects her investment in expanding access to cultural power, identifying sources of knowledge that escaped canonization. It also offers a new entry point into canonization. The archive's implicitly horizontal structure of association replaces the hierarchy of the canon with the network of the document. Self-archiving becomes an act of self-construction, and digital publication a self-education.

The networked paradigm shifts processes of canon formation. "Water" was taught in college classrooms prior to its publication in print, as an already-remediated and revised version of itself. Canonization now responds to entextualization: the remediation of familiar texts enables us to reimagine the relationship between writer and reader. Digital publication platforms, and particularly social media, create a new system for the production and dissemination of cultural capital. And, though not perfectly liquid, that capital has its own power. Celebrity brands can catalyze meaningful change: during the 2020 coronavirus pandemic, Putuma and Mashile used their platforms to call for governmental and institutional support for South African artists, paving the way for programs like Hear My Voice's Poetry Fund and, eventually, pressuring the government to provide direct support for artists. The popular is now a key site for the production, evaluation, and adjudication of cultural values and literary canons. The traditional spaces of the classroom, the publishing house, and the literary festival still manage literary capital, yet they do so increasingly in response to popular and market pressures.

The journey of Putuma's *Collective Amnesia* and her feature in the *Forbes Africa* "Under 30 Creatives" article together demonstrate how poetic canons are formed today: in response to shifting media norms, which demand multimodal, popular poetry. This is not to suggest, however, that traditional forms of canon formation have disappeared. The underlying economic structures that support literary institutions retain power, as does the global marketplace in which postcolonial poetry is situated. Access to prominent university spaces, expensive recording technologies, and the eyes (or Twitter feeds) of influential gatekeepers can have substantial impact on an artist's early success.

Despite these technological revolutions, culture still follows the market—even more so as internet access increasingly defines cultural access. Access to capital from the Global North, including both literary prizes and creative writing degree programs, have spurred the careers of prize-winning, best-selling "Afropolitan" writers, including Chimamanda Adichie, Teju Cole, and Nnedi Okorafor; they have become "an integral part of a financialized creative class." This trend led Kalyan Nadiminti to single out "the American MFA program as an ideological site of global South literary production." Nadiminti echoes ongoing debates about the cultural impact of CIA- and UN-funded artistic programs when they argue that these programs engender a widespread embrace of "vernacular anglophone realism," marking "a decisive shift from the revolutionary but often compromised postcolonial novel to a professionalized and market-driven global novel."[72] Nadiminti's focus on US-based MFA programs belies a much broader trend, as regional economic hubs can serve similar roles in focusing literary energies and forcing a performative authenticity. The still-tiny global marketplace for poetry means such a "market-driven global poetics" may never emerge in quite the same form. Yet the insularity of this network creates heightened effects, ensuring outsized attention to those few artists who can access the dominant universities, corporations, and associated literary structures of a regional economic hub like South Africa.

Even as digital media reconfigure poetic circulations and community formation, they remain beholden to long-standing hierarchies and political structures. These forces can feel inescapable, reproducing colonial knowledge structures: this book, for instance, aimed to highlight lesser-known poets but prioritized writers whose work was most accessible to me as a scholar from the United States.[73] And, while COVID-19 brought more poets online, it also limited my capacity to engage with those poets for whom data costs proved prohibitive. In writing about, and teaching, some poets and not others, scholarly work inevitably contributes to the canonization of these algorithmic aesthetics. The links any given writer draws between poets transform their names into key words connected through Google search results. These search algorithms prioritize those names that appear in more places—so that, as Hear My Voice cofounder Ishmael Sibiya puts it, the African literary sphere appears reduced to a select group of eight.[74]

Once a poem has gone viral or begun to appear on many sites at once, other poets seeking similar fame (or simply inspired by the work) will be more likely to reproduce elements of its theme or form. The seeming democracy of digital publication obscures the extent to which largely opaque systems like YouTube's and Google's algorithms structure reception. Designed, rehearsed, and reinforced by programmers in the Global North, these algorithms determine what texts are prioritized. Extrahuman gatekeepers shape the production and dissemination of knowledge; their influence on literary norms and aesthetics will grow only stronger. Yet their drive is purely quantitative: the sign and the spring of success are one. Badilisha, Sapitwa Poetry, Brittle Paper, and similar independent organizations, founded by and speaking to artists from the Global

South, intervene in the algorithm as pre-springs, creating direct forces and quantitative value that the algorithms then reproduce and expand.

Nonetheless, the power to promote particular artists remains with those institutions that retain both cultural and material capital. The historic gatekeepers of literary access—publishing houses, radio shows, arts festivals—retain primacy in the hypothetically open digital realm precisely because of their market power and brand recognition. At the time of writing, the two largest publicly available archives of African performance poetry (digital or traditional) were Poetry Africa's YouTube channel and Badilisha Poetry X-Change; six weeks later, Badilisha disappeared, pointing to the instability of the broader landscape. Both organizations are based in South Africa, which has become the region's economic and cultural hub over the past twenty-five years. Both are founded on principles defined in part by YouTube's algorithms, and both rely on outside sites to host their corpuses, making them vulnerable to corporate whims. Such sites are shaping contemporary poetry; integrating text, video, and sound recordings; and inviting direct audience feedback in forms immediately familiar to social media users. Based on norms established by programmers in the Global North, the sites risk reproducing colonial epistemologies if we fail to recognize and support the alternative aesthetic structures emerging from the Global South.[75]

African Literature's Digital Futures

Prestige is, as Hernstein-Smith and James English have amply demonstrated, cyclical. The forums through which poets first encounter poetry create models of successful poetry. Those models, in turn, determine which works garner future attention, reproducing the colonial logic of an extractive publishing industry. Blending popular and elite literary forms across media paradigms enables African writers to navigate local and global networks. It sets Koleka Putuma's work within a canon of twentieth-century African poetry: her work to address queerphobia and Afrophobia in new media paradigms echoes Alfred Qabula's integration of protest poetry into urban settings; Jack Mapanje's into print politics; and Christopher Okigbo's into the dense imagery of the modernist tradition. Putuma, Chiwamba, and Sky—in bringing together vernacular and popular imagery with emerging modes of literary circulation—follow in these footsteps. But rather than subject their work to the extroverted gaze of publishers based in the Global North, they draw on local communities and platforms to build an audience and gain recognition—or, in Chiwamba's case, build their own.

These platforms remain at the mercy of algorithmic aesthetics and new media norms. Digital spaces that profess to democratize access to the arts instead replace human gatekeepers with algorithmic ones. Of the platforms discussed throughout this book, only Sapitwa offers a fully populist approach to literary curation—and its relatively stagnant front page and early demise profess the limits of such an approach. Instead, we are left with a series of platforms designed in the Global North, curated by algorithms created and maintained by programmers based largely in the United States and China. And these algorithms determine not only what videos rise to the top of our YouTube feeds but also what poems appear in our Google searches. Poetry is shaped by digital engagement, and that engagement is defined, in large part, by the programmer's invisible hand.

The imbalance of representation and recognition online is especially important because most audiences of performance poetry in southern Africa remain offline, without recourse to digital commentary or responsiveness and yet affected by it: as of January 2019, only 38 percent of Malawians had cell phones; 40.2 percent of Zimbabweans had regular internet access; and 28 percent of South Africans regularly used social media. These numbers have increased rapidly since lockdowns in response to the COVID-19 pandemic concentrated energies online. Nonetheless, these minority populations, largely occupying privileged urban positions, drive regional literary production through social media's network effects.[76] Digital poetry publication is thus a double-edged sword: it opens up a wider, broadly regional or diasporic audience to more artists and yet changes the art that is widely available, placing it at the mercy of such largely unknowable corporations as Facebook and Google. Nonetheless, it represents a sea change in the publication and circulation of African literary and cultural productions, supporting South-South channels of distribution and disrupting commonplace ideas about the role of poetry in everyday life.

In part, this is what has made Putuma's success so striking. She built personal networks from her digital success; used the public promotion of Twitter and Facebook, as well as TEDx and poetry slams, to drive attention to her personal blog and literary work; and brought those spaces together to market the collection, which was published by the South African press uHlanga. *Collective Amnesia* is, indeed, a signal of how African poetry books can be marketed today: built on the author's cross-platform brand, it draws on her social media audience, performance network, and personal connections to elicit a new audience for poetry. The success of *Collective Amnesia* thus signals a new direction for the establishment and dissemination of cultural capital, one marked first by popular success and only secondarily authorized by elite platforms, which themselves rely on the quantifiable metrics of digital spaces to maintain legitimacy.

CODA

Digital Poetry and the Global Creative Economy

P OETRY MATTERS. Despite the endless elegies, poetry matters, and its influence is growing. In the mottos that comfort, the slogans that sell, the chants that unite, and the allusions that connect, poetry shapes our cultural imagination, helping us understand what's possible and expanding our sense of what might yet be. Protest chants amplify disparate voices. Spoken word stages underrepresented stories. Visual poetry on Instagram encapsulates common experiences. These poetic forms help young people locate their own stories in broader communities.

But poetry matters differently, depending on who you are and where you stand. In the ten years since I began the project that became this book, the rise of popular poetic forms has engendered endless elegies for poetry in the Anglophone press. The same worries that led Stanley Kenani to dismiss spoken word poets as "jokers" in 2015 reemerged in the American press in 2022, when the centenary of T. S. Eliot's *The Waste Land* prompted major outlets to publish articles with titles like "Poetry Died 100 Years Ago This Month."[1] These articles express anxieties about the passing of a particular form of poetry tied to cultural conservatism. Poetry has been used as a marker of cultural capital to uphold colonial hierarchies; canonized into curricula, it has been used to justify formal limitations and, incorporated within persuasive rhetoric, to maintain capitalist structures. Digital self-publishing, together with the user-driven curations of social media platforms, accelerates poetry's move into the popular sphere and thus further threatens to disrupt poetry's conservative role. As mobile networks and digital platforms broaden opportunities for publication, this liberating function grows. Poetry is, or has become again, a youth-driven form.

In southern Africa, I contend, that transformation has largely been shaped by the interplay of two emergent processes in the social production of poetry. The first, "networked poetics," draws on Mizuko Ito's conception of the networked public sphere to suggest that the connective logics of digital media communication inflects contemporary artistic production offline as well.[2] The second, "algorithmic aesthetics," refers to a secondary effect of that process: the aesthetic norms established by and in response to the curatorial algorithms that organize social media newsfeeds. These processes follow common patterns around the world: WhatsApp groups offer continuous forums for literary debate; live tweeting remediates prior broadcast patterns; live streaming transforms the audiences for local open mics. But they unfold in locally specific ways: WhatsApp groups in Malawi debate the relationship between poetic form and generational concerns, whereas South African groups consider the role of local identity. Studying the two together reveals the interplay between local agency and media effects: social media creates new possibilities for local and regional groups to connect—and, with those possibilities, new constraints on the connections that form.

These effects are especially acute in southern Africa, where poetry's historical power, the rise of a new political generation, and the focus on mobile communication have together fostered an intense focus on digital media as a space of artistic production. But the broader patterns resound across the continent: Shola Adenekan's work on Kenya and Nigeria illustrates how digital platforms enable transnational literary networks; James Yékú's engagement with "digital netizenship" in Nigeria speaks to the shifting formal structures of popular literature online; Meg Arenberg's work maps the role of digital networks on Swahili poetry in Tanzania.[3]

Across Africa, the underdevelopment of literary publishing led writers to adopt digital self-publication relatively quickly. Long histories of migration within the continent also led to the relatively fast adoption of mobile networks for communication. Because African countries skew extremely young, youth culture can have outsized impacts on the broader economy. Because of the underdevelopment of the continent's publishing industries, African writers were quick to adopt social media publication. And African literary forms shaped the work they produced online. The intensity of digital literary production in Africa led literary scholar and founder of the blog Brittle Paper,

Ainehi Edoro-Glines to remark, "Contemporary African literature offers a uniquely rich archive on the impact of social media on literary discourse. In the African context where the internet was a welcome intervention in a struggling print culture, the uptake of social media in the literary community was early and rapid. [...] After all, African literature's recent non-codex, non-print, and mostly oral past makes it a particularly powerful site for interpretive interventions in digital culture."[4]

The rich history of oral and performance literatures has made poets and scholars of African literature more attentive to the multimodal flow of literature online. Moreover, suspicion about received forms and Europhone traditions renders literary forms online of both an experimental and an alternative nature. Those trends, so pronounced in an African context, echo globally: Pallavi Rao and Urvashi Sahni detail the use of YouTube to host dissident feminist poetries in India; Veena Mani has shown how digital poetry encourages confessional modes in Kashmir; Kate Kovalik and Jen Scott Curwood argue that Instagram forms affect community identity among urban youth in England.[5] Digital communication networks move across global channels, linking expressive communities and constructing connections across diasporic networks.[6] And, in the Global North, where poetry has been largely relegated to the schoolroom, these changes catalyze new conversations about what public art can do. Analyzing shifting literary cultures in southern Africa illustrates how poetry's political potential emerges anew as it enters the digital public sphere.

On 20 January 2021, shock over these changing structures of cultural capital launched debates across the United States about what poetry is—and who it is for. At Joe Biden's inauguration as forty-sixth president of the United States, he followed his Democratic Party predecessors in inviting a poet to read an inaugural poem. But Biden's selection of poet—the slam poet and first National Youth Poet Laureate Amanda Gorman—reflected poetry's changing social position, bringing in a popular form largely removed from academic and institutional apparatuses. Gorman's poem, "The Hill We Climb," drew its style from spoken word, relying heavily on wordplay and repetition to emphasize the contradictions at the heart of the American national project. Its references drew on Lin-Manuel Miranda's popular musical *Hamilton*, recent US history, and American political rhetoric to create a universalizing "we," suddenly and remarkably healed (or, perhaps, bereft) of difference and division. It draws together popular references and a sense of urgency to bring its audience into a very particular vision of the future—in this case, one of national unity and solidarity, notably in line with the Biden campaign's promises.

Such spectacular co-optation of poetry to nationalist ends has not, historically, been especially well received by cultural commentators in the United States: Elizabeth Alexander's "Praise Song for the Day," performed at Barack Obama's inauguration in 2009, was called "public in the worst sense—inauthentic, bureaucratic, rhetorical," and even "prosaic."[7] The critical discontent with Alexander's poem reflects a frustrated questioning of poetry's place in society: Do we seek the reflecting lyric? The rousing protest poem? How can either of these two models fit into the placatory, routinized celebrations of the inauguration? But where these previous debates focused on poetry's role in society, Gorman's poem catalyzed tensions over the nature of poetry itself. Critics on social media demanded: Was this poetry or not? Was it good poetry or not? And who, exactly, was eligible to adjudicate it?

The conversation stood out to me for two reasons: first, because I had seen how poets in southern Africa had found power through these critiques; and second, because I was teaching a new class on "Poetry and Performance" in January 2021, and our first session began just two hours after the inauguration. The poem became our entry point into the seminar's central questions of poetry's role in the world. We watched Gorman's performance twice. After the first viewing, when we discussed the poem as a whole, the students' responses followed the terms of the debate unfolding online. Several loved the poem immediately: they were drawn in by its wordplay, its palpable emotions, its approachability. A few were more skeptical. While the poem may be fun, they questioned its purpose: Was the poet's role to uphold the rhetoric of politicians? Surely her skills could be put to better use than placating political masses? And several more objected to the form itself: if this was poetry, it was not the kind that interested them.

Challenged, in the second viewing, to select one particular set of sounds, gestures, or lines to celebrate or critique, the students identified something else in the poem: its attention to audience, both those locally present at the inauguration and the broader American public viewing the broadcast. They noted the participatory gesture of the collective "we" that interweaves the poet's more personal reflections; Gorman's use of her hands to conduct audience responses, following her own rising and falling intonations; the way her use of wordplay set up and then subverted their expectations. They came to appreciate her use of performance to create poetic effects and solicit direct participation.

Gorman's performance had a tremendous effect on the commercial landscape of US poetry. The following month, she became the first poet to ever perform at the Super Bowl, the country's largest annual media event. The Super Bowl—the culmination of an annual sports competition that highlights regional divides—has, since the 1970s, functioned as one of the country's most significant performances of national pride and unity: the event begins with a performance of the national anthem; the president and vice president traditionally participate; and time is set aside to celebrate the military. It is also a major commercial platform: because of its unusually large broadcast audience—consistently the largest television event each year in the United States—it attracts huge amounts of advertising money. The same commercial promise has been extended to musical artists: since 1991, the Super Bowl's "halftime" show has also featured performances by popular musicians and singers promoting upcoming tours or albums. Gorman's performance at the 2021 Super Bowl, together with her performance at the inauguration, would launch her commercial presence: her first poetry collection was the best-selling book in the country for weeks after the event—even though it would not be released for another eight months.

I am less interested here in the specifics of Gorman's poem or her performance than in what it signals about poetry's place in the public sphere. Gorman's trajectory—exceptional though it is—reflects the broader shifts that I have tracked in this book. Her work began in the institutional spaces of academia but flourished as activism. The work is tied to audiovisual modes, offering lyrical rhetoric that sits within her filmmaker-sister's pieces on social justice and activism. She draws on popular references, youth culture, and the oratorical style of slam poetry—itself drawn from African American and Latinx literary forms—to reimagine the occasional poem for the contemporary moment. She wrote a popular poem for an elite space. And as the culmination of decades of collaborative work and collective pushes to reimagine poetry's place in public life, her performance realized Q Malewezi's declaration at the 2013 Lake of Stars festival: "Poetry is on the main stage. Poetry wins."[8]

But which poetry, specifically, wins? On whose terms? And to what ends? Social media platforms draw together diverse communities, open new publishing venues, and displace traditional centers of power. But social media algorithms have rushed into the seeming power vacuum of the early internet to create new gatekeeping forces that structure new aesthetic forms. Networked poetics are shaped by new forces for the production of cultural capital: the quantifiability of the popular vies with traditional gatekeepers to mark cultural significance and enable in-the-know audiences to use that knowledge for their benefit.

The global circulation of poetic rhetoric has changed how we make and mark history: statues fall, voices rise, and connections grow through literary rhetoric that takes shape online. Networked media collapse context, flattening time and enabling an intense focus on individual words and phrases. As Nancy K. Baym and danah boyd argue of what they call "socially mediated publics," "Social media blur boundaries [. . .] affecting how old patterns should be understood and raising new challenges and opportunities for people engaging others through new technologies."[9] These new engagements, in turn, challenge conceptions of self and community, forging new forms of sociality: digitally engaged audiences "become more aware of themselves relative to visible and invisible audiences and more aware of the larger publics to which they belong and which they seek to create. They negotiate collapsed contexts, continuously shifting power dynamics, and an open-ended timeframe." In the end, "offline contexts permeate online activities, and online activities bleed endlessly back to reshape what happens offline."[10] These changes are unfolding globally, as social media networks and popular culture shift processes of cultural capital formation. The self-publishing structures of digital media encourage a participatory poetics. Social media platforms' algorithmic curation demands popular poetics.

Artists rely on collaborations, on the kinds of networks described in the second chapter of this volume. Their collaborations are engaged in the very disintegration of the private and public. And, as shown through the third and fourth chapters, these networks have tangible effects on the poetry that artists produce and that institutions reward. At the highest levels of artist legitimation, from the university classroom to the presidential stage, popular poetry is rising to the fore. The public sphere to which poetry increasingly speaks is, itself, a networked public sphere—and the poetry that speaks to it a networked poetics.

NOTES

INTRODUCTION: POETRY IN MOTION

1. Nathan Suhr-Sytsma, *Poetry, Print, and the Making of Postcolonial Literature* (Cambridge: Cambridge University Press, 2017), 10. Twitter was rebranded as X in summer 2023; however, it is still more commonly referred to by its previous name.
2. James Yékú, *Cultural Netizenship: Social Media, Popular Culture, and Performance in Nigeria* (Bloomington: Indiana University Press, 2022).
3. Building on Ruth Finnegan's foundational *Oral Literature in Africa* (London: Clarendon Press, 1970), Leroy Vail and Landeg White's *Power and the Praise Poem* (Charlottesville: University of Virginia Press, 1991) lays out the particular forms through which poetry fostered social capital development in southern Africa: the use of complaint songs, for instance, to solicit higher wages (198–220); of royal praises to shape political tenure (84–100); and of folk songs to create collective memory (231–50). Each of these enabled disempowered individuals and communities to launch claims of political and material restitution against empowered groups.
4. For an overview of the "mobile revolution" in Africa, see Mirjam de Bruijn and Inge Brinkman, "Mobile Phone-Communication in the Mobile Margins of Africa," *Palgrave Handbook of Media and Communication Research in Africa*, ed. Bruce Mutsvairo (London: Palgrave Macmillan, 2018), 225–41, and Sebastiana Etzo and Guy Collender, "The Mobile Phone 'Revolution' in Africa: Rhetoric or Reality?," *African Affairs* 109, no. 437 (2010): 659–68.
5. This "underdevelopment" of publishing in Africa, to borrow Sarah Brouillette's term (*Underdevelopment and African Literature: Emerging Forms of Reading* [Cambridge: Cambridge University Press, 2021]), has been widely documented. See also Caroline Davis, *Creating African Literature: African Writers and British Publishers* (London: Palgrave Macmillan, 2013); Walter Bgoya and Mary Jay, "Publishing in Africa from Independence to the Present Day," *Research in African Literatures* 44, no. 2 (Summer 2013): 17–35; Francis B. Nyamnjoh, "From Publish or Perish to Publish and Perish," *Journal of Asian and African Studies* 39, no. 5 (2004): 331–35; and Apollo Amoko, "The Problem with African Literature" (PhD diss., University of Michigan, 2002).
6. My use of "orature" follows from Ngũgĩ wa Thiong'o's adoption of Pio Zirimu's term for oral literature. For Ngũgĩ, as for Zirimu, "orature" ensures the oral and performative elements are not subordinated to the primary noun of "literature," as in the adjectival formation. F. Abiola Irele, *The African Imagination: Literature in Africa and the Black Diaspora* (Bloomington: Indiana University Press, 2001), 9, 11.
7. Ngũgĩ wa Thiong'o, *Penpoints, Gunpoints, and Dreams: Towards a Critical Theory of the Arts and the State in Africa* (London: Clarendon Press, 1998), 105, 111.

8. Robert Pinsky, *The Sounds of Poetry: A Brief Guide* (New York: Farrar, Straus and Giroux, 1998), 8.
9. Ngũgĩ wa Thiong'o, *Penpoints, Gunpoints, and Dreams*, 111; April Sizemore-Barber, *Prismatic Performances: Queer South Africa and the Fragmentation of the Rainbow Nation* (Ann Arbor: University of Michigan Press, 2020), 7, 8.
10. Reuters, "South African Lawmakers Chant 'Pay Back the Money' at Zuma," 21 August 2014, https://www.reuters.com/article/uk-safrica-politics-idAFKBN0GL1HM20140821.
11. Lupenga Mphande. "If You're Ugly, Know How to Sing: Aesthetics of Resistance and Subversion," in *Songs and Politics in Eastern Africa*, ed. Kimani Njogu and Hervé Maupeu (Dar es Salaam, Tanzania: Mkuki ya Nyota, 2007), 387.
12. Lupenga Mphande, "Ngoni Praise Poetry and the Nguni Diaspora," *Research in African Literatures* 24, no. 4 (Winter 1993): 99–122; Ari Sitas, "Traditions of Poetry in Natal," *Journal of Southern African Studies* 16, no. 2 (June 1990): 307–26.
13. Ari Sitas, personal conversation with the author, 23 November 2016.
14. Alfred Temba Qabula, *Black Mamba Rising: South African Worker Poets in Struggle* (Johannesburg: COSATU, 1986). For more on the relationship between poetry and the labor movement in South Africa, see Ari Sitas's "Traditions of Poetry in Natal," *Journal of Southern African Studies* 16, no. 2 (1990): 307–26.
15. Pungwe refers to an all-night political vigil and the dances performed at them. As early as 1994, Stephen Chifunyise argued, "An all-night song-dance-political rally called pungwe became the medium for the dramatization of the people's struggle (Chimurenga) and the inevitable defeat of colonialism in Zimbabwe." See his "Trends in Zimbabwean Theatre since 1980," in *Politics and Performance: Theatre, Poetry, and Song in Southern Africa*, ed. Liz Gunner (Bloomington: Indiana University Press, 1994), 55–75, quotation on 55. For a longer history of the development and cooptation of *chimurenga* music, see John Kaemmer, "Social Power and Music Change among the Shona," *Ethnomusicology* 33, no. 1 (1989): 31–45; for more on its development into the twenty-first century, see Wendy Willems, "Risky Dialogues: The Performative State and the Nature of Power in a Postcolony," *Journal of African Cultural Studies* 27, no. 3 (2015): 356–69.
16. Mbumba, which refers to the matrilineal relationship structure between children and their maternal uncle, was a popular dance form developed under Banda as a way of demonstrating women's allegiance to him as the symbolic head of their family. John Lwanda provides the most thorough histories of the Nyasaland African Congress's use and cooptation of music in his *Music, Culture, and Orature: Reading the Malawian Public Sphere, 1949–2006* (Zomba, Malawi: Kachere Press, 2008).
17. Meg Arenberg, "The Digital Ukumbi: New Terrains in Swahili Identity and Poetic Dialogue," *PMLA* 131, no. 5 (2016): 1344–60; Kelly Askew, *Performing the Nation: Swahili Music and Cultural Politics in Tanzania* (Chicago: University of Chicago Press, 2002). Taarab is a music genre which blends Swahili and Arab-style tunes; its spread reflects the movement of Swahili people through East Africa.
18. Flora Veit-Wild traces the transnational development of independence chants in her *Patterns of Poetry in Zimbabwe* (Gweru, Zimbabwe: Mambo Press, 1988).
19. Raphael d'Abdon, "The Commercialization of Celebratory Poetry: A Critical Examination of Zolani Mkiva's Post-Apartheid Praise Poetry (Izibongo)," *African Identities* 12, no. 3–4 (2014): 323.
20. Susanna Sacks, "The Poetics of Dictatorship: Speech, Song, and Sound in H. K.

Banda's 'Tenth Republic Anniversary Tour,'" *Research in African Literatures* 50, no. 4 (2019): 55–71.
21. Winston Mano, "Scheduling for Rural and Urban Listeners on Bilingual Radio Zimbabwe," *Radio Journal* 3, no. 2 (2005): 102–3.
22. For more on radio's role in creating national and social frameworks across Africa, see *Radio in Africa: Publics, Cultures, Communities*, ed. Liz Gunner, Dina Ligaga, and Dumisani Moyo (Johannesburg: Wits University Press, 2011).
23. Made up of sixteen southern African states, SADC is among the strongest intergovernmental cooperations in Africa. It has mandated a Free Trade Area since 2008, as well as legally binding protocols on energy, gender and development, and politics, defense, and co-security.
24. Chichewa and English remain the country's official languages and the only two in which schooling is offered. However, as of 2009, only about half of Malawi's population spoke Chichewa as a home language; Lomwe, Tumbuka, and Yao—spoken, respectively, by 12 percent, 8 percent, and 6 percent of the population—have no official recognition. To understand how disenfranchised these linguistic groups are, consider that in August 2018, a range of newspapers took note when a Chichewa-speaking politician bothered to give any of his speech in Chitumbuka while campaigning in the heavily Tumbuka northern region.
25. According to the World Bank, only 10 percent of Malawians used the internet as of 2016, putting it in the bottom twenty countries for internet usage worldwide. By 2021, that rate had increased to 24 percent. See https://data.worldbank.org/indicator/IT.NET.USER.ZS?year_high_desc=false.
26. Until 2016, Malawian students were instructed in their mother tongues until Primary Grade 4; recent policy changes, however, now mandate English instruction beginning in Primary Grade 1, although studies suggest teachers still translanguage. For more, see Sam Mchombo, "Politics of Language Choice in African Education: The Case of Kenya and Malawi," *International Relations and Diplomacy* 5, no. 4 (2017): 181–204, and USAID, *Language of Instruction Country Profile: Malawi*, March 2021, https://pdf.usaid.gov/pdf_docs/PA00XFMV.pdf.
27. International Telecommunication Union, "Individuals Using the Internet (% of Population)—Zimbabwe," World Bank, 2022, accessed 16 March 2023, https://data.worldbank.org/indicator/IT.NET.USER.ZS?locations=ZW.
28. World Bank, "Literacy rate, adult total (% of people ages 15 and above)—Zimbabwe," UNESCO Institute for Statistics, accessed 17 July 2023, https://data.worldbank.org/indicator/SE.ADT.LITR.ZS?locations=ZW.
29. For more, see Human Rights Watch, "Zimbabwe: Events of 2016," Human Rights Watch, 2017, https://www.hrw.org/world-report/2016/country-chapters/zimbabwe; Bruce Mutsvairo and Lys-Anne Sirks, "Examining the Contribution of Social Media in Reinforcing Political Participation in Zimbabwe," *Journal of African Media Studies* 7, no. 3 (2015): 329–44; and Shepherd Mpofu, "Social Media and the Politics of Ethnicity in Zimbabwe, *African Journalism Studies* 34 no. 1 (2013): 115–22.
30. For more on the adoption of English by South African radicals via Black Consciousness literatures, see Mafika Gwala, "Writing as a Cultural Weapon," in *Momentum: On Recent South African Writing*, ed. M. J. Daymond, J. U. Jacobs, and Margaret Lenta (Durban: University of KwaZulu-Natal Press, 1984), 37–53, and N. Barney Pityana, Mamphela Ramphele, Malusi Mpumlwana, and Lindy Wilson, eds., *Bounds*

of Possibility: The Legacy of Steve Biko and Black Consciousness (Cape Town: New Africa Books, 1991).
31. Caroline McKinney, *Language and Power in Post-colonial Schooling: Ideologies in Practice* (New York: Routledge, 2016).
32. IMF World Economic Outlook, January 2021, accessed 2 June 2021, https://www.imf.org/en/Publications/WEO/weo-database/2020/October.
33. Drawn from indexes like *U.S. News and World Report*'s "Best Global Universities in Africa" and *Times Higher Education*'s "Best Universities in Africa," these rankings imply both Eurocentric presumptions about the structure and goals of higher educations and an implicit bias toward Anglophone institutions. For more on the history and limitations of university rankings, see Bill Readings, "The Idea of Excellence," in *The University in Ruins* (Cambridge, MA: Harvard University Press, 1996), 21–43.
34. Arenberg, "Digital Ukumbi," 1344–60.
35. Stephanie Bosch Santana, "From Nation to Network: Blog and Facebook Fiction from Southern Africa," *Research in African Literatures* 49, no. 1 (2018): 187–208.
36. The killings are often attributed to witchcraft practices that use the bones of people with albinism. In addition to a range of popular news articles on the subject, the United Nations–recognized expert on injustice toward people with albinism, Ikponwosa Ero, has called albinos living in Malawi, Tanzania, and Mozambique—where the crisis is most acute—an "endangered people." See her "In Malawi, People with Albinism Face 'Total Extinction'—UN Rights Expert," *UN News*, 29 April 2016, https://news.un.org/en/story/2016/04/528082).
37. Karin Barber, *The Anthropology of Texts, Persons, and Publics* (Cambridge: Cambridge University Press, 2007), 139.
38. Emmanuel Ngara, *Ideology and Form in African Poetry* (London: James Currey, 1990), 15.
39. See Suhr-Sytsma, *Making of Postcolonial Literature*.
40. Eileen Julien, "The Extroverted African Novel," in *The Novel*, vol. 1, ed. Franco Moretti (Princeton, NJ: Princeton University Press, 2008), 685, 689.
41. Tsitsi Jaji illustrates the potent history of these print networks in her study of reader engagement in midcentury small magazines, in "Our Readers Write: Mediating African Poetry's Audiences," *Research in African Literatures* 51, no. 1 (2020): 70–93.
42. Moradewan Adejunmobi. "Revenge of the Spoken Word? Writing, Performance, and New Media in Urban West Africa," *Oral Tradition* 26, no. 1 (2011): n.p., fifth page of pdf.
43. Jahan Ramazani, *A Transnational Poetics* (Chicago: University of Chicago Press, 2009), 4.
44. Zeynep Tufekci, *Twitter and Teargas: The Power and Fragility of Networked Protest* (New Haven, CT: Yale University Press, 2017), 18.
45. Michael Warner, *Publics and Counterpublics* (New York: Zone Books, 2002), 72.
46. Yékú, *Cultural Netizenship*, 6.
47. Ian Watt, *The Rise of the Novel* (Oakland: University of California Press, 2001). For more on the role of literature and performance in South African anti-colonial movements, see Michael Chapman, ed., *The "Drum" Decade: Stories from the 1950s* (Scottsville, South Africa: University of KwaZulu-Natal Press, 1989); Daniel Magaziner, *The Law and the Prophets: Black Consciousness in South Africa, 1968–1977* (Athens: Ohio University Press, 2010); and Harri Englund, *Human Rights and the African Airwaves:*

Mediating Equality on the Chichewa Radio (Bloomington: Indiana University Press, 2011).
48. Lynn Hunt, *Inventing Human Rights* (New York: W. W. Norton, 2007); Brian Larkin, *Signal and Noise: Media, Infrastructure, and Urban Culture in Nigeria* (Durham, NC: Duke University Press, 2008).
49. Centre for Creative Arts, "Q Malewezi at POETRY AFRICA 2014," YouTube, 13 February 2015, 22:11–22:15, https://www.youtube.com/watch?v=4pX1d2mS3UI.
50. Safiya Umoja Nobel, *Algorithms of Oppression: How Search Engines Reinforce Racism* (New York: New York University Press, 2018).
51. Nick Seaver, *Computing Taste: Algorithms and the Makers of Music Recommendation* (Chicago: University of Chicago Press, 2022).
52. Jahan Ramazani's *Poetry and Its Others* (Chicago: University of Chicago Press, 2014) highlights poetry's long-standing interactions with other genres, arguing that "all genres are ineluctably intergeneric" (5). Despite acknowledging poetry's particular connections to oral forms like song and prayer though, Ramazani neglects its ongoing connection to performance through genres like the slam poem, arguing that "poetry, having long been in its literary forms an art for limited and specialized audiences in the English-speaking world, became even more so after modernism made it still more difficult and forbidding, and even the abundance of slams and the explosion of online resources are unlikely to reverse its fortune" (18). Such dismissals of this major shift is typical of contemporary poetry scholarship from the Global North, suggesting a political imbalance between the "high art" distinction typically reserved for print poetry and the "explosion" of works derided as popular culture. By attending to those works specifically, I question and resist those presumptions and prejudice that dismiss oral, performance, and digital works as unworthy of sustained scholarly attention.
53. "Netnography" refers to the ethnographic methods adapted to the study of digital communities. The term was coined by Robert Kozinets and was elaborated in "Netnography: Doing Ethnographic Research Online" (London: SAGE, 2010).
54. Lev Manovich, *The Language of New Media* (Cambridge: MIT Press, 2002), 33.
55. Jacob Pousher and Russ Oates, "Cell Phones in Africa: Communication Lifeline," PEW Research Center, 15 April 2015, https://www.pewresearch.org/global/2015/04/15/methods-in-detail-19/.
56. GSMA, "The Mobile Economy: Sub-Saharan Africa 2022," GSMA Intelligence, 2022, accessed 16 March 2023, 10, https://www.gsma.com/mobileeconomy/wp-content/uploads/2022/10/The-Mobile-Economy-Sub-Saharan-Africa-2022.pdf; Manovich, *Language of New Media*, 11, 17.
57. For more, see chapter 2 of this volume; see also Susanna Sacks, "Developing a Poetics of Connections: Constructing Literary Community through Lockdown Poetry Performances from South Africa," *Interventions*, forthcoming 2024.
58. Santana, "From Nation to Network," 190.

CHAPTER 1: HASHTAGS BECOME CHANTS

1. The relationship between Zimbabwe's political repression and its media landscape has been extensively documented. See, for example, Winston Mano, "Renegotiating

Tradition on Radio Zimbabwe," *Media, Culture, and Society* 26, no. 3 (2004): 315–36); Memory Mabika and Abiodun Salawu "A Tale of Failure: Indigenous Language Radio Broadcasting in Zimbabwe," *Mediterranean Journal of Social Sciences* 5, no. 20 (September 2014): 2391–2401); Selina Mudavanhu, "The Politics of 'Patriots' and 'Traitors' on Radio Zimbabwe," *Journal of African Media Studies* 6, no. 3 (September 2014): 327–43; and Everette Ndlovu, "The Role of Diasporic Media in Facilitating Citizen Journalism and Political Awareness in Zimbabwe" (PhD diss., University of Salford, 2014).

2. Levi Obijiofor, "New Technologies as Tools of Empowerment: African Youth and Public Sphere Participation," in *Popular Media, Democracy and Development in Africa*, ed. Herman Wasserman (New York: Routledge, 2011), 208.

3. Rekopantswe Mate, "Youth Lyrics, Street Language and the Politics of Age: Contextualizing the Youth Question in the Third Chimurenga in Zimbabwe," *Journal of Southern African Studies* 38, no. 1 (March 2012): 107–27, quotation on 109.

4. Mate, "Youth Lyrics," 112.

5. Elizabeth Losh, *Hashtag* (New York: Bloomsbury Press, 2020), 63.

6. Eunsung Kim, "The Politics of Trending," Model View Culture, March 19, 2015, https://modelviewculture.com/pieces/the-politics-of-trending.

7. Reginald Gibbons and Terrence Des Pres, "An Interview with Thomas McGrath, January 30–February 1, 1987," *Triquarterly Journal* (1987): 38.

8. Uhuru Phalafala, "Going Back to Black with Spoken Word in South Africa," in *The Spoken Word Project*, ed. Mbongeni Buthulezi, Christopher Ouma, and Katleho Shoro (Munich: Goethe-Institut, 2014), 28–55, quotation on 39.

9. Leroy Vail and Landeg White, *Power and the Praise Poem* (Charlottesville: University of Virginia Press, 1981).

10. Lupenga Mphande, "If You're Ugly, Know How to Sing," in *Songs and Politics in Eastern Africa*, ed. Kimani Njogu and Hervé Maupeu (Dar es Salaam, Tanzania: Mkuki ya Nyota, 2007), 377.

11. Karin Barber, *A History of African Popular Culture* (Cambridge: Cambridge University Press, 2018), 12.

12. Phalafala, "Going Back to Black," 40.

13. Shirli Gilbert, "Singing against Apartheid: ANC Cultural Groups and the International Anti-Apartheid Struggle," *Journal of Southern African Studies* 33, no. 2 (2007): 421–41.

14. Augusto Boal, *Theatre of the Oppressed*, trans. Charles A. McBridge and Maria-Odilia Leal McBridge (New York: Theatre Communications Group, 1979), 53.

15. Mphande, "If You're Ugly, Know How to Sing," 377.

16. For more on this, see John Lwanda, "Mother's Songs: Male Appropriation of Women's Music in Malawi and Southern Africa," *Journal of African Cultural Studies* 16, no. 2 (2004): 119–31, and Reuben Chirambo "'The Sinking Cenotaph': Jack Mapanje's and Steve Chimombo's Contestation of Monumentalised Nationalist Public Memories of Malawi's President Banda," *Social Dynamics* 36, no. 3 (September 2010): 547–64.

17. For more on the use of chimurenga music to support the regime and the risk of censorship that attaches to it, see Wonderful Bere, "Urban Grooves: The Performance of Politics in Zimbabwe's Hip Hop Music" (PhD diss., New York University, 2008), and Winston Mano, "Renegotiating Tradition on Radio Zimbabwe," *Media, Culture, and Society* 26, no. 3 (2004): 315–36.

18. For more on Zuma's strategic use of izibongo, see Raphael d'Abdon, "The Commercialization of Celebratory Poetry: A Critical Examination of Zolani Mkiva's Post-Apartheid Praise Poetry (*Izibongo*)," *African Identities* 12, no. 3–4 (2014): 314–25.
19. John Lwanda, *Music, Culture, and Orature: Reading the Malawian Public Sphere, 1949–2006* (Zomba, Malawi: Kachere Press, 2008).
20. Benedict Anderson, *Imagined Communities: Reflections on the rign and Spread of Nationalism* (New York: Verso, 1983), 145.
21. Fred Cummins, "Rhythm as Entrainment: The Case of Synchronous Speech," *Journal of Phonetics* 37, no. 1 (2008): 16–28, quotations on 22, 23.
22. Losh, *Hashtag*, 65.
23. Nathan Rambukkana, introduction to *Hashtag Publics: The Power and Politics of Discursive Networks*, ed. Nathan Rambukkana (New York: Peter Lang, 2015), 30, 31.
24. Khumo Sebambo, "Azania House as a Symbol of the Black Imagination," *Johannesburg Salon* 9 (2015): 108.
25. Leketi Makalela, "'Our academics are intellectually colonised': Multilanguaging and Fees Must Fall," *Southern African Linguistics and Applied Language Studies* 36, no. 1 (2018): 1–11, quotation on 1.
26. For a more detailed history of these early protests, see Susan Booysen, ed., *Fees Must Fall: Student Revolt, Decolonisation and Governance in South Africa* (Johannesburg: Wits University Press, 2016); Francis B. Nyamnjoh, *#RhodesMustFall: Nibbling at Resilient Colonialism in South Africa* (Bamenda, Cameroon: Langaa Research & Publishing, 2016); and Robyn Baragwanath, "Social Media and Contentious Politics in South Africa," *Communication and the Public* 1, no. 3 (September 2016): 362–66.
27. The phrase refers to American feminist writer Flavia Dzodan's famous blog post "My Feminism Will be Intersectional or It Will Be Bullshit," *Tiger Beatdown* (blog), 10 October 2011, http://tigerbeatdown.com/2011/10/10/my-Feminism-will-be-intersectional-or-it-will-be-bullshit/), a phrase that has spread widely on internet forums devoted to issues of social justice.
28. Tshirelesto Mati reports further on the use of chants in the Fallist protests in "Understanding the Struggle Songs of Fees Must Fall," *Media for Justice* (blog), 2 February 2016, https://www.mediaforjustice.net/understanding-the-struggle-songs-of-fees-must-fall/. For more on the role of anthems in global Black protest, see Shanaa Redmond, *Anthem: Social Movements and the Sound of Solidarity in the African Diaspora* (New York: New York University Press, 2013).
29. Kelwyn Sole quoted in Mark Nowak, *Social Poetics* (Minneapolis, MN: Coffee House Press, 2020), 67.
30. Ari Sitas, interview by the author, 23 November 2016.
31. Alfred Themba Qabula, Mi S'dumo Hlatshwayo, and Nise Malange, *Black Mamba Rising: South African Worker Poets in Struggle*, ed. Ari Sitas (Dalbridge, Durban: Worker Resistance and Culture Publications, 1986).
32. Bhekizizwe Peterson, "Apartheid and the Political Imagination in Black South African Theatre," in *Politics and Performance: Theatre, Poetry and Song in Southern Africa*, ed. Liz Gunner (Johannesburg: Witwatersrand University Press, 1994).
33. Gilbert, "Singing against Apartheid," 424.
34. Daniele de Kadt, "This Data Confirms South Africa's Ruling Party Initially Ignored Mass Protests," Monkey Cage (blog), *Washington Post*, 23 October 2015, https://

www.washingtonpost.com/news/monkey-cage/wp/2015/10/23/this-data-confirms-south-africas-ruling-party-initially-ignored-mass-protests/.
35. Geert Lovink, *Networks without a Cause: A Critique of Social Media* (Cambridge: Polity Press, 2011).
36. Kim, "Politics of Trending."
37. Theresa Sauter and Axel Bruns, "#auspol: The Hashtag as Community, Event, and Material Object for Engaging with Australian Politics," in *Hashtag Politics*, ed. Nathan Rambukkana (New York: Peter Lang, 2015), 48.
38. #FeesMustFall had been used by students protesting fee hikes at the University of California in 2014. The earlier use further marked the link between the South African protests and global protests against austerity measures. Algorithmically, too, its earlier use meant the hashtag trended more quickly and broadly than it otherwise would have, bringing #FeesMustFall South Africa to the attention of a global audience.
39. Siphokazi Jonas, interview by the author, 22 November 2016.
40. Siphokazi Jonas and Kyle Louw, "Spoken Word Poem: Books Not Bullets—Kyle Louw/Siphokazi Jonas (#FeesMustFall)," YouTube, 3:53, 26 November 2015.
41. Michael Schaub, "Malala Yousafzai Wants Leaders to Invest in #booksnotbullets," *Los Angeles Times*, 8 July 2015. The phrase was widely embraced by student protesters in South Africa: shortly after Jonas and Louw's poem was published, the Johannesburg-based spoken word organization Hear My Voice began a campaign soliciting poetry under the same title.
42. Jonas and Louw, "Spoken Word Poem," https://www.youtube.com/watch?v=SleCjOmWhGw. Quoted lines below are from this video on YouTube.
43. Judith Butler, *Excitable Speech: A Politics of the Performative* (New York: Routledge, 1997), 2.
44. Gillian Godsell, Refiloe Lepere, Swankie Mafoko, and Ayabonga Nase, "Documenting the Revolution," in *Fees Must Fall: Student Revolt, Decolonization, and Governance in South Africa*, ed. Susan Booysen (Johannesburg: Wits University Press, 2016).
45. Evan Mawarire. "#ThisFlag: The 1st Video That Started It All," YouTube, 19 May 2017, https://www.youtube.com/watch?v=7dF-6uR4a88. The original video is no longer on Facebook.
46. Simon Gukurume, "#ThisFlag and #ThisGown Cyber Protests in Zimbabwe: Reclaiming Political Space," *African Journalism Studies* 38, no. 2 (2017): 49–70.
47. Wendy Willems, "Risky Dialogues: The Performative State and the Nature of Power in a Postcolony," *Journal of African Cultural Studies* 27, no. 3 (2015): 356–69, quotation on 357.
48. BlackPearl, PoetryAfricaperformance, CentreforCreativeArts, "BlackPearlatPOETRY AFRICA 2014," YouTube, 10 February 2015, https://www.youtube.com/watch?v=CMom3wRw3Jw.
49. This phenomenon has been widely documented. See, for example, Willems, "Risky Dialogues"; Samuel Ravengai, "Performing the Subversive: Censorship and Theatre Making in Zimbabwe," *Studies in Theatre and Performance* 35, no. 3 (2010): 237–50; and Bere, "Urban Grooves."
50. John E. Kaemmer. "Social Power and Music Change among the Shona," *Ethnomusicology* 33, no. 1 (1989): 31–45, quotation on 39.

NOTES TO PAGES 41–45

51. Stephen Chifunyise, "Trends in Zimbabwean Theatre since 1980," in Gunner, *Politics and Performance*, 54.
52. Bere, "Urban Grooves," 71.
53. Chifunyise, "Trends in Zimbabwean Literature," 54.
54. Jonathan Moyo, Twitter, 14 May 2016.
55. The appropriation of state rhetoric by activists has been widely documented throughout Africa. See, for example, Barber, *History of African Popular Culture*. This has been an especially popular strategy in Malawi, as detailed by Reuben Chirambo in "'The Sinking Cenotaph': Jack Mapanje's and Steve Chimombo's Contestation of Monumentalised Nationalist Public Memories of Malawi's President Banda, *Social Dynamics* 36, no. 3 (2010): 257–64, and Lwanda, *Music, Culture, and Orature*.
56. This move was magnified in January 2019, when the Zimbabwean government ordered state-controlled internet companies to shut down to avert rising protests. During the week-long internet shutdown, Zimbabwe security forces are alleged to have rounded up and abused hundreds of protesters and dissidents, according to a letter published by the Zimbabwe Human Rights NGO Forum, https://www.hrforumzim.org/daysofdarkness2/, 18 January 2019.
57. Exact estimates of the number of Zimbabweans living abroad are hard to find, in part because of the high rates of informal migration to South Africa and Botswana. According to the 2015 report of the International Organization on Migration Zimbabwe, "It is currently estimated that between 500,000 and 3 million Zimbabweans are residing outside Zimbabwe." See Martin Ocaga, "IOM Zimbabwe Annual Report, 2015," International Organization for Migration, 2016, https://www.iom.int/sites/g/files/tmzbdl486/files/country/docs/zimbabwe/IOM-Zimbabwe-AR-25Aug2016.pdf, 5.
58. Gukurume, "#ThisFlag," 58.
59. Born in 1977, Mawarire was thirty-nine at the time of the protests, an age that places him within Zimbabwean youth politics.
60. The latter is a regionally common way of communicating laughter online.
61. While Zimbabwe has 16 official languages, Cheshona and Sindebele are the two most widely spoken languages in Zimbabwe.
62. Amanda Habane, "Feeling Emotional. Being Tear Gassed in My Own Country. #ThisFlagzw," YouTube, 6 September 2016, https://www.youtube.com/watch?v=_0ELb-bax8U&t=94s.
63. Habane's video moves between English and Cheshona as she emotionally recounts what happened to her. However, I have focused on the English, here, in part to capture the parallels with Mawarire's video and in part because of my own limited capacities in Cheshona.
64. World Bank, "Internet Users for Zimbabwe," retrieved from FRED, Federal Reserve Bank of St. Louis, 16 March 2023, https://fred.stlouisfed.org/series/ITNETUSERP2ZWE.
65. Zeynep Tufekci, *Twitter and Tear Gas: The Power and Fragility of Networked Protest* (New Haven, CT: Yale University Press, 2017), 6.
66. Xolelwa Siyamthanda Dwesini and Mncedi Eddie Magade, "Mapping Audience Perceptions of How Digital Media Impacts the Reception of News from Traditional Media Sources," *Global Media Journal* 19, no. 6 (2021): 1–11.
67. Lars Kamer, "Percentage of Population Using the Internet in Malawi from 2000

to 2019," *Statista*, 13 December 2022, https://www.statista.com/statistics/640140/malawi-internet-penetration/.
68. Kudzai Mashininga, "President Slashes University Fees after Student Protests," *University World News*, 17 August 2016, https://www.universityworldnews.com/post.php?story=20160817101205675.
69. See, for example, Jay David Bolter and Richard Grusin, *Remediation: Understanding New Media* (Cambridge, MA: MIT Press, 2000), 6.
70. Philip Auslander, *Liveness: Performance in a Mediatized Culture* (New York: Routledge, 1999), 7.
71. Reuben Chirambo, "Protesting Politics of 'Death and Darkness' in Malawi," *Journal of Folklore Research* 38, no. 3 (2001): 205–27.
72. David Kerr, "Playing the Tyrant Away: Creative Academic Resistance to Dictatorship in Malawi," *Journal of Arts & Communities* 2, no. 3 (2012): 215–25, quotation on 219.
73. Benedicto Wokomatani Malunga, interview by the author, 17 August 2015.
74. Joey Power, *Political Culture and Nationalism in Malawi: Building Kwacha* (Rochester, NY: University of Rochester Press, 2010), 136–56.
75. Reuben Chirambo, Max Iphani, and Zondiwe Mbano, *The Unsung Song: An Anthology of Malawian Writing in English* (Zomba, Malawi: Chancellor College Publications, 2001), ix.
76. Pascal Kischindo, "Recurrent Themes in Chichewa Verse in Malawian Newspapers," *Nordic Journal of African Studies* 12, no. 3 (2003): 327–53; "Malawi Data—2015," *World Bank*, http://data.worldbank.org/country/malawi.
77. Lwanda quoted in Kerr, "Playing the Tyrant Away," 222.
78. Robert Chiwamba, interview by the author, 15 December 2016.
79. Barber, *History of African Popular Culture*, 8.
80. Yankho Seunda, interview by the author, 29 July 2016.
81. Felicia Miyakawa, "'I Can't Breathe': Protest Music Now," *Avid Listener*, 24 July 2020, https://theavidlistenerblogcom.wordpress.com/2020/07/24/i-cant-breathe-protest-music-now/ (emphasis in original).
82. For more on the use of WhatsApp in popular protests globally, see, for example, Paolo Gerbaudo, *Tweets and the Streets* (London: Pluto Press, 2012); Emiliano Treré, "Reclaiming, Proclaiming and Maintaining Collective Identity in the #YoSoy132 Movement in Mexico," *Information, Communication and Society* 18, no. 8 (2015): 901–15; and Brian Pindayi, "Social Media Uses and Effects in Africa: The Case of WhatsApp in Africa," in *Impacts of the Media on African Socio-economic Development*, ed. Nelson Okorie and Biodun Salawu (Hershey, PA: IGI Global, 2017).
83. Facebook appears to be planning to change this through targeted advertising, but as of 2018, WhatsApp had not been monetized.
84. Lovink, *Networks without a Cause*, 11.

CHAPTER 2: COMMENTING IN COMMUNITY

1. Howard Becker, *Art Worlds* (Oakland: University of California Press, 1982), 4. Nicole Starosielski details the role of material infrastructures in constructing networked communities in *The Undersea Network: Sign, Storage, Transmission* (Durham, NC: Duke University Press, 2015). More recently, scholarship has turned to consider the

relationship between digital platforms and communication infrastructures broadly; see, for example, Jean-Christophe Plantin, Carl Lazoge, Paul N. Edwards, and Christian Sandvig, "Infrastructure Studies Meet Platform Studies in the Age of Google and Facebook," *New Media & Society* 20, no. 1 (2018): 293–310.

2. Stephanie Bosch Santana, "The Story Club: African Literary Networks Offline," in *Routledge Handbook of African Literature*, ed. Moradewun Adejunmobi and Carli Coetzee (New York: Routledge, 2019), 385–99.
3. Linda Gabriel, interview by the author, 14 December 2016.
4. Eiko Ikegami, *Bonds of Civility: Aesthetic Networks and the Political Origins of Japanese Culture* (Cambridge: Cambridge University Press, 2005). Although the specific forms of aesthetic training and civic engagement Ikegami describes are particular to sixteenth-century Japan, the role of in-group training to produce cross-class aesthetic affiliations is useful for understanding the nature of these connections.
5. Santana, "Story Club," 396.
6. Examples of this phenomenon abound. Meg Arenberg's study of Swahili poetry WhatsApp groups ("Swahili Poetry's Digital Geographies: WhatsApp and the Forming of Cultural Space," *Postcolonial Text* 15, nos. 3 and 4 [2020]) provides an especially vivid and careful account of the development of formal norms in Tanzania.
7. vangile gantsho, interview by the author, 8 August 2020. Lisa McCormick's "Marking Time in Lockdown: Heroization and Ritualization in the UK during the Coronavirus Pandemic," *American Journal of Cultural Sociology* 8 (2020): 324–51, further theorizes the use of performance to structure daily life under lockdowns.
8. See chapter 3 of this volume for more on Malewezi's organizing work.
9. An image with text superimposed over it. For more on the cultural significance of image macros in the twenty-first century, see Marta Dynel, "'I have seen image macros!' Advice Animal Memes as Visual-Verbal Jokes," *International Journal of Communication* 10 (2016): 660–68. See also Akin Adesokan, "The Remix: Of New Identities and Technologies of Reuse," in *Everything Is Sampled: Digital and Print Mediations in African Arts and Letters* (Bloomington: Indiana University Press, 2023), chapter 6.
10. Binyavanga Wainaina, *One Day I Will Write about this Place* (Minneapolis, MN: Graywolf, 2011), 173–76, 188–89.
11. Shola Adenekan, *African Literature in the Digital Age: Class and Sexual Politics in New Writing from Nigeria and Kenya* (New York: Routledge, 2021), 10.
12. Adekenan, *African Literature in the Digital Age*, 118–19.
13. Ikegami, *Bonds of Civility*, 4.
14. Patrick Jagoda, Network Aesthetics (Chicago: University of Chicago Press, 2016), 8, 102.
15. Ben Etherington, "Against Network Thinking," *Affirmations of the Modern* 6, no. 1 (2019): 30–44, quotation on 40.
16. Sarah Brouillette, *Underdevelopment and African Literature: Emerging Forms of Reading* (Cambridge: Cambridge University Press, 2020), 1.
17. Adenekan's *African Literature in the Digital Age* offers a detailed outline of this process, focusing on Nigerian and Kenyan literary networks. "Digital Africas," ed. Shola Adekenan, Rhonda Cobham-Sander, Stephanie Bosch Santan, and Kwabena Opoku-Agyemang, special issue, *Postcolonial Text* 15, nos. 3 and 4 (2020), draws together further examples from Francophone Africa, Ghana, South Africa, East Africa, Uganda, and Kenya to suggest the breadth of this pattern.

18. For more on the effects of these algorithmic biases, see, for example, Safiya Noble, *Algorithms of Oppression* (New York: New York University Press, 2016); Ruha Benjamin, *Race after Technology* (Princeton, NJ: Princeton University Press, 2019); and Sasha Costanza-Chock, *Design Justice: Community-Led Practices to Build the Worlds We Need* (Cambridge, MA: MIT Press, 2020). Nick Seaver's ethnographic study of programmers in *Computing Taste: Algorithms and the Makers of Music Recommendation* (Chicago: University of Chicago Press, 2022) helps illustrate the social and cultural processes that feed into this divide. Although these scholars focus on the US context, the phenomena they identify are broadly applicable, in large part because so much software design and development is concentrated in the United States, as Roopika Risam argues in *New Digital Worlds: Postcolonial Digital Humanities in Theory, Praxis, and Pedagogy* (Evanston, IL: Northwestern University Press, 2018).
19. Frank Pasquale, *The Black Box Society: The Secret Algorithms That Control Money and Information* (Cambridge, MA: Harvard University Press, 2015), points out that this illegibility is a deliberate design decision.
20. Mike Chasar, *Poetry Unbound: Poems and New Media from the Magic Lantern to Instagram* (New York: Columbia University Press, 2020), 190.
21. Dwaine Plaza and Lauren Plaza, "Facebook and WhatsApp as Elements in Transnational Care Chains for the Trinidadian Diaspora," *Genealogy* 3, no. 2 (2019): 1–20, quotation on 15.
22. See chapter 1 of this volume for further discussion.
23. Sapitwa Poetry Artists, WhatsApp, 26 October 2016. Unless otherwise noted, all translations are my own; all social media messages reproduced as closely as possible. Ellipses as is in the original.
24. Sapitwa Poetry Artists, WhatsApp, 31 October 2016.
25. Karin Barber, *The Anthropology of Texts, Persons and Publics: Oral and Written Culture in Africa and Beyond* (Cambridge: Cambridge University Press, 2007), 161, 164.
26. Shola Adenekan's study of "network thinking" in *African Literature in the Digital Age* highlights the way literary networks—from listservs to Facebook groups—have affected digitally engaged writing in Nigeria and Kenya.
27. Observations are based on messages observed between 19 September and 29 December 2016, during which period the groups generated 2,440 and 3,134 messages, respectively. These two groups have comparable numbers of participants and rates of participation—with 189 and 254 members, respectively, and an average participation rate of 26.9 percent and 24.8 percent in the observed period.
28. Barber, *Anthropology of Texts, Persons and Publics*, 137.
29. Heather Inwood, *Verse Going Viral: China's New Media Scenes* (Seattle: University of Washington Press, 2014), 115.
30. Critical feedback accounts for approximately 4 percent of messages sent in Living Room and 15 percent in Sapitwa.
31. Sapitwa Poetry Artists, 10 February 2017.
32. Bonaventure Mkandawire and Reuben Chirambo have each suggested that Chewaization in Malawi—enforced, among other ways, through national education in Chichewa, despite the country's many major languages—has been a lasting violence of Hastings Banda's regime of cultural and political oppression. For more, see Bonaventure Mkandawire, "Ethnicity, Language, and Cultural Violence: Dr. Hastings Kamuzu Banda's Malawi, 1964–1994," *Society of Malawi Journal* 63, no. 1 (2010):

23–42, and Rueben Chirambo, "Malawain Literature under Dr. Kamuzu Banda and Its Place in the New Malawi," *Tizame* 6 (1998): 28–32.
33. Sam Hinton and Larissa Hjorth, *Understanding Social Media* (Thousand Oaks, CA: Sage, 2013).
34. Becker, *Art Worlds*, 42.
35. Sapitwa Poetry Artists, WhatsApp chat.
36. In February 2016, when these groups were active, WhatsApp limited group size to 256 members; as of 2022, that limit had expanded to 1,024.
37. Henry Jenkins's *Convergence Culture: Where Old and New Media Collide* (New York: New York University Press, 2006) foundationally describes digital media as creating "participatory cultures."
38. Kate Crawford, "Following You: Disciplines of Listening in Social Media," *Continuum* 23, no. 4 (2009): 525–35, quotation on 528.
39. Max Bearak, "'Shut Down Zimbabwe' Protests Are Met with Internet Blackouts and Arrests," *Washington Post*, 6 July 2016, https://www.washingtonpost.com/news/worldviews/wp/2016/07/06/shut-down-zimbabwe-protests-are-met-with-internet-blackouts-and-arrests/; Camila Domonoske, "American Woman Faces Charges in Zimbabwe over Tweets about Mugabe," NPR, "The Two-Way," 10 November 2017, https://www.npr.org/sections/thetwo-way/2017/11/10/563285405/american-woman-faces-charges-in-zimbabwe-over-tweets-about-mugabe.
40. For more on the use of digital poetry to promote political action in Zimbabwe, see Susanna L. Sacks, "Evan Mawarire's #ThisFlag as Tactical Lyric: The Role of Digital Speech in Imagining a Networked Zimbabwean Nation," *African Studies Review* 63, no. 2 (June 2020): 238–57.
41. Shepherd Mpofu, "Social Media and the Politics of Ethnicity in Zimbabwe," *Ecquid Novi: African Journalism Studies* 34, no. 1 (2013): 115–22, quotations on 116, 115.
42. The separation between WhatsApp and Facebook is more illusory than this implies: Facebook acquired WhatsApp in February 2014, and several features encourage cross-platform sharing. However, daily use appears unaffected by this link, as Facebook's acquisition had, as of December 2017, had little direct impact on WhatsApp's user interface; in 2022, though, Meta updated the application to include features found on other social media platforms, including video status updates similar to those on Instagram.
43. Although Facebook had previously allowed pseudonymous accounts, in 2016 its policies changed to require that all users identify themselves under their full, legal names.
44. Eldred Masunungure, "Nation-Building, State-Building, and Power Configuration in Zimbabwe," *Conflict Trends* 1 (2006): 3–8.
45. Mbizo Chirasha, "In Solidarity," Facebook, 12 October 2017.
46. Pierre Bourdieu, *The Rules of Art: Genesis and Structure of the Literary Field*, trans. Susan Emmanuel (Redwood City, CA: Stanford University Press, 1996), 53.
47. Morset Billie, interview by the author, 11 December 2016.
48. Becker, *Art Worlds*, 48.
49. The group's name refers to the Canada-based international 100 Thousand Poets for Change network, which seeks to mobilize poets and artists under their political vision for "peace & sustainability." The network understands effective work to occur at local and regional levels and supports the work of poets in cities and towns across the world. See https://100tpc.org/.

50. Sydney Saize, "They Need Cyber Security in a Nation That Guaranteed Safety," Facebook post, *100 Thousand Poets for Peace-Zimbabwe*, 17 November 2017.
51. Bwesigiye Bwa Mwesigire, "What Is Literary Activism (Or Who Keeps the Housekeepers' House?)," *Eastern African Literary and Cultural Studies* 7, no. 1–2 (2021): 10–22.
52. IGTV predated Reels, which Instagram introduced in 2021.
53. Urayoán Noel, "The Queer Migrant Poemics of #Latinx Instagram," *New Literary History* 50, no. 4 (2019): 531–57, quotation on 544.
54. vangile gantsho, interview by the author, 24 July 2021.
55. Instagram, Frequently Asked Questions, 2019.
56. Chantal Stanfield, Twitter, 3 March 2020, https://twitter.com/chantalstan.
57. Noel, "Queer Migrant Poemics of #Latinx Instagram."
58. Timothy Yu, "Instagram Poetry and Our Poetry Worlds," Poetry Foundation, 24 April 2019, https://www.poetryfoundation.org/harriet/2019/04/instagram-poetry-and-our-poetry-worlds.
59. Chasar, *Poetry Unbound*, 190.

CHAPTER 3: INSTITUTIONALIZING ALGORITHMIC AESTHETICS

1. Vusumuzi Mpofu, "Foreign Searching for Rain," Facebook, 16 November 2016, https://www.facebook.com/vusumuzi.mpofu.395/posts/555487841315807.
2. In this chapter, I use the term *slam poetry* to denote the styles of poetry commonly performed at competitive poetry slams. *Spoken word poetry* refers more broadly to contemporary styles of performance poetry, including (and often influenced by) but not limited to slam poetry.
3. Doreen Strauhs, *African Literary NGOs: Power, Politics, and Participation* (London: Palgrave Macmillan, 2013).
4. Susan B. A. Somers-Willet's *The Cultural Politics of Slam* (Ann Arbor: University of Michigan Press, 2010) was among the first histories of slam's development and spread in the United States. For a discussion of the form's relation to Blackness and identity production, see Javon Johnson's *Killing Poetry: Blackness and the Making of Slam and Spoken Word Communities* (New Brunswick, NJ: Rutgers University Press, 2017), and for a broader analysis of its formal engagements, see Kevin Coval's introduction to *The BreakBeat Poets: New American Poetry in the Age of Hip-Hop*, ed. Kevin Coval, Quraysh Ali Lansana, and Nate Marshall (London: Haymarket Press, 2015).
5. Scott Woods, "Poetry Slams: The Ultimate Democracy of Art," *World Literature Today* 82, no. 1 (2008): 16–18, quotation on 16.
6. Woods, "Poetry Slams," 18.
7. Johnson, *Killing Poetry*, 89.
8. Kila van der Starre, "How Viral Poems Are Annotated: On 'OCD' by Neil Hillborn," *Performance Research* 20, no. 6 (2015): 58–64, quotation on 58.
9. Susan Weinstein details a similar phenomenon among American youth poets, in *The Room Is on Fire: The History, Pedagogy, and Practice of Youth Spoken Word Poetry* (Albany: State University of New York Press, 2018). *Louder than a Bomb*, directed by Greg Jacobs and Jon Siskel, Siskel/Jacobs Productions, 2010.

10. Mbongeni Buthulezi, Christopher Ouma, and Katleho Shoro, "Spoken Word in Sub-Saharan Africa: Past, Present, and Future," in *The Spoken Word Project: Stories Travelling Through Africa*, ed. Mbongiseni Buthelezi, Christopher Ouma, and Katleho Shoro (Lektora: Der Poetry-Slam-Verlag, 2014), 14, 19.
11. Jules Banda, interview by the author, 2 August 2015.
12. Moses Serubiri, "The Self-Making of Spoken Word Poets in Kampala," in Buthelezi, Ouma, and Shoro, *Spoken Word Project*, 100–115, quotation on 100.
13. Siphokazi Jonas, interview by the author, 22 November 2016.
14. Susan Weinstein notes a similar phenomenon in the Louisiana youth slams, where she guides students to present work attentive to their audience's needs, rather than their own.
15. For more on the cultural context of homophobia in Malawi, see C. Biruk, "'Aid for Gays': The Moral and the Material in 'African Homophobia' in Post-2009 Malawi," *Journal of Modern African Studies* 42, no. 3 (2014): 447–73. For more on the prominence of homophobia in Malawian spoken word poetry specifically, see Harri Englund, "Love and Homophobia in Malawi's Spoken Word Poetry Movement," *Africa* 91, no. 3 (2021): 361–87.
16. Mwaura Samora, "A Fast and Furious African Generation of Poets Says Goodbye to Shakespeare," *Nation*, updated 21 June 2020, https://nation.africa/kenya/indepth/africa-insight/a-fast-and-furious-african-generation-of-poets-says-goodbye-toshakespeare-shakespeare-614408.
17. Johnson, *Killing Poetry*, 91.
18. Moradewun Adejunmobi, "Revenge of the Spoken Word? Writing, Performance, and New Media in Urban West Africa," *Oral Tradition* 26, no. 1 (2011): p. 8 of PDF.
19. Many scholars highlight the formal attributes of slam as connected to more diffuse interpersonal networks, acknowledging the institutional spread of slam while focusing on its cultural implications and attachments. Often, the local rise of slam poetry appears within a broader trend in cosmopolitan media and educational standards, as in Jonathan Gray's study of cultural influence in Malawian media ("Scales of Cultural Influence: Malawian Consumption of Foreign Media," *Media, Culture, and Society* 36, no. 7 [2014]: 982–97), or Natalia Molebatsi and Rafael d'Abdon's study of youth "floetry" in South Africa ("From Poetry to Floetry: Music's Influence in the Spoken Word Art of Young South Africa," *Muziki* 4, no. 2 [2007]: 171–77). Otherwise, scholars figure slam poetry's spread through the lens of global Blackness, as in Karen Flynn and Evelyn Marrast's study of Canadian slam poetry ("Spoken Word from the North: Contesting Nation, Politics, and Identity," *Wadabegei: A Journal of the Caribbean and Its Diasporas* 11, no. 2 [2008]: 3–24); Bronwen Low's analysis of televised slam poetry ("Poetry on MTV? Slam and the Poetics of Popular Culture," *JCT* 22, no. 4 [2006]: 97–112); and Kelly Josephs's reading of Staceyann Chin's poetry ("Dissonant Desires: Staceyann Chin and the Queer Politics of a Jamaican Accent," *Mosaic: A Journal for the Interdisciplinary Study of Literature* 42, no. 2 [2009]: 153–70).
20. Urayoán Noel, *In Visible Movement: Nuyorican Poetry from the Sixties to Slam* (Iowa City: University of Iowa Press, 2014), 141.
21. Madhu Krishnan, *Contingent Canons: African Literature and the Politics of Location* (Cambridge: Cambridge University Press, 2019), 77.
22. Vera Chisvo, interview by the author, 15 December 2016.

23. The slams faded after Paul Brickhill's death in 2014 but were restarted by Morset Billie as monthly events beginning in 2017.
24. Linda Gabriel, interview by the author, 14 December 2016.
25. PerchTV—Zimbabwe, "Sins of Mothers: Poem by Linda Gabriel," YouTube, 1 September 2014, https://www.youtube.com/watch?v=0BQ5P5rl1D4&pp=ygUdbGluZGEgZ2FicmllbCBzaW5zIG9mIG1vdGhlcnM%3D.
26. Linda Gabriel, interview by the author, 14 December 2016.
27. Johnson, *Killing Poetry*, 92.
28. For more on the Spoken Word Project, see the commemorative volume, Buthelezi, Ouma, and Shoro, eds., *The Spoken Word Project*.
29. Stephanie Bosch Santana, "The Story Club: African Literary Networks Offline," in *Routledge Handbook of African Literature*, ed. Moradewun Adejunmobi and Carli Coetzee (New York: Routledge, 2019), 385–99.
30. Christian de Beukelaer and Justin O'Connor, "The Creative Economy and the Development Agenda: The Use and Abuse of 'Fast Policy,'" in *Contemporary Perspectives on Art and Development*, ed. Polly Stupples and Katerina Taeiwas (New York: Routledge, 2017): 27–47.
31. Krishnan, *Contingent Canons*, 77.
32. Weinstein, *Room Is on Fire*, 67. Mirjam de Bruijn details a parallel situation in Chad, where slam "festivals can exist only with support from outside, which often involves an arduous search for funding" ("Slam Poetry in Chad: A Space of Belonging in an Environment of Violence and Repression," *Conflict and Society: Advances in Research* 8 (2022): 242–57, quotation on 244.
33. "Tasks and Targets," Goethe-Institut, 13 March 2023, https://www.goethe.de/ins/za/en/ueb/auf.html.
34. For a history of politically efficacious performance poetry in Malawi, see Leroy Vail and Landeg White, *Power and the Praise Poem: South African Voices in History* (Charlottesville: University of Virginia Press, 1991), and John Lwanda, "Mother's Songs: Male Appropriation of Women's Music in Malawi and Southern Africa," *Journal of African Cultural Studies* 16, no. 2 (December 2003): 119–41), as well as chapter 1 of this volume.
35. Lake of Stars, "Q Malewezi at National Library," YouTube, 9 October 2013, https://www.youtube.com/watch?v=2F8Q82jl2Pc.
36. Lupenga Mphande, "If You're Ugly, Know How to Sing: Aesthetics of Resistance and Subversion," in *Songs and Politics in Eastern Africa*, ed. Kimani Njogu and Hervé Maupeu (Dar es Salaam, Tanzania: Mkuki ya Nyota, 2007), 377.
37. Malewezi Qabaniso, "'People' by Qabaniso Malewezi," YouTube, 17 March 2016, https://www.youtube.com/watch?v=KQwOPK3MR_M.
38. Banda is among the most common surnames in Malawi, but most people with the name are not closely related. For clarity, I refer to poets with the surname "Banda" by both their given and surnames.
39. SapitwaPoetry.com was founded by Robert Chiwamba in late 2015. Modeled on the highly successful MalawiMusic.com, Sapitwa Poetry allows poets to directly upload recordings of their work to the site, where fans can then listen to and download the work. Before the platform closed in 2022, Chiwamba had planned to monetize the site by requiring users to pay a nominal fee (approximately one dollar) to download

a poem. This would have addressed the problem of monetization that plagues poets who publish digitally.
40. Weinstein, *The Room Is on Fire*, 23. Maureen Perry, "Resources for Your Rhymes: Sites for Slam/Spoken Word/Performance Poetry," *College & Research Libraries News* 72, no. 3 (2011): 143–46; Mia Fiore, "Pedagogy for Liberation: Spoken Word Poetry in Urban Schools," *Education and Urban Society* 47, no. 7 (2015): 813–29; and Valerie Chepp, "Activating Politics with Poetry and Spoken Word," *Contexts* 15, no. 4 (2016): 42–47, have identified similar pedagogical uses of slam poetry in the United States, suggesting that the form's open-endedness makes it particularly suited for eliciting and supporting youth voices and movements.
41. For more on the role of the World Bank in cultural development, see Isaac Kamola, *Making the World Global* (Durham, NC: Duke University Press, 2019).
42. Phindu Banda, "Nothing People," Lake of Stars, 1 October 2016 (Chintheche Inn, Chintheche, Nkhata Bay, Malawi).
43. Stanley Kenani, *Nation*, 22 July 2016.
44. Robert Chiwamba, interview by the author, 23 July 2016.
45. Benedicto Malunga, interview by the author, 17 August 2015.
46. Harri Englund, "Love and Homophobia in Malawi's Spoken Word Poetry Movement," *Africa* 91, no. 3 (2021): 361–87, esp. 365.
47. Linda Gabriel, interview by the author, 14 December 2016.
48. Afrikaaps refers to the style of Afrikaans spoken in the Cape Flats, a predominantly mixed-race area.
49. Mbongeni Nomkonwana, launch event for Carolyn McKinney's *Language and Power in Postcolonial Schooling*, the Book Lounge, Cape Town, 24 October 2016.
50. Mbongeni Nomkonwana, interview by the author, 31 October 2016.
51. Jahan Ramazani, *The Hybrid Muse: Postcolonial Poetry in English* (Chicago: University of Chicago Press, 2001), 36.
52. Mbongeni Nomkonwana, *Umzila ka Moya*, reading and performance at the Poetry Foundation, Chicago, IL, 18 April 2018.
53. Katleho Shoro, *Umzila ka Moya*, reading and performance at the Poetry Foundation, Chicago, IL, 18 April 2018.
54. Mbongeni Nomkonwana, email to author, 2017.
55. Mpofu, "Foreign Searching for Rain."

CHAPTER 4: MIGRATING MOVEMENTS

1. James Yékú, *Cultural Netizenship: Social Media, Popular Culture, and Performance in Nigeria* (Bloomington: Indiana University Press, 2022), 3.
2. UN High Council on Refugees, "Malawi Factsheet August 2021," 8 September 2021, https://data.unhcr.org/en/documents/details/88529.
3. Eileen Julien, "The Extroverted African Novel," in *The Novel*, vol. 1, ed. Franco Moretti (Princeton, NJ: Princeton University Press, 2006), 682.
4. John Lwanda, in "Mother's Song: Male Appropriation of Women's Music in Malawi and Southern Africa," *Journal of African Cultural Studies* 16, no. 2 (2003): 119–41, details the significance of poetry performance in Malawian national culture.
5. For more on the use of performance poetry in European contexts, see David Aberbach's

work in "The Poetry of Nationalism," *Nations and Nationalism* 9, no. 2 (2003): 255–75, and "The British Empire and Revolutionary National Poetry," *Nations and Nationalism* 16, no. 2 (2010): 220–39; in the US context, see Tyler Hoffman, *American Poetry in Performance: From Walt Whitman to Hip Hop* (Ann Arbor: University of Michigan Press, 2011).

6. Pascale Casanova, *The World Republic of Letters*, trans. M. B. DeBevoise (Cambridge, MA: Harvard University Press, 2004), 84, 105.

7. David Aberbach's work highlights the contradictory position of the poet relative to the nation. In "Poetry of Nationalism," Aberbach highlights poets' role supporting nineteenth-century European nationalism; in "British Empire and Revolutionary National Poetry, though, he emphasizes the role of revolutionary poets in resisting British imperialism. In each case, poetry offers a cultural touchstone to unite disparate communities, a role discussed further in chapter 1 of this book.

8. Matthew Hart, *Nations of Nothing but Poetry: Modernism, Transnationalism, and Synthetic Vernacular Writing* (New York: Oxford University Press, 2010).

9. Angela Bartie, *The Edinburgh Festivals: Culture and Society in Post-War Britain* (Edinburgh: Edinburgh University Press, 2013).

10. For more on the use of poetry in Malawian independence movements, see John Lwanda, "Poetry, Culture and Orature: A Reappraisal of the Malawi Political Public Sphere, 1953-2006," *Journal of Contemporary African Studies* 26, no. 1 (2014); for its use in South Africa, see Jeff Opland, *Xhosa Poets and Poetry* (Cape Town: David Philip Publishers, 1998).

11. See chapter 1 of this volume for more on the historical deployment of poetry to political ends in southern Africa.

12. Kwame Dawes, "Meeting at the Crossroads: Mapping Worlds and World Literature," *Comparatist* 36 (2012): 292–99, quotations on 295. Many of these arguments build on Gauri Viswanathan's foundational study of English literary instruction in India in *Masks of Conquest: Literary Study and British Rule in India* (New York: Columbia University Press, 1989); for more on its deployment in southern Africa, see Isabel Hofmeyr, *The Portable Bunyan: A Transnational History of the Pilgrim's Progress* (Princeton, NJ: Princeton University Press, 2004).

13. Daniel Magaziner, *The Law and the Prophets: Black Consciousness in South Africa, 1968–1977* (Athens: Ohio University Press, 2010).

14. Ari Sitas, "The Making of the 'Comrades' Movement in Natal, 1985–91," *Journal of Southern African Studies* 18, no. 3 (1992): 629–41.

15. In a Francophone context, Kristen Stern provocatively argues that the festival's branding processes should be read through a performance lens, highlighting the constrained position of the contemporary author. See "Disidentifying African Authors at a French Literary Festival: Mabanckou and Miano at Étonnants Voyageurs," *Research in African Literatures* 50, no. 2 (2019): 49–67.

16. Norie Neumark's "Doing Things with Voices: Performativity and Voice," in *Voice: Vocal Aesthetics in Digital Arts and Media*, ed. Norie Neumark, Ross Gibson, and Theo van Leuven (Cambridge, MA: MIT Press, 2010), attaches digital anxieties about authenticity to the performer's voice specifically.

17. Mary Louise Pratt, *Imperial Eyes: Travel Writing and Transculturation* (New York: Routledge, 2007), 7.

18. Heather Inwood, *Verse Going Viral: China's New Media Scenes* (Seattle: University of Washington Press, 2014), 8.
19. Yékú, *Cultural Netizenship*.
20. Neil Lazarus, "Cosmopolitanism and the Specificity of the Local in World Literature," *Journal of Commonwealth Literature* 46, no. 1 (2011): 119–37, quotation on 119–20.
21. Bhekizizwe Peterson, "Apartheid and the Political Imagination in Black South African Theatre," in *Politics and Performance: Theatre, Poetry and Song in Southern Africa*, ed. Liz Gunner (Johannesburg, South Africa: Witwatersrand University Press, 1994), 39.
22. For more on the role of censorship in Black theater in South Africa, see Janet Suzman, "Stage Directions in South Africa," *Index on Censorship* 43, no. 2 (2014): 158–63, and Bhekizizwe Peterson, "Apartheid and the Political Imagination in Black South Africa Theatre," *Journal of Southern African Studies* 16, no. 2 (1990): 229–45.
23. Ari Sitas, "Traditions of Poetry in Natal," in Gunner, *Politics and Performance*, 138.
24. Jill Dolan, *Utopia in Performance: Finding Hope at the Theater* (Ann Arbor: University of Michigan Press, 2010), 164.
25. Richard Bauman and Charles Briggs, "Poetics and Performance as Critical Perspectives on Language and Social Life," *Annual Review of Anthropology* 19 (1990): 59–88, quotations on 70, 73.
26. Peter Middleton describes this standard "poetry voice" in *Distant Reading: Performance, Readership, and Consumption* (Tuscaloosa: University of Alabama Press, 2005).
27. Roché Kester, "Premium Poes," *Poetry Africa 2016*, at the Elizabeth Sneddon Theatre, University of KwaZulu-Natal, Durban, South Africa, 10 October 2016. Unless otherwise noted, all transcriptions are my own.
28. Kester, "Premium Poes." The word "punani" is Hindi-derived Jamaican slang for female genitalia.
29. For more on the structure and influence of slam poetry and debates over its cultural position as literature in southern Africa, see chapter 3 of this book.
30. Wegerif has since gained widespread acclaim for her musical performances as Sho'Majozi.
31. Bronwyn Williams, "The World on Your Screen: New Media, Remix, and the Politics of Cross-Cultural Contact," in *New Media Literacies and Participatory Popular Culture across Borders*, ed. Bronwyn T. Williams and Amy A. Zenger (New York: Routledge, 2012), 17–32, quotations on 18 and 21.
32. Lily Banda, "New Shoes," *Lake of Stars*, Mangochi, Malawi, 25 September 2015.
33. Jahan Ramazani, *Poetry and Its Others: News, Prayer, Song, and the Dialogue of Genres* (Chicago: University of Chicago Press, 2013), 10.
34. "About," *Lake of Stars*, https://lakeofstars.org/about, accessed 2 December 2020. This information was removed from the page in 2022.
35. These numbers come from the festival's own reporting.
36. "About," https://lakeofstars.org/about.
37. Hector Macpherson, interview by the author, 30 August 2018.
38. Shadreck Chikoti, interview by the author, 22 July 2016. His book is *Imagine Africa 500*, ed. Billy Kahora (Lilongwe, Malawi: Pan African Publishing House, 2016).
39. Lake of Stars, "Q Malewezi at National Library," YouTube, 9 October 2013, https://www.youtube.com/watch?v=2F8Q82jl2Pc.

40. 88th StaR, "Great Poet—Qabaniso "Q" Malewezi's Live Performance @ LOS.3GP," YouTube, 21 January 2012, https://www.youtube.com/watch?v=WhQd1Kgw7Fg.
41. "Malawian Poets Can Do Better, Says Q. Malewezi," *Nyasa Times*, 29 October 2013, https://www.nyasatimes.com/malawian-poets-can-do-better-says-q-malewezi/.
42. "About," https://lakeofstars.org/about, accessed 2 December 2020. This information was removed from the page in 2022.
43. For more on Project Project, see chapter 3 of this volume; for more on the Living Room Poetry Club, see chapter 2.
44. Sarah Nuttall, "Reading Recognition, and the Postcolonial," *Interventions* 3, no. 3 (2001): 391–404, quotation on 395.
45. Cindy Wong, "Publics and Counterpublics: Rethinking Film Festivals as Public Spheres," in *Film Festivals; History, Theory, Method, Practice*, ed. Marijke de Valk, Brendan Kredell, and Skadi Loist (Routledge, 2016), 83–99, quotation on 89.
46. Sitas, "Traditions of Poetry," 150.
47. Bartie, *The Edinburgh Festivals* (2013), tracks this focus in her history of the Edinburgh International Festival.
48. Or "age, sex, location."
49. Black Pearl's poetry here and below from Centre for Creative Arts, "Black Pearl at POETRY AFRICA 2014," YouTube, 10 February 2015.
50. Anita Howarth, "Foreign Policy, Identity and the Media: Contestation over Zimbabwe," in *Power, Politics and Identity in South African Media*, ed. Adrian Howland, Eric Louw, Simphiwe Sesanti, and Herman Wasserman (Pretoria, South Africa: HSRC Press, 2008), 290–311, quotation on 290.
51. For more on the role of international funding bodies in African literary production, see Doreen Strauhs, *African Literary NGOs: Power, Politics, and Participation* (London: Palgrave, 2013), and Madhu Krishnan, *Contingent Canons: African Literature and the Politics of Location* (Cambridge: Cambridge University Press, 2018).
52. Tyler Hoffman, *American Poetry in Performance: From Walt Whitman to Hip Hop* (Ann Arbor: University of Michigan Press, 2011), 229.
53. See Javon Johnson, *Killing Poetry: Blackness and the Making of Slam and Spoken Word Communities* (New Brunswick, NJ: Rutgers University Press, 2018).
54. For an overview of the legal position of refugees in Malawi, see Miriam Reiboldt, "On the Legal and Social Labels of Asylum-Seekers and Refugees: A Case Study in Malawi" (master's thesis, Utrecht University, 2019); for more on the role of Dzaleka and Tumaini in particular, see Catherine Makhumula, "Re-imagining *Dzaleka*: The *Tumiaini* Festival and Refugee Visibility," *Eastern African Literary and Cultural Studies* 5, no. 1 (2019).
55. Lazarus, "Cosmopolitanism," 120.
56. Paul Gilroy, "A New Cosmopolitanism," *Interventions* 7, no. 3 (2005): 287–92, quotation on 292.
57. Tumaini Letu, "Tumaini Festival 2021 at Dzaleka Refugee Camp," *Kickstarter*, 1 November 2021, https://www.kickstarter.com/projects/tumaini21/tumaini-festival-2021-at-dzaleka-refugee-camp.
58. Tumaini Letu, "Tumaini Festival 2021."
59. Edward Said, *Reflections on Exile, and Other Essays* (Cambridge, MA: Harvard University Press, 2000), 144, 137–38. Ramazani, *Poetry and Its Others*, 3.
60. Ramazani, *Poetry and Its Others*, 3.
61. Ramazani, *Poetry and Its Others*, 10.

CHAPTER 5: BUT CANONS CONTINUE

1. Lindsay Thomas theorizes this shift through her analysis of BookTok recommendation videos. For more, see Thomas, "BookTok and the Rituals of Recommendation," in "Reading with Algorithms," ed. Sarah Brouillette and Susanna Sacks, special cluster, *Post45 Contemporaries*, December 2023.
2. Ruha Benjamin, *Race After Technology: Abolitionist Tools for the New Jim Code* (New York: Polity Press, 2019), details the widespread reproduction of racial bias through algorithmic decision-making; more recently, Nick Seaver, *Computing Taste: Algorithms and the Makers of Music Recommendation* (Chicago: University of Chicago Press, 2023), has shown how programmers' cultural norms shape music curation algorithms, specifically. Together with Safiya Noble's foundational work in *Algorithms of Oppression: How Search Engines Reinforce Racism* (New York: New York University Press, 2016), these books suggest the widespread reproduction of social injustice through algorithmic decision-making.
3. Pierre Bourdieu, *The Rules of Art: Genesis and Structure of the Literary Field* (Redwood City, CA: Stanford University Press, 1996).
4. Economists Tyler Cowen and Alexander Tabarrok attributed the growing division between elite culture and popular markets through the second half of the twentieth century to artists' "pursuit of the nonpecuniary benefits of high satisfaction art," while acknowledging that this division reproduces inequitable access to the arts, as "family funds, bequests, and other lump-sum grants have been important encouragements to the careers of many artists" ("An Economic Theory of Avant-Garde and Popular Art, or High and Low Culture," *Southern Economic Journal* 67, no. 2 [2000]: 232–53, quotation on 234).
5. Forbes Africa, "Under 30 Creatives," 4 June 2018, https://www.forbesafrica.com/under-30/2018/06/04/under-30-creatives/.
6. Putuma recounted her experience in "An Open Letter to TEDxStellenbosch," published on the blog of the Word N Sound Literature Movement on 15 December 2015, https://wordnsoundlivelit.wordpress.com/2015/12/15/an-open-letter-to-tedxstellenbosch-by-koleka-putuma/.
7. Barbara Hernstein-Smith, *Contingencies of Value: Alternative Perspectives for Critical Theory* (Cambridge, MA: Harvard University Press, 1991), 23.
8. For more on the use of literary instruction to further English imperial rule, see Gauri Viswanathan, *Masks of Conquest* (New York: Columbia University Press, 1989). In Africa specifically, see Apollo Amoko, "The Problem with English Literature in Africa" (PhD diss., University of Michigan, 2002); Ngũgĩ wa Thiong'o, *Decolonising the Mind: The Politics of Language in African Literature* (Rochester, NY: James Currey, 1986), and *Penpoints, Gunpoints, and Dreams* (Oxford: Clarendon Press, 1998); and Abiola Irele, *The African Imagination* (Oxford: Oxford University Press, 2001).
9. Stephanie Rudwick, *The Ambiguity of English as a Lingua Franca* (New York: Routledge, 2022); Gregory Kamwendo, "The New Language of Instruction Policy in Malawi: A House Standing on a Shaky Foundation," *International Review of Education* 62 (2016): 221–28. See also Colin Reilly, Elvis ResCue, and Jean Josephine Chavula, "Language Policy in Ghana and Malawi: Differing Approaches to Multilingualism in Education," *Journal of the British Academy* 10, s. 4 (222): 69–95.

10. See, for example, Laura Heffernan and Rachel Sagner Buurma, *The Teaching Archive* (Chicago: University of Chicago Press, 2020).
11. For more, see Pierre Bourdieu, *Distinction* (Cambridge, MA: Harvard University Press, 1979).
12. For more on literary activism and "gateopening" in Africa, see Bwesigye Bwa Mwesigire, "What Is Literary Activism? (Or Who Keeps the Housekeepers' House?)," *Eastern African Literary and Cultural Studies* 7, nos. 1–2 (2021): 10–22.
13. Koleka Putuma, "Water," InZync Poetries, *YouTube*, 27 June 2016.
14. The line order here reflects the video-poem, which differs from the version of "Water" published in Koleka Putuma, *Collective Amnesia* (Durban, South Africa: uHlanga Press, 2017), 96–100. The published version reads, "And I often hear this joke / about Black people not being able to swim, / or being scared of water. [. . .] Yet every time our skin goes under, / it's as if the reeds remember that they were once chains."
15. Isobel Hofmeyr, "Provisional Notes on Hydrocolonialism," *English Language Notes* 57, no. 1 (2019): 11–20, quotation on 13.
16. The Company's Garden, established by the Dutch East India Company, extends through the central business district of Cape Town, connecting the National Gallery, the National Library, Parliament, and Tuynhuys. Even as it is a central space of governance for the country, its structure (and unique resident squirrel population) retains the markers of South Africa's colonial past. Again, the line order varies in the video from the printed version, which reads, "Another one (who looks like me) was murdered today // May that be the conversation at the table" (100).
17. Pumla Gqola's *Rape: A South African Nightmare* (Johannesburg: Jacana Media, 2015) helped draw widespread attention to the country's unusually high rates of violence against women and queer people, and particularly rape, kidnapping, and murder.
18. Jürgen Habermas, *The Structural Transformation of the Public Sphere*, trans. Thomas Burger and Frederick Lawrence (Cambridge, MA: MIT Press, 1989).
19. Michael Warner, *Publics and Counterpublics* (Brooklyn, NY: Zone Books, 2002), 51, 62.
20. Denise Newfield and Rafael d'Abdon, "Reconceptualizing Poetry as a Multimodal Genre," *TESOL Quarterly* 49, no. 3 (2015): 510–32, quotation on 515.
21. Here, I reprise F. Abiola Irele's argument in *The African Imagination: Literature in Africa and the Black Diaspora* (Oxford: Oxford University Press, 2001).
22. Pierre Bourdieu, "The Market of Symbolic Goods," *Poetics* 14, nos. 1–2 (1985): 13–44.
23. Rachel Sagner Buurma and Laura Heffernan, *The Teaching Archive: A New History for Literary Study* (Chicago: University of Chicago Press, 2020).
24. Kimberly Quiogue Andrews refers to this tendency as "the viral esoteric," in "A Little Bit of Cold Plums in My Life: 'This Is Just o Say' on the Internet" (presentation, MLA Annual Convention, 4 January 2019, Hyatt Regency Hotel, Chicago).
25. This artistic trajectory is, of course, not limited to poetry: Kenyan writer and arts organizer Binyavanga Wainaina details his own artistic coming-of-age in parallel terms in his memoir *One Day I Will Write about This Place: A Memoir* (Minneapolis, MN: Graywolf Press, 2011), where he discusses the power of digital forums and listservs for his own development as a writer and even his publication of the Caine Prize–winning story that helped fund *Kwani?*
26. Hua Hsu describes the centrality of rivalry to literary branding in a US context

through their analysis of H. T. Tsiang's opposition to Pearl S. Buck and Frank Chin's and Maxine Kingston's rival productions ("Varieties of Ether: Toward a History of Creativity and Beef," *Lapham's Quarterly*, 23 September 2018, https://www.laphams quarterly.org/rivalry-feud/varieties-ether).

27. John Guillory, *Cultural Capital: The Problem of Literary Canon Formation* (Chicago: University of Chicago Press, 1993), 55.
28. Leketi Makalela, "'Our academics are intellectually colonised': Multi-languaging and Fees Must Fall," *International Review of Education* 64 (2018): 823–43.
29. Stephanie Bosch Santana, "From Nation to Network: Blog and Facebook Fiction from Southern Africa," *Research in African Literatures* 49, no. 1 (2018): 187–208.
30. Thomas, "BookTok and the Rituals of Recommendation."
31. Roopika Risam, *New Digital Worlds: Postcolonial Digital Humanities in Theory, Praxis, and Pedagogy* (Evanston, IL: Northwestern University Press, 2018), 34.
32. Santana, "From Nation to Network," 190.
33. Koleka Putuma quoted in Ainehi Edoro, "Koleka Putuma Could Change How We Sell Books," Brittle Paper (blog), 24 August 2017.
34. Sarah Brouillette, *Postcolonial Writers in the Global Literary Marketplace* (London: Palgrave Macmillan, 2007); Ariel Bookman, "Commodity Fictions" (PhD diss., Northwestern University, 2016); Nathan Suhr-Sytsma, *Poetry, Print, and the Making of Postcolonial Literature* (Cambridge: Cambridge University Press, 2018).
35. Walter Bgoya and Mary Jay's "Publishing in Africa from Independence to the Present Day," *Research in African Literatures* 44, no. 2 (2013), illustrates the difficulties faced by independent, indigenous publishers seeking to enter a market dominated by and oriented toward multinational publishers of textbooks; for more on the social impact of these structures, see Abebe Zegeye and Maurice Vambe, "Knowledge Production and Publishing in Africa," *Development Southern Africa* 23, no. 3 (November 2006): 333–49.
36. Madhu Krishnan, *Contingent Canons: African Literature and the Politics of Location* (Cambridge: Cambridge University Press, 2019), 5.
37. Rachel Mennies, "Paying to Play: On Submission Fees in Poetry Publishing," *The Millions*, 3 January 2018, https://themillions.com/2018/01/paying-to-play-on-solvency-and-submissions-fees-in-poetry-publishing.html.
38. Mark McGurl, *The Program Era: Postwar Fiction and the Rise of Creative Writing* (Cambridge, MA: Harvard University Press, 2009).
39. Doseline Kiguru, "Literary Prizes, Writers' Organisations and Canon Formation in Africa," *African Studies* 75, no. 2 (2016): 202–14, quotation on 205.
40. James English, *The Economy of Prestige: Prizes, Awards, and the Circulation of Cultural Value* (Cambridge, MA: Harvard University Press, 2005), 269.
41. Hernstein-Smith, *Contingencies of Value*, 52.
42. Graham Huggan, *The Postcolonial Exotic: Marketing the Margins* (New York: Routledge, 2002), 105.
43. Kiguru, "Literary Prizes," 208.
44. Krishnan, *Contingent Canons*, 61.
45. My use of "underdeveloping African literature" here draws on Sarah Brouillette's claims in *Underdevelopment and African Literature: Emerging Forms of Reading* (Cambridge: Cambridge University Press, 2021). Brouillette's argument, which focuses on the tension between traditional publishing structures and informal,

popular (or demotic) forms of reading, parallels the tension this chapter identifies between elite and popular gatekeeping structures.
46. Badilisha Poetry X-Change, "We Are," www.badilishapoetry.com/we-are (no longer available). Badilisha's own trajectory illustrates the fragility of these institutions. Between Between October 2022, when I began final revisions on this book, and March 2023, when I completed them, the site went offline.
47. Badilisha Poetry X-Change, "Why We Do It," www.badilishapoetry.com/why-we-do-it (no longer available).
48. Huggan, *Postcolonial Exotic*, 50–68.
49. Henry Chakava, quoted in Bgoya and Jay, "Publishing in Africa," 19.
50. Brouillette, *Underdevelopment and African Literature*, 18; Huggan, *Postcolonial Exotic*, 51.
51. Bgoya and Jay, "Publishing in Africa, 25–26.
52. Shola Adenekan, *African Literature in the Digital Age: Class and Sexual Politics in New Writing from Nigeria and Kenya* (Rochester, NY: Boydell & Brewer, 2021), 13.
53. In their 2019–20 survey of African literature professors in the United States, Lily Saint and Bhakti Shringarpure identify a near-identical distribution: "45 of the 54 countries that make up the African continent made the cut [into university syllabuses]: South Africa dominated with 106 authors on the list, followed by Nigeria (62) and Kenya (30)." See their *African Literature Is a Country*, August 2020, https://africasacountry.com/2020/08/african-literature-is-a-country. Zimbabwe comes in fifth on their list; however, its geographic proximity to South Africa—where Badilisha is based—may account for some of the difference. Even as Badilisha opens up publishing to more poets, then, the geopolitical distribution of literature remains more or less consistent.
54. Badilisha Poetry X-Change, "Submit," www.badilishapoetry.com (no longer available).
55. This is not a commonly used term, yet the dominant national publishing countries in Anglophone Africa—South Africa, Nigeria, Kenya, Zimbabwe, and Uganda—do happen to be a quintet.
56. Chiwamba's work on Sapitwa is discussed in more detail in chapter 2 of this volume.
57. Robert Chiwamba, interview by the author, 15 December 2016. See also Harri Englund, "Love and Homophobia in Malawi's Spoken-Word Poetry Movement," *Africa* 91, no. 3 (2021): 361–87, esp. 363.
58. For the past four years, the "Hottest" video has always been Robert Chiwamba's *Flames Sidzamva*, indicating the persistence of the bestseller effect.
59. Nikitta Dede Adjirakor, "Fieldwork as Decolonising African Literary Studies: Researching Tanzanian Hip-Hop and Spoken Word Poetry as a Ghanaian" (working paper, African Studies, University of Bayreuth, Bayreuth, Germany, 2021), 40–54, quotation on 42.
60. For an overview of this debate in a US context, see Timothy Yu, "Instagram Poetry and Our Poetry Worlds," Poetry Foundation, 24 April 2019, https://www.poetryfoundation.org/harriet-books/2019/04/instagram-poetry-and-our-poetry-worlds. Jacquelyn Ardam sympathetically summarizes the tension many scholars experience when approaching internet poetry: "Many poets, critics, and scholars find these internet poems banal and trite. My instinct is to also find them banal and trite, but I am trying to put these judgments aside, to see these poems for what they are: not experimental works that push the boundaries of language and sense and politics (my preference) but poems to read at the end of a long day when you might want to be

seen or comforted or validated." See Ardam, *Avidly Reads Poetry* (New York: New York University Press, 2022), 121–22.
61. Newfield and d'Abdon, "Reconceptualizing Poetry," 511.
62. Jahan Ramazani, *Poetry and Its Others: News, Prayer, Song, and the Dialogue of Genres* (Chicago: University of Chicago Press, 2013), 6–7.
63. The nostalgic styling reflects a tendency Seth Perlow identifies as "the handwritten styles of Instagram poetry," which, he argues, "ironically use Instagram to reassert the traditional notion that genuine poetic expression looks inky and papery"; see "The Handwritten Styles of Instagram Poetry, *Post45 Contemporaries*, 17 September 2019, 2. This concern for the materiality of text, represented digitally, echoes broader trends toward what Jessica Pressman calls "bookishness" in the theoretically post-book digital age. See her *Bookishness: Loving Books in a Digital Age* (New York: Columbia University Press, 2019).
64. Adenekan *African Literature in the Digital Age*, 3.
65. Ainehi Edoro-Glines, "Unruly Archives: Literary Form and the Social Media Imaginary," *ELH* 89, no. 2 (2022): 523–46, quotation on 526.
66. Edoro-Glines, "Unruly Archives," 527.
67. Putuma, *Collective Amnesia*, 5–6.
68. Putuma, 57.
69. Putuma, "Lifeline," in *Collective Amnesia*, 85, emphasis in original.
70. Putuma, "Black Joy," in *Collective Amnesia*, 12, emphasis in original.
71. Putuma, "Teachings," in *Collective Amnesia*, 79, emphasis in original.
72. Kalyan Nadiminti, "The Global Program Era: Contemporary International Fiction in the American Creative Economy," *Novel* 51, no. 3 (2018): 375–96 (quotations on 376, 377, 394).
73. For more on the position of African literary studies in US and African higher education, see Apollo Amoko, "The Problem with English Literature" (PhD diss., University of Michigan, 2002).
74. Ishmael Sibiya, interview by the author, 20 July 2020.
75. Roopika Risam, "Insurgent Academics," in *The SAGE Handbook of Media and Migration*, ed. Kevin Smetts, Koen Leurs, Myria Georgiou, Saskia Witteborn, and Radhika Gajjala (Thousand Oaks, CA: Sage, 2019).
76. GSMA, "The Mobile Economy: Sub-Saharan Africa 2022," GSMA Intelligence, 2022, accessed 16 March 2023, 10, https://www.gsma.com/mobileeconomy/wp-content/uploads/2022/10/The-Mobile-Economy-Sub-Saharan-Africa-2022.pdf.

CODA: DIGITAL POETRY AND THE GLOBAL CREATIVE ECONOMY

1. Stanley Kenani, *Nation*, 16 July 2015; Matthew Walther, "Poetry Died 100 Years Ago This Month," *New York Times*, 29 December 2022.
2. Mizuko Ito, introduction to *Networked Publics*, ed. Kazys Varnelis (Cambridge, MA: MIT Press, 2012), 1–7.
3. Shola Adenekan, *African Literature in the Digital Age* (Rochester, NY: Boydell & Brewer, 2021); James Yékú, *Cultural Netizenship* (Bloomington: Indiana University Press, 2022); Meg Arenberg, "Swahili Poetry's Digital Geographies: WhatsApp and the Forming of Cultural Space," *Postcolonial Text* 15, nos. 3–4 (2020).

4. Ainehi Edoro-Glines, "Unruly Archives: Literary Form and the Social Media Imaginary," *ELH* 89, no. 2 (2022): 523–46, quotation on 527–28.
5. Pallavi Rao, "#Patriarchykapacup: Mediating Sexual Discourse and the Casteless Feminist Subject in Indian Performance Poetry," *Porn Studies* 9, no. 3 (2022): 365–83; Veena Mani, "Poets of Circumstances: Love, Trauma and Death in Digital Poetry," *South Asian Review* 43, nos. 1–2 (2022): 121–31; Urvashi Sahni, "Methodology as 'Resistance Aesthetics': Young Girls in Lucknow, India Talk Back to Patriarchy," in *Global Youth Citizenry and Radical Hope: Enacting Community-Engaged Research through Performative Methodologies*, ed. Kathleen Gallagher, Dirk J. Rodricks, and Kelsey Jacobson (New York: Springer, 2020), 67–88; Kate Kovalik and Jen Scott Curwood, "#poetryisnotdead: Understanding Instagram Poetry within a Transliteracies Framework," *Literacy* 53, no. 4 (2019): 185–95.
6. See, for example, Silas Udenze and Bibian Ugoala, "Building Community and Construction Identity on WhatsApp: A Netnographic Approach," *World of Media* (2019), and Dwaine and Lauren Plaza, "Facebook and WhatsApp as Elements in Transnational Care Chains for the Trinidadian Diaspora," *Genealogy* 3, no. 2 (2019): 15.
7. Adam Kirsch, "Adam Kirsch on Elizabeth Alexander's Bureaucratic Verse," *New Republic*, 20 January 2009, https://newrepublic.com/article/47178/adam-kirsch-elizabeth-alexanders-bureaucratic-verse; David L. Ulin, "Inaugural Poem Is Less Than Praiseworthy," *Los Angeles Times*, 21 January 2009, https://www.latimes.com/archives/la-xpm-2009-jan-21-na-inaug-poet21-story.html; for a rare counterpoint, see Moira Weigel, "'I hear America singing,'" *Guardian*, 30 January 2009, https://www.theguardian.com/books/2009/jan/31/inauguration-poetry-reading.
8. Lake of Stars, "Q Malewezi at Malawi National Library," YouTube, 9 October 2013, https://www.youtube.com/watch?v=2F8Q82jl2Pc.
9. Nancy K. Baym and danah boyd, "Socially Mediated Publicness: An Introduction," *Journal of Broadcasting & Electronic Media* 56, no. 3 (2012): 320–29, quotation on 320.
10. Baym and boyd, "Socially Mediated Publicness," 325, 327.

INDEX

Adejunmobi, Moradewan, 13, 98
Adenekan, Shola, 59, 168
Adichie, Chimamanda, 174, 178
aesthetic networks, 55–59; algorithmic forms, 58–62; contemporary poetry as social network, 88–89; networked publics, 62–70; picturing pandemic poetry in South Africa, 79–88; securing publication of Zimbabwean poetry, 70–79
Africa: book accessibility in, 59–60; poetry in, 4–11
Africa Centre, 167
Africalia, 102
African literary production, 13, 79, 164
African literature, 12, 59, 121, 123; contemporary, 175, 184; digital future of, 180–81; neocolonial ventures and, 167–68; prize economies and, 166; term, 164
African National Congress (ANC), 7, 28, 33
Afrophobia, 147, 180
AKO Caine Prize, 164–65
albinism, 192n36
Alexander, Elizabeth, 185
algorithmic aesthetics, 3, 19, 62, 70, 73, 90, 92, 97, 170, 179–80, 183
algorithmic forms, aesthetic networks and, 58–62
algorithms of oppression, 17
Alliance Française, 102, 106
ambassador, festival poet as, 145–52
Anderson, Benedict, 29
Arenberg, Meg, 183
Around the Fire (play), 85–86
Atan, Mata-Uiroa Manuel, 131
audiences: creation of, 129–38; negotiating demands of, 145–52; organizing responses of, 138–45
authenticity, 19, 88, 95, 97, 121–24, 127, 137, 144, 149, 150, 157, 178
Azania House, 31, 34

Badilisha Poetry X-Change, 167–71, 179–80
Banda, Hastings "Kamuzu," 7–9, 28, 46, 47, 113
Banda, Jules, 150
Banda, Lily, 109, 138
Banda, Phindu, 110, 150
Barber, Karin, 11–12, 63
Bauman, Richard, 132
Baym, Nancy K., 187
Becker, Howard, 76–77
Bere, Wonderful, 42
Bgoya, Walter, 168
Biden, Jill, 51
Biden, Joe, 184
Billie, Morset, 72, 74–76
Black Mamba Rising (Qabula), 6, 33
Black Pearl (Chirirui, Wadzanai), 145–48
Blaq Perl, 114
Boal, Augusto, 28
Book Café, community center, 101–2, 106
Bookman, Ariel, 164
"Books Not Bullets" (Louw), 35–38
BookTok, 162, 209n1
born-free writers, 2
Bourdieu, Pierre, 73
boyd, danah, 187
Brathwaite, Kamau, 125
Brickhill, Paul, 102
Brickhill, Tomas, 102
Briggs, Charles, 132
British Empire, 126
Brittle Paper, 163, 166, 179, 183
Brouillette, Sarah, 60, 164
Buthulezi, Mbongeni, 95–96
Button Poetry, 168
Buurma, Rachel Sagner, 161

call-and-response poem, 49
canon reform, limits of, 177–80

215

Cape Town Ultimate Slam Championship, 83
Cape Town, South Africa, 19, 31–32, 36, 83, 90–91, 94, 114–19, 134, 136, 159
Cape Youth Poetry Hub for Expression and Rhythm (CYPHER), 117–18
Carlton, Terri, 77
Casanova, Pascale, 124–25
Censorship Board, 47
Centre for the Creative Arts (CCA), 129, 136
Chakava, Henry, 167
chants: hashtags and, 27–31; hashtags as poetry, 31–38; as networked poetics, 45–52; poetry as hashtag, 38–45
Chasar, Mike, 61–62, 83–84
Chichewa, language, 9, 21, 48, 51, 63–68, 113, 191n24
Chifunyise, Stephen, 41–42
Chikoti, Shadreck, 140–41
Chimombo, Steve, 99
chimurenga, 7, 28–29, 41–42, 194n17
Chirasha, Mbizo, 71–73, 77, 78
Chisvo, Vera, 102
Chiwamba, Robert, 48–49, 66, 109–10, 112–13, 150, 169–70, 180
co-performers. *See* Poetry Africa, creating audiences at
Coldplay, 99
Cole, Teju, 178
Collective Amnesia (Putuma), 155–57, 163, 165, 175, 178, 181; economies of prestige and, 161–66; evaluating technological epistemes, 157–61; marketing of, 164
collective intentionality, 30
Collinson Trust, 102
Comrade Fatso, 102
conscience, slam poetry, 112–15
contemporary festival, development of, 124–29
"Conversations about Home (at a Deportation Centre)," 1, 10, 16
cosmopolitanism, contemporary festival and, 125–29. *See also* festivals, poetry
COVID-19, 21, 57, 62, 76, 79, 170, 179, 181
Crawford, Katie, 69
Crenshaw, Kimberlé, 176
critique, aestheticizing, 145–48
cultural capital: changing media landscapes, 171–77; creating new networks, 166–71; digital futures, 180–81; emphasizing author function, 174–75; limits of canon reform, 177–80; networked poetry, 157–61; overview of, 154–57; prestige economies, 161–66
cultural netizen, 15
Cummins, Fred, 30
Current State of Poetry, 106
Curwood, Jen Scott, 184

d'Abdon, Rafael, 160–61, 171
Daily Times, 46
Dawes, Kwame, 126, 169
Def Jam Poetry, 136
Democratic Republics of Congo, 122
digital aesthetic networks. *See* aesthetic networks
digital cosmopolitanism, troubling, 152–53
digital media, 5, 11, 14, 16, 19–20, 32, 43, 45, 54–55, 93, 97–98, 101, 108
digital netizenship, 183
digital network, 10–11
digital platforms, support of, 2–3
digital poem, 124
digital publication, tension of, 104–5
digital slam, 86–87
Dolan, Jill, 132
Dzaleka Refugee Camp, 110, 122–23, 149

echo chamber, 3
Economic Freedom Fighters (EFF), 5
Edinburgh International Festival, 126
Edoro-Gaines, Ainehi, 174–75, 184
Elhillo, Safia, 154
Eliot, T. S., 182
Elizabeth Sneddon Theatre. *See* Poetry Africa
English, James, 180
Englund, Harri, 113

Facebook, 34, 51, 57, 58, 136; algorithmic forms and, 58–62; amplifying voices on, 73–74; feed-based organization on, 79; forming aesthetic networks on, 76–78; hashtags and shares on, 74; image macros on, 74–76; Instagram *versus*, 79–88; marking shared knowledge system on, 77–79; privacy on, 72–73; publication options of, 70–79; rewarding works

INDEX

soliciting engagement, 74; self-broadcast format, 71–72
Fallism, movement, 8, 18
#FeesMustFall, 31–38, 46, 53, 196n38
festivals, poetry: audience creation, 129–38; contemporary festival development, 124–129; digital engagement, 128–29; directing audiences, 138–45; establishing cosmopolitan ideal of literature, 125–26; negotiating audience demands, 145–52; poets as ambassadors, 145–52; proliferation of, 126–27; in southern Africa, 126; staging tensions, 121–24; structure, 148–49; transnational audience-poet interactions, 126–29; troubling digital cosmopolitanism, 152–53
"Flames Sidzamva" (Chiwamba), 109
Forbes, 154–56
Forbes Africa, 154, 178
Ford Foundation, 102
"Foreign Searching for Rain" (Mpofu), 90–91, 118

Gabriel, Linda, 55, 101–7
gatekeeping, 3, 20, 135–36, 144, 154, 157, 161–64, 186, 212n45
gateopening, 157
Gilroy, Paul, 150
GivingWay, 152
global creative economy, poetry and, 182–87
Global North, 3, 92, 97, 102, 107, 119, 154, 162, 166–69, 178–80, 184, 193n52
Global South, 59, 93, 125, 164, 178–79
Goethe-Institut Südafrika, 102, 104, 107
Gorman, Amanda, 184–86
Guillory, John, 162

Habane, Amanda, 44–45
Hart, Matthew, 125
hashtags, 22–27; hashtag publics, 30; as poetry, 31–38; poetry as, 38–45; tactical poetics of protest, 27–31
Hear My Voice, 56, 178–79, 196n41
Heffernan, Laura, 161
Heinemann African Writers Series, 167
Herderian nationalism, 125
Hernstein-Smith, Barbara, 156, 165, 180
Hilborn, Neil, 95
Hlatshwayo, Mi S'dumo, 6, 33

Hofmeyr, Isobel, 158–59
House of Hunger Poetry Slam, 101–7, 170
"How to Be a Feminist" (Adichie), 174–76
Howart, Anita, 147
Huggan, Graham, 165
Hunt, Lynn, 15
hydrocolonialism, 158–59

iimbongi, 133
Ikegami, Eiko, 56–57
Ikpi, Bassey, 136
Imagine Africa 500 (Chikoti), 141
imphepo press, 57
inaugurations, performing poetry at, 184–85
individual performance, success or failure, 103
Instagram (IG), 57, 139, 157, 162 182, 172, 184; atomistic community of, 82; cross-posting as key to use of, 85–88; individually curated feeds on, 84–86; picturing pandemic poetry on, 79–88; poemics on, 82–84; presuming identities, 81–82; prioritizing individual content creator, 88; resistance to appropriation on, 83–84; transition to digital-first network, 79–81
Instagram TV (IGTV), 79
Instapoetry, 3
Institutions: algorithmic aesthetics, 90–120; cultural institution, 97–98, 130, 154, 163; digital, 171–77; slam poetry, 101–7; support of, 98, 106, 178; universities, 45–52
international governmental organizations (IGOs), 8
Inwood, Heather, 65
Irele, F. Abiola, 4
isiZulu, 6, 132–33
Ito, Mizuko, 183
izibongo, 5–7, 28, 33

Jagoda, Patrick, 60
Jahan, Ramazani, 151
Jameson, Leander Starr, 35
Jameson, Will, 139, 150–51
Jay, Mary, 168
Joburg Theatre Youth Development, 106
Johannesburg Review of Books, 166
Johnson, Javon, 95

Jonas, Siphokazi, 35–38, 82–85, 96
Julien, Eileen, 12–13, 140

kaBhekuzulu, Goodwill Zwelethini, 131
Kaemmer, John, 41
Kai, Jambiya, 78
Kamlongera, Christopher, 47
Kaur, Rupi, 60, 86
Kenani, Stanley, 112, 182
Kerr, David, 47–48
Kester, Roché, 133–36
Kgositsile, Keorapetse William, 169
Knowles, Beyoncé, 162, 169
Koinange, Wanjiru, 167
Kovalik, Kate, 184
Krishnan, Madhu, 107, 164, 166
Kwa-Haraba Open No-Mic Night, 98–101
KwaHaraba Art Gallery and Café, 99
Kwani?, 59

Lake of Stars Festival, 123–24, 138–45, 186; cultural representation at, 144–45; digital aesthetic network influence in, 139; Malawianness insistence, 140; origins, 139–40; performer statistics, 140; poetry inclusion at arts festivals, 138–39; Q Malewezi event at, 141–43; reflecting festival logic, 140–41; social media at, 141; as training ground for poetry reception, 143–45
Larkin, Brian, 15
Lazarus, Neil, 128, 149–50
"Lifeline" (Putuma), 176–77
limits, canon reform, 177–80
Lingua Franca Spoken Word Collective, 94
Lingua Franca Spoken Word Movement: and *Umzila ka Moya* ("Spirit's Path"), 115–19
literacy production, 4
literary NGOs (LiNGOs), 93
literary production, 3–4, 19, 59, 66, 88, 94, 98, 106, 113, 127, 137, 157, 161–62, 164, 168, 170, 175, 178, 181, 183
literary public sphere, networked poetry in, 157–61
literature, access to, 168
Living Room (Lilongwe Living Room Poetry Club), 64–68, 144
Lorde, Audre, 176
Louder than a Bomb (documentary), 95

Louw, Kyle, 35–38
Lovink, Geert, 52

Macpherson, Hector, 140
Madzitatiguru, 102
Mahon, Derek, 12
Makalela, Leketi, 31
Malange, Nise, 6, 33
Malawi, 3, 7–9; cell phones in, 181; conscience of slam poetry in, 112–15; extreme censorship in, 167–68; Facebook contacts in, 57; funding poetry in, 110–11; Lake of Stars in, 138–45; language use in, 66–67; listening for poetic voice, 11, 16; melding dual roles in, 48–49; poetry performance surge, 48; popular poetry in, 49; slam poetry in, 96; slam scene in, 107–12; spread of poetry in, 109–10; Tumaini Festival in, 121–24; university crisis of, 45–52; WhatsApp features used in, 62–70
Malawi Congress Party, 8
Malawi News, 46
Malawi Writers' Group, 47–48
Malewezi, Qabaniso "Q," 16, 58–59, 93–94, 107–12, 141–43, 186
Malunga, Benedicto, 113
Mani, Veena, 184
Mano, Winston, 8
Mapanje, Jack, 47
Maravi Post, 46, 52
Marikana Massacre (2012), 33
Mashile, Lebogang, 174–75, 178
Masunungure, Eldred, 72
Mawarire, Evan, 38–45
Mbangeni, Jessica, 133
mbumba, poetic form, 6–7, 28, 190n16
McGurl, Mark, 165
Mennies, Rachel, 164
Meta. *See* WhatsApp
Mfecane, 6, 8
micro-poems, 3, 62
migration, 6
Miles Moreland Foundation, 102
Miranda, Lin-Manuel, 184
Miyakawa, Felicia, 50
Mkiva, Zolani, 7
Mnthali, Felix, 47
Moyo, Jonathan, 42

INDEX

Mozambique, 122
Mphande, Lupenga, 5–6, 28
Mpofu, Shepherd, 71
Mpofu, Vusumuzi, 90–92, 118
Mugabe, Grace, 72
Mugabe, Robert, 8, 28–29, 39–40, 43, 70, 148
multicentricity, 13–14
Mussa, Faith, 122
Mutharika, Peter, 24, 46, 49–50
Muyanga, 99–100
Mwesigire, Bwesigye Bwa, 79

Nadiminti, Kalyan, 178
naked storytelling, 117–18
Nation, 112
National Poetry Slam Championship, 155–56
Ndlovu, Malika, 167, 176
netnography, 193n53
networked poetics: chant as, 45–52; collective poetics of protest, 23–24; concept, 14; cultural capital, 154–81; digital aesthetic networks, 57–88; digital cosmopolitanism, 121–53; global creative economy, 182–87; reading for performance in digital age, 1–22; site-based readings of, 18–20; slam poetry networks, 90–120
networks, creating, 166–71
New Digital Worlds, 162
new nation, poetry festival and, 124–29
Newfield, Denise, 160–61, 171
Ngara, Emmanuel, 12
Nigeria, 183
Noble, Safiya, 17
Noel, Urayoán, 81–82, 83, 98
Nomkonwana, Mbongeni, 114
nongovernmental organizations (NGOs), 93, 98, 107–10, 118, 120, 139, 150
Nuttall, Sarah, 144

Obama, Barack, 185
Okigbo, Christopher, 12–13, 180
Okorafor, Nnedi, 178
100,000 Poets for Peace-Zimbabwe, 77
"Online" (Putuma), 175–76
Open Book Festival, 115
orature, 4, 28, 118, 189n6
Ouma, Christopher, 95–96

Pamberi Trust, 74
pandemic, poetry regarding, 79–88
paravirtual networks, 26, 55, 57, 90, 106
pay back the money, poetic speech act, 5
PEN Student Writing Prize, 155–56
"People" (Malewezi), 109, 111
performance, 4–5
performance poetry, 2, 5, 8, 11–13, 28, 34–35, 48, 89, 96–99, 115, 119, 141, 144, 169–70, 179, 181
Perry, Jacie Hill, 99–100
Peterson, Bh ekizizwe, 130
Phalafala, Uhuru, 163–64
Pinsky, Robert, 4
Plume, Menes La, 150
poem-video, 35, 42
poemics, 82–84
poet-refugee, 149–52
poetic form, 2–6, 10–12, 20, 22, 28, 32, 72, 92, 99, 108, 120, 158, 170, 172, 182–83
poetry: analyzing digital media influence on, 16–17; circulating through digital spaces, 100–101; circulation of, 2; collective poetics of protest, 23–54; cultural capital and, 154–81; cultural engagement presumed by, 114–15; digital aesthetic networks, 55–89; economies of prestige, 161–66; embracing "universal" themes, 48; festivals of, 121–53; formal structure of, 12; global creative economy and, 182–87; as hashtag, 38–45; hashtag as, 31–38; imagined sound of, 30; impact on community life, 163; inclusion at arts festivals, 138–39; making risks, 145; multicentricity of, 13–14; nationalist, 7–8; political stakes, 113; political uses of, 4–11; publics and, 22; remediation of, 12–13; scholarship on, 12; site-based readings, 18–20; as social form, 52–54; as social network, 88–89; term, 112–13; as vectorized movement, 14; voice in networked public sphere, 11–18
Poetry Africa, 16, 19, 123–24, 179
Poetry Africa, creating audiences at, 129–38; audience interactions shaping event, 132–33; celebrating Pan-African cosmopolitanism, 131–32; opening night, 133–36; origins, 129–31; tensions, 131; YouTube presence, 136–38
poetry cycle, 67–69

Poetry dot Slam, 106
"Poetry for a Cause," event, 11
Poetry Slam, Inc. (PSI), 94, 97
poetry slam. *See* slam poetry
Poets to the People, 33
praise poetry, 6, 47, 96, 126
"Praise Song for the Day" (Alexander), 185
Pratt, Mary Louise, 127
"Premium Poes" (Kester), 133–36
prestige, economies of, 161–66
prize, economies of, 164–66
Project Project, 107–12, 144
protest, collective poetics of: chant as networked poetics, 45–52; hashtags, 22–27; hashtag as poetry, 31–38; poem as social form, 52–54; poetry as hashtag, 38–45; tactical poetics, 27–31
publics: literary public sphere, 157–61; networked, 14–15; poets and, 22
Pungwe, 190n15
pungwe, poetic forms, 6
Putuma, Koleka, 154–55, 169, 172, 174, 178, 180

Q Malewezi. *See* Living Room
Qabula, Alfred, 6, 33, 180

Ramazani, Jahan, 13–14, 116, 139, 172, 193n52
Rambukkana, Nathan, 30
Rao, Pallavi, 184
reception, importance of, 128
refugees. *See* poet-refugee
representation, imbalance of, 181
Risam, Roopika, 162–63
Rothenberg, Michael, 77
Rubadiri, David, 13
Rwanda, 122

Sahni, Urvashi, 184
Santana, Stephanie Bosch, 10, 55
Sapitwa (Sapitwa Poetry's Artists), 64–68
Sapitwa Poetry, 169–71, 179
SapitwaPoetry.com, 109, 204n39
Schroder, Kurt, 99
scope, 20–22
Sebambo, Khumo, 31
self-as-citizen, performance of, 147–48
Serubiri, Moses, 96
Seunda, Yankho, 49

Shire, Warsan, 1, 60, 169
Shoro, Katleho, 95–96
Shoro, Katleho Kano, 117
Sibiya, Ishmael, 179
Sindaphi, Lwanda, 114, 115
"Sins of Our Mothers" (Linda), 103–4
Sitas, Ari, 6
site-based readings, network poetics, 18–20
Siwani, Buhlebezwe, 176
Sizemore-Barber, April, 5
Sky, Nomonde, 172–75, 180
slam poetry: aesthetics of, 100–101; capsule quality, 95; community desires shaping, 97; conscience of, 112–15; digital spread of, 98–101; emergence in Malawi, 108; formal attributes, 203n19; global networks of, 94–98; institutionalizing algorithmic aesthetics in, 90–94; institutions of, 101–107; localizing spoken word, 115–19; managing spread of, 97–98; personal poetics, 107–12; regional networks of, 119–120; WhatsApp and, 97
social form, poem as, 52–54
social media, 2–3; #ThisFlag movement and, 42–45; aesthetic networks and, 55–59; algorithmic networks and, 58–62; fantasy of publishing on, 61–62; logics of, 46–47; in Malawi, 45–52
Sol Plaatje European Union Poetry Award, 83
song, embodied collectivity of, 29–30
South Africa, 3, 9–10; picturing pandemic poetry in, 79–88; Poetry Africa in, 129–38; political uses of poetry in, 4–11; social media usage in, 181; Zimbabwean poetry in, 145–48
South African Broadcasting Corporation (SABC), 34
Southern African Development Community (SADC), 8–10
spoken word: localizing, 115–19; organizations, 19, 110, 196n41; poetry, 90, 97, 105, 107, 110, 119, 202n2
Spoken Word Project, 104–7
Stanfield, Chantal, 83
Starre, Kila van der, 95
Strauhs, Doreen, 93
Suhr-Sytsma, Nathan, 2, 12, 164
Sydney Saize, pseudonym, 77–78
synthetic vernaculars, 125

taarab, genre, 6
tactical poetry, 26–27, 53
talk values, 14
Tanzania, 5–7, 11
TEDxStellenbosch, 156, 162
Tembo, Lucky, 133
Thiong'o, Ngũgĩ wa, 4
#ThisFlag, movement, 38–45
"This Flag: A Lament for Zimbabwe," poem, 38–45
Tolson, Melvin, 125
Traveling Theatre, 47
trending topic, concept, 30
Trump administration, 1
Tufekci, Zeynep, 14, 45
Tumaini Arts Festival, 149–52
Tumaini Festival, 121–23
Tupac, 99
24News Malawi, 46
Twitter, 2, 3, 10, 16–17, 19, 32, 34, 51, 70, 137, 157; algorithmic networks and, 58–62; Instagram *versus*, 79–88

Uganda, 122
uHlanga, 163, 164, 181
Umzila ka Moya ("Spirit's Path"), 116–19
UN Millennium Goals, 143
underdevelopment, 189n3
universal themes, print poetry, 48
university crisis, Malawi, 45; background of, 46–49; collective chanting, 49–51; opening first national university, 46; organizing grounded action, 51–52; student protests, 46–47; turning to public-facing networks, 51
University of Cape Town (UCT), 32
University of KwaZulu Natal (UKZN), 129–30
University of Malawi, 23, 47, 96, 113

Vail, Leroy, 28
vernacular anglophone realism, 178
Vili, Xabiso, 87–88
voluntourism, 122

Walcott, Derek, 12
Warner, Michael, 14, 160
"Water" (Putuma), 155–56; bridging discursive fields, 160; canon formation, 177–78; centering sea in, 158–59; narrow allusions in, 159–60; prize eligibility of, 165; rejecting colonialism in, 159; speaker-space relationship in, 158; success of, 161
#WeAreDyingHere (production), 82–83
Wegerif, Maya, 136
WhatsApp, 2, 32, 51, 57, 76, 109, 183; always-on capacities of, 65–66; background listeners, 69; conversation and feedback patterns, 64–65; emphasis on written commentary on, 66; engraining patterns, 63–64; features of, 62–63; Instagram *versus*, 79–88; networked publics and, 62–70
White, Landeg, 28
"Why You Talk So White" (Wegerif), 136
"Wikipedia" (Malewezi), 16, 142–43
Wong, Cindy, 144
Woods, Scott, 94
Word N Sound, 87
World Bank, 9, 21, 110, 191n25
World Republic of Letters (Casanova), 124–25
World War II, 125

Yékú, James, 2, 15, 121, 183
YouTube, 16, 44, 58, 70, 109, 157; algorithmic forms and, 58–62; Poetry Africa on, 136–38

Zambia, 5
Zimbabwe, 3, 9; internet access in, 181; poetry networks of, 101–7; poetry performance in South Africa, 145–48; securing publication of poetry, 70–79; typewriter aesthetic from, 172–73
Zimbabwean African National Union-Patriotic Front (ZANU-PF), 7, 9, 28–29, 102; "This Flag" and, 39–42
Zuma, Jacob, 5, 7, 29

SUSANNA L. SACKS is assistant professor of English at Howard University, where she teaches courses in comparative literature, focusing on contemporary poetry and Afro-diasporic literatures. Prior to joining Howard, she taught at the College of Wooster (OH) and at Northwestern University (IL), where she completed her PhD in 2019. Her research focuses on contemporary African poetry, with emphases on performance, audience formation and response, new media, and the politics of speech, including language policy and political rhetoric. This work has received awards from the African Literature Association and the African Studies Association. She lives in Washington, D.C., with two needy cats.